The American Impact on
Postwar Germany

THE AMERICAN IMPACT ON POSTWAR GERMANY

edited by
Reiner Pommerin

Berghahn Books
Providence • Oxford

First published in 1995 by
Berghahn Books
Revised edition 1997

Editorial offices:
165 Taber Avenue, Providence, RI 02906, USA
Bush House, Merewood Avenue, Oxford, OX3 8EF, UK

© Reiner Pommerin 1995
All rights reserved.
No part of this publication may be reproduced in any form or by any means without the written permission of Berghahn Books.

Library of Congress Cataloging-in-Publication Data
The American impact on postwar Germany / edited by
Reiner Pommerin.
    p.   cm.
   Includes bibliographical references.
   1. United States—Foreign Relations—Germany. 2. Germany—Foreign relations—United States. 3. Germany—Politics and government—1945–1990. 4. German reunification question (1949–1990) 5. United States—Cultural policy. 6. Adenauer, Konrad, 1876–1967.
   I. Pommerin, Reiner, 1943-
   E183.8.G3A625   1994
327.73043—dc20   94-27019
                                                             CIP
   ISBN 1-57181-095-1

British Library Cataloguing in Publication Data
A catalogue record for this book is available from the British Library.

Printed in the United States on acid-free paper.

Table of Contents

Foreword *Peter Schmitt*	VII
Introduction *Reiner Pommerin*	IX
1. **Konrad Adenauer and the United States** *Gordon A. Craig*	1
2. **The United States and the Armament of the Federal Republic of Germany** *Reiner Pommerin*	15
3. **Ambivalence and Attraction: The German Social Democrats and the United States, 1945–1974** *Dietrich Orlow*	35
4. **The Genesis of American Policy toward the GDR: Some Working Hypotheses** *Gerald R. Kleinfeld*	53
5. **West German Reconstruction and American Industrial Culture, 1945–1960** *Volker R. Berghahn*	65
6. **Daily Life and Social Patterns** *Hermann Glaser*	83

7. REBELS WITH A CAUSE? AMERICAN POPULAR CULTURE, THE 1956 YOUTH RIOTS, AND NEW CONCEPTIONS OF MASCULINITY IN EAST AND WEST GERMANY   93
   Uta G. Poiger

8. CULTURE AS AUTHORITY: AMERICAN AND GERMAN TRANSACTIONS   125
   Peter K. Breit

9. EQUALITY, DIFFERENCE, AND THE GRUNDGESETZ: WOMEN, FAMILIES, AND THE FEDERAL REPUBLIC'S BASIC LAW   149
   Robert G. Moeller

10. CINEMA, SPECTATORSHIP, AND THE PROBLEM OF POSTWAR GERMAN IDENTITY   165
    Heide Fehrenbach

NOTES ON THE CONTRIBUTORS   197

Foreword

The Goethe-Institut has been involved in numerous programs and conferences dealing with the Weimar Republic, with National Socialism, and with the former GDR, and these historical subjects will continue to be of importance in our work. But with the unification of the Germanys, the postwar Federal Republic itself has also become history, and it is time to reexamine its beginnings. The younger generation of today is little aware of how much West German society was influenced by America, not only through the close ties of American politics and economics but also through the presence of hundreds of thousands of Americans in Germany during the postwar decades.

The intensity and significance of the "Americanization" of West Germany in the fifties and sixties was the subject of a symposium organized by Prof. Dr. Reiner Pommerin, Dresden, the History Department of Dartmouth College, and the Goethe-Institute Boston. During the symposium, an examination of American influence on the Federal Republic's general political and economic development provided the overarching context for studies of specific cultural and social changes during the early nation's history. This American influence extended to all levels of culture and into many aspects of daily life and mass consumption.

The youth of West Germany were most open to "Americanization." American films, jazz, and casual manners changed the lifestyle of the fifties. The economic and cultural influence of America also left its mark on contemporary theater, postwar literature, architecture, and city planning, as well as on consumer attitudes and modern modes of production and distribution.

Have the Germans really become "children of an American civilization," as Klaus Harpprecht once wrote? Should we agree with the answer

Paul Theroux gave in the eighties to his question: what's German culture? "These days it's American culture—the same books, the same music, the same movies, even the same clothes"? These are the questions critically examined by the symposium. Yet another question is whether "Americanization"—be it in culture, economics, or other areas—should be considered only in regard to Germany. The German response is part of a larger phenomenon that Ralph Willet has pointedly called the "global process of Coca-Colonization." The historical inquiry into the beginnings of this process after the second World War enlarges our understanding of the complex relationship between Germany and the United States today.

Peter Schmitt
(Goethe-Institut Boston)

INTRODUCTION

In October 1993 a colloquium on "The American Impact On Postwar Germany" took place at Dartmouth College in New Hampshire. The event was organized by Michael Ermarth and the editor. It was sponsored by the Goethe-Institute Boston and its director, Peter Schmitt, who originated the idea of a conference on this theme. This volume unites the papers given at Dartmouth with two additional articles by Robert Moeller and Uta Poiger written especially for this book.

Following the unexpected reunification of Germany and the collapse of the Soviet Bloc, a fresh debate has been unleashed in the Federal Republic on what it means to be German and on where the Germans belong culturally and ideologically. Above all, there is the question of whether Germany's western orientation since 1945 provides the only viable cultural identity. In the 1950s, when the Federal Republic was still trying to become a part of the "Atlantic Community," this western orientation appeared to many Germans tantamount to "Americanization." Many conservatives today argue that West Germans abandoned their identity to the United States in what they call "Hollywood hegemony," and they are critical of this development. We therefore are facing a trendy anti-Americanism in the western parts of the Federal Republic alongside the traditional anti-Americanism in the new states in the east. The following contributions try to throw new light on the political, industrial, cultural, social, and psychological impact of the United States on postwar Germany in the fifties and early sixties.

In his contribution entitled "Konrad Adenauer and the United States" Gordon A. Craig (Stanford University) examines the ambivalent relationship between the first chancellor of the Federal Republic and the United States. It was a marriage of political convenience that was never free from strain and finally ended in an atmosphere of alienation and mounting suspicion on the part of Adenauer. Reiner Pommerin's (TU Dresden) "The United States and the Armament of the Federal Republic of Germany" illuminates American thought on the possibility of disarming the western part of Germany and the ultimate decision not to do so. As a consequence of the Cold War, the Federal Republic of Germany was armed, with the United States strongly promoting Bonn's membership in NATO. "Ambivalence and Attraction: The German Social Democrats and the United States, 1945–1974" is the title of Dietrich Orlow's (Boston University) contribution. While many left-wing scholars portrayed the Americans as villains who prevented the establishment of democratic socialism in Germany after 1945, conservative American scholars mistrusted the SPD. Orlow comes up with a fascinating new, and somewhat revisionist, view of the relations between the United States and the SPD. Gerald R. Kleinfeld (Arizona State University) describes, in "The Genesis of American Policy toward the GDR: Some Working Hypotheses," the various reasons why the GDR was a nonentity as far as the foreign policy of the United States was concerned.

Volker Berghahn (Brown University) does not approach the history of the reconstruction of the western parts of the defunct German Reich from the usual political perspective. He looks at "West German Reconstruction and American Industrial Culture," analyzing German-American industrial symbiosis and partial assimilation. Berghahn shows that America had a tangible influence on the development of West Germany's industrial system by virtue of its hegemonic position in the world economy.

In "Daily Life and Social Patterns," Hermann Glaser (TU Berlin) examines the terrible circumstances and conditions of daily life in Germany after the second World War. But he also describes the cultural euphoria that prevailed and shows that cultural "westernization" really meant, to a large extend, "Americanization." Uta G. Poiger (Brown University), writing on "Rebels with a Cause? American Popular Culture, the 1956 Youth Riots, and the New Conception of Masculinity in East and West Germany," explains that the debate about *Halbstarke* and American influences played a crucial part in the complex process of reconstructing Germanness in both parts of Germany. It is interesting to learn how authorities in East and in West Germany translated their perceptions into public policy and pushed cultural forms that did not pose challenges to gender norms in the reconstruction of a German national identity in East and West. Peter Breit (University of Hartford) looks at

"Culture as Authority: American and German Transactions." He underscores the fact that America's cultural transactions and the Cold War, more by happenstance than by intention, fostered in the Federal Republic a society that, because of its materialism, its uncertain attitude toward its past, and the frequency with which it was periodically disoriented by the flow of events—most recently in 1989—now confronts the first real test of America's largely shapeless cultural legacy. Breit's hypothesis is that American culture had no deep and long effect on Germany but did have an effect when it was necessary. Robert G. Moeller (University of California, Irvine) in "Equality, Difference, and the *Grundgesetz*: Women, Families, and the Federal Republic's Basic Law" comes to the conclusion that laws alone cannot construct social reality. Nevertheless, the passages defining the status of women in the Basic Law were important in that they brought into sharp focus competing conceptions of how best to reconstruct gender differences in the wake of National Socialism. He identifies the family and the status of women as central concerns of the postwar era. Last but not least, Heide Fehrenbach (Colgate University) demonstrates in her article "Cinema, Spectatorship, and the Problem of Postwar German Identity" how much many German teenagers admired the youthful, confident, uninhibited—even informal—masculinity embodied in their favorite Hollywood stars. Like their young male counterparts, teenage girls turned to American-style culture and consumer goods to construct new social and sexual identities.

Thanks are due to the contributors and also to the publisher, Marion Berghahn. Without the engagement and support of Dr. Peter Schmitt, this book could not have appeared. Throughout his career till his retirement in the fall of 1994 he worked hard to bring a better understanding of German culture and mentalities to other nations. His untiring efforts to this end are the reason this book is dedicated to him.

Reiner Pommerin
Dresden, September 1994

1. KONRAD ADENAUER AND THE UNITED STATES

Gordon Craig

Not so long ago, I was invited by the German-American Culture Fund and the Library of Congress to give a so-called Carl Schurz Lecture on Konrad Adenauer. I felt at the time, and told my audience, that this was perhaps a not very fortunate combination of names. Carl Schurz, perhaps the most brilliant and attractive of the German liberals who came to this country in the wake of the failed revolutions of 1848, loved the United States with a great passion and served it, in the field and in public life, with loyalty and enthusiasm for the rest of his life. Konrad Adenauer's relationship with the United States was always ambivalent, a marriage of political convenience that was never free from strain, and—as I shall endeavor to make clear—ended in an atmosphere of alienation.

But then Konrad Adenauer was ambivalent about many things. Three years ago, when Germany was reunified, the German people remembered what they owed to him, and there were many encomia in the press, among them one by the political scientist Christian Hacke, who wrote in the pages of the Hamburger weekly *Die Zeit* that Adenauer was:

> a foreign-political revolutionary. He led the former Federal Republic from its old geopolitical position into the political modernity of Atlantic civilization. Since unification, Germany—with a democratic constitution and integrated in the West—has become the beacon of hope for those Europeans who were deprived of freedom, well-being, and human dignity. It is this new vision that makes Adenauer the greatest European of the twentieth century.

One could not agree with this without being struck at the same time by the paradox that the man whose leadership and long tenure of office contributed so much to the establishment of a democratic state that is the freest in German history, had so little personal faith in the future of German democracy. As a survivor of the failed Weimar Republic and the twelve years of Nazi rule, he always took a dark view of life and had a deep awareness of the frailties of human beings. Indeed, his view of his fellows bordered on cynicism—he once said that it was a pity that God had put limits on human percipience but not upon human stupidity—while encouraging him at the same time to develop arts of persuasion, dissimulation, and obstinacy that might be used to win their support or to manipulate them. It must be said that he employed these skills for objectives that were for the most part neither selfish nor narrowly nationalistic. Nevertheless, ingrained suspicion and distrust, that were the concomitants of his political style, were often a great trial to his allies.

It is true that in 1949, when Adenauer became Federal Chancellor, he had good reason for his pessimism. If the German people were beginning to recover from the postwar trauma and the rigors of the years of military government, they were still confused, volatile, and without clear direction. As Adenauer told Secretary of State Dean Acheson during their first meeting at the end of 1949, his fellow countrymen were in such a state of "mental instability" as a result of the events of the past thirty-five years that no one could tell how susceptible they would be to what the French called their familiar demons—nationalism and submissiveness to authority. This condition made the task of governing them extremely difficult, the more so because Adenauer's position was hardly a commanding one. He was the head of an uneasy parliamentary coalition of four parties without common policy objectives, a coalition that had elected him to office by only one vote and that was opposed by a well-organized Socialist opposition with a strongly nationalistic leader. He was 73 years old, two years short of the age at which Bismarck left office, so he was not expected to last long and hence had many rivals within his own coalition. Essentially, his ability to carry out any policy was dependent upon the assent of the Allied High Commissioners; but they represented governments and peoples that remembered the war and hated and distrusted the Germans. If we remember how, in 1989, when it suddenly became clear that German unification was imminent, a writer in *The Times* of London wrote that the Fourth Reich was coming, with a statue of Hitler in every German town, and the American press broke out in a rash of cartoons showing Helmut Kohl wearing jackboots and giving the Hitler salute, we can imagine the intensity of anti-German feeling forty years earlier. All in all, the difficulties facing the new Bundeskanzler were enough to make an ordinary politician's heart quail.

In dealing with these difficulties, Adenauer turned away from anything resembling traditional nationalism. To dedicate his energies to an effort to win reunification was bound, he felt, to be feckless, given the nature of Soviet policy (the Berlin blockade was fresh in memory), and would probably annoy the British and alarm the French. In addition, it would run counter to his own profound feelings about where Germany's future lay. "When you fall from the heights as we Germans have done, " he said on one occasion, "you recognize that it is necessary to break with what has been. We cannot live fruitfully with false illusions." The day of the Great German Reich was over. The times called for a policy of collaboration with the West and, by this means, the regaining of West German sovereignty. The ultimate goal must be western European unity.

In retrospect, the genuineness of Adenauer's European convictions are evident enough. A Rheinlander and a Catholic, he had, since the early twenties, thought of Germany as part of a West European community based upon a thoroughgoing reconciliation with France and the development of joint economic, political, and cultural agencies that would attract other European nations as collaborators. In 1949, this was not so clearly recognized and, in the wake of twelve years of Nazi terror and aggression, persuading the Allies of Germany's good faith and inducing them to enter into a process of mutual concession with West Germany did not promise to be easy. One of Adenauer's parliamentary critics joked that he was ideally suited for the task because he was "more untrustworthy than a Frenchman, more mendacious than an Englishman, more brutal than an American, and more impenetrable than a Russian." That of course trivialized the problem by suggesting that success lay in demonstrating a superiority in character faults. Adenauer knew that it was not that simple, for he was aware, as a result of his dealings with the High Commissioners, of the depth of anti-German feeling in London and Paris. And this led him to the conclusion that he must, above all, seek the confidence and support of the United States, which alone had the means of persuading the British and the French to agree to a faster rate of German recovery than they desired.

More specifically, Adenauer saw his problem as one of persuading the Americans first of all that, for the protection of their own interests, he was the most reliable German leader and that, unless they strengthened his hand, he was likely to be replaced by people who would be willing to negotiate with the Soviets for reunification at the price of neutralization or worse. He had to convince them that he was willing to make economic and territorial concessions in return for alleviations of Germany's present condition, such as the end of dismantling, and he had to attempt also to exploit the growing concern they felt in 1949 and 1950 about the defensibility of Western Europe by suggesting that he would be ready, and able, to raise a military contingent for any international force assembled to protect against incursions from the east. (Such intimations he had begun to make secretly well in advance of the outbreak of the Korean War.) And while he pursued this diplomatic course, he had to keep all the threads of policy in his own hands, excluding his own cabinet and the Foreign Affairs Committee of the Bundestag from any knowledge of the pledges he was making in the country's name, lest a premature disclosure cause a parliamentary firestorm.

This, in general, was the nature of Konrad Adenauer's diplomacy in his first and most brilliant period, from the Petersburg Protocols of 1949, which ended dismantling, at the price of West Germany's adhesion to the Ruhr Statute, establishment of the Coal and Steel Community, and the signing of the European Defence Community Treaty and the so-called General Treaty of 1952, at the price of accepting the Saar Statute, which gave that territory a semi-autonomous status in economic union with France, although this proved in the end to be temporary. There is no doubt that Adenauer's tactical virtuosity contributed a great deal to these diplomatic successes, but the basic reason for success was the relationship he was able to establish with the United States. This was by no means the natural development that it may have seemed later.

In 1949, John J. McCloy, the U.S. High Commissioner, was not an Adenauer admirer. Indeed, he was often annoyed by the Chancellor's constant complaints and his ability to make every concession a platform for new demands and would have agreed with the French High Commissioner, Andre Francois-Poncet, who, after Adenauer had haggled for a full day over the wording of the final communique of the Petersburg negotiations, sighed, "It is a very hard task making presents to the Germans. It is also a very thankless task." McCloy was also doubtful of Adenauer's staying power and at one time believed that a Great Coalition between Adenauer's party and the SPD of Kurt Schumacher might give the country a more effective government, surely not one of his better ideas. But in time, the American High Commissioner became persuaded of the genuineness of Adenauer's European sentiments and his desire for a broad-based agreement with France, not least of all because of the positive way in which the Chancellor responded to Robert Schuman's proposal of a Coal and Steel Community, and, as one who believed that Europe could be defended only if German troops were part of the Western battle line, McCloy became convinced that Adenauer was the leader most likely to win the support of the German people for rearmament. As for Secretary of State Dean Acheson, he had been impressed by Adenauer from the moment of their first meeting, and his faith in the old man does not seem to have wavered.

As a result, in the heated inter-allied debates of 1949 to 1952, the Americans generally came down on the German side in moments of near stalemate. Alan Bullock's account of Ernest Bevin's term as Foreign Secretary makes it clear that in 1949 Bevin greatly resented American pressure to end dismantling, believing that the Germans had not yet earned the right to the concessions made in the Petersburg Protocols, but in the end he was persuaded by the Americans to go along. In the same way, Acheson was the key figure in putting an end to French footdragging in 1952, and in pushing forward the signature of both the EDC Treaty and the General Treaty between the Western Allies and the Federal Republic in March 1953.

The partnership with Adenauer became even stronger when Eisenhower came to power in January 1953. Indeed, in April of that year, when Adenauer made his first visit to the United States, bringing assurance that the ratification of the treaties by parliament was a certainty, the new administration received him as a hero and a trusted ally, arranging any number of flattering public appearances, including a ceremony at Arlington National Cemetery in which the Chancellor stood by the tomb of the Unknown Soldier while the U.S. Marine Band played "The Star Spangled Banner" and "Deutschlandlied." The effect that this had upon German public opinion was reflected in Adenauer's great victory in September when his coalition won an absolute majority in the Bundestag. This was a result so greatly desired by the U.S. government that three days before the election Secretary of State John Foster Dulles did not hesitate to say, in response to a question raised at a press conference, that a defeat of Adenauer's coalition would have "catastrophic results for German prospects of full sovereignty" and that, if Adenauer ceased to be Chancellor, it "could cause such confusion that a further slowing down of progress toward reunification and freedom would be inevitable."

These remarks were not without effect in Germany, thanks to the outrage expressed by the SPD and ensuing discussion in the press. A year later, when the French Assembly refused to ratify the EDC treaty, Dulles again stepped into the breach for his German partner, and—after threatening the French with an "agonizing reappraisal" of the European position of the United States—collaborated with Anthony Eden to bring the crisis under control and to force through the allied treaties that brought Western Germany into NATO and restored its full sovereignty.

The German-American partnership was symbolized by the relationship between Dulles and Adenauer, the two champions of the "policy of strength", which held that Western unity and military power would not only preserve Western freedom but in the end roll back the advanced frontiers of the Soviet Empire and in the process liberate East Germany. Adenauer not only admired Dulles but had a deep personal affection for him. I once witnessed a striking, even if rather comical, example of this. In March 1960, there was a conference on German affairs at Princeton University that the distinguished Germanist Viktor Lange and I had organized, and the university invited the Chancellor, who was planning a trip to the United States, to come to Princeton on the opening evening to receive an honorary degree and make an address. He accepted, and his address, a rather prosaic and uninspiring affair, was sent to Princeton in advance so that Lange could translate it and read it after the Chancellor had delivered it in German. On the appointed evening, after receiving the degree, the Chancellor drew the speech from his pocket, looked at it as if he had never seen it before, and began to read it. He then paused, as if struck by a sudden thought, perhaps—at least this was my belief—that Princeton was the alma mater of Dulles, who had died the previous May. Decisively, he pushed the manuscript aside and delivered an extemporaneous eulogy of Dulles as statesman, as European, and as friend. I was very moved by it. Lange was less so. He was sitting in the front row with the translation of the speech that had not been delivered and, since he had no other option, when the Chancellor sat down, he got up and dutifully read it.

The intimacy of the relationship between the governments of West Germany and the United States, which reached its height during the fifties, is generally the first thing we remember about the Adenauer regime. It is only very recently, indeed only within the last two years, that we have learned about the extent to which Adenauer himself developed doubts about the partnership. In the second volume of his remarkable biography of Adenauer, based upon the Chancellor's personal papers and CDU and other archives that have not been available to other scholars, Hans-Peter Schwarz shows how Adenauer's deep pessimism about the human condition and potentiality, about which I spoke briefly at the beginning of these remarks, affected his judgement and reduced his policy in his last years to an incoherence that dismayed his friends and brought his career to an end. Schwarz, a great admirer of the Chancellor, intimates that part of the trouble was that Adenauer was always a *Besserwisser* who was convinced that other people, even when they were heads of government in other countries, did not understand their own interests as well as he did (his inability to keep this view to himself caused Prime Minister Harold MacMillan to write in his diary, not once but frequently, "Adenauer is half mad!"). This was compounded by an obsessive conviction that any overtures to the Soviet Union were by their very nature, dangerous, and any agreement potentially disastrous.

In December 1955, the German ambassador in London, Hans Herwarth von Bittenfeld, had a talk with Ivone Kirkpatrick of the British Foreign Office about the British position at the recent Foreign Ministers Conference in Geneva, which had been that the Western Powers would be willing to conclude any reasonable security arrangement with the Soviet Union, provided it grant free elections in Germany and assure any future united German government of complete freedom for its domestic and foreign policy. Herwarth said he had talked with Adenauer about this and that the Chancellor wanted the British government to know that he did not think much of it. He had no confidence in the German people and regarded the integration of Germany in the West as more important than reunification.

Adenauer was flattered to hear that, in a pause during the Geneva meeting, Dulles had said to the German observer, "If we love Germany, it is because we have unlimited confidence in the Federal Chancellor," but this did not prevent him from becoming increasingly critical of American policy. Even his friend Dulles was not exempt from this criticism. Dulles traveled too much, he said, implying that he was not intent enough on the German question; and, when Dulles pointed out to him, on one occasion, that the United States, as a world power could not confine its concerns to Europe alone, he was deeply worried. He became affected by a nagging premonition that the superpowers were bent on making an arrangement at Germany's expense. Almost everything that happened in the world he saw in German terms and found suspicious. The Austrian State Treaty of 1955, which freed Austria from Soviet occupation at the cost of neutralization, was a *Schweinerei* that would encourage people to seek a similar solution for Germany.

The plan of the Polish Foreign Minister Adam Rapacki for a nuclear-free zone in Germany and Poland he regarded as a Russian trap, and the fact that George F. Kennan devoted his 1957 Reith Lectures to this plan and the disengagement idea in general struck him as an ominous circumstance. The collaboration of the United States and Soviet Union in the United Nations to force British and French troops out of Suez in 1956 he regarded as either politically naive on the part of the United States or an indication that it was contemplating a division of the world between the two superpowers. He began to lose his faith in Eisenhower, who, he believed, now that Dulles was ill, had fallen under the influence of his brother Milton, who wanted a deal with the Soviet Union. In any case, he grumbled, Eisenhower, like most of the people around him, was lazy and inattentive and had allowed the Soviet Union to win virtual nuclear parity with the United States because he hadn't been watching.

At the same time, the successful launching of the Soviet Sputnik in 1957 convinced him that the United States was falling behind in the race for world mastery, and that in these circumstances German dependence on the United States was dangerous. He began to become preoccupied with the idea of West Germany acquiring a nuclear capacity of its own, perhaps in collaboration with France. Adenauer, to be sure, didn't know much about nuclear weapons, as his statement (at a press conference in April 1957) that tactical nuclear weapons were merely an extension of artillery, made clear; and, in any case, his tentative plan for developing nuclear weapons with the French died when de Gaulle came to power in June 1958. But his nuclear fixation was a sign of his growing doubts about the reliability of the Americans.

Five months later, the diplomatic dovecotes were fluttered with a vengeance by Khrushchev's note, demanding that the Western Allies withdraw their forces from Berlin and announcing that Soviet functions in the city would be turned over to the East German government; and the next four years were never entirely free from the possibility that the Russians really meant what they said and would use force if they were resisted. In this period, Adenauer's faith in the Anglo-Saxon powers steadily dwindled. His friend Dulles seemed bereft of expedients and vacillated between devising elaborate legal schemes that would give the Russians what they wanted without admitting it and blood-curdling brinkmanship scenarios that risked the use of nuclear weapons in Berlin. President Eisenhower, without much reflection on the matter, suggested to Harold MacMillan that a willingness to recognize the

Oder-Neisse line might be useful in solving the crisis. MacMillan himself embarked on a personal visit to Moscow to sound out the Soviet leaders and see what he could come up with. All of this seemed to confirm Adenauer's darkest suspicions. In his mind, the Anglo-Saxon powers were bent on appeasement.

Here is not the place to try to tell the complicated story of the series of Berlin crises of the years from 1958 to1962. In his summary statement about them, Hans-Peter Schwarz ventures the opinion that, "with a combination of stubbornness and intermittent hints of willingness to compromise, the Chancellor in fact succeeded in preserving the city unscathed through four years of intense Soviet pressure."

This is certainly an over-statement. That Berlin was not lost during this difficult period was due to a number of complicated factors, which included Khrushchev's disinclination to push things to a point that would threaten hostilities; his mistake, after the U-2 incident, of breaking up the Paris summit in 1960, where he might indeed have gotten much of what he wanted (Adenauer remarked after the summit's collapse, "Wir haben nochmals fies Jlück jehabt!"); his decision in August 1961 to settle for half of what he wanted by authorizing the building of the Wall; and his subsequent folly in abandoning a concentrated strategy for a diffuse one and becoming involved in the Cuban affair. Seen against this background, Adenauer's role was minor, although certainly not unimportant. He contributed to the final result by stubborn opposition and detailed criticism of all Allied plans for meeting the Soviets halfway, by producing elaborate but generally impracticable solutions of his own, consideration of which slowed the process, and perhaps also by hinting that he might meet with Khrushchev himself if worse came to worst, which would have alarmed his Western Allies. The German ambassador in Moscow, Hans Kroll, kept reporting that Khrushchev had told him repeatedly that the whole Berlin business could be solved quite handily if he and Adenauer could sit down together. The Chancellor had no desire for such a tête-à-tête, but he may have suggested artfully that he had the option.

However that may be, in the course of these dangerous four years, Adenauer's suspicion of London and Washington grew darker. This was particularly true in the Kennedy years. The Chancellor was not able to establish a relationship of confidence with the young president and the people around him, who, John McCloy told him rather indiscreetly in January 1962, were a bunch of professors who had perhaps earlier had to decide whether someone got an honorary degree or became a full professor but had never in their lives been confronted with a decision that posed a dilemma. On their part, the President and his advisers had little patience with the old man in Rhondorf, who seemed to them to represent an age long past, and, shaken up as they were by the building of the Wall and suspecting that worse was to come, they were over-anxious to reach an agreement. In April 1962, Alan Lightner, the U.S. Minister in Berlin, told me gloomily that he had the gravest fears that President Kennedy would be gulled by the Soviets into giving up the city, and added, "We've just got to get Bobby Kennedy over here to see what the situation's really like." Later that month, a new American negotiation paper intended as a basis for talks between Dean Rusk and Ambassador Dobrynin caused consternation in Bonn, leading Adenauer to tell Paul Nitze that it was equivalent to granting East Germany de facto recognition. An unedifying squabble ensued, with Rusk accusing the Germans of leaking exaggerated versions of the paper to the press and making it clear that he could no longer work with the German ambassador, Wilhelm Grewe.

The peaceful ending of the Cuban missile crisis and Kennedy's visit to Berlin in June 1963 lowered the temperature of international affairs and brought things back into perspective. But Adenauer's faith in the United States did not recover. In his view, the only truly faithful ally had been de Gaulle, who had steadfastly refused to consider any negotiations on Berlin until the Soviet threat was withdrawn and had been openly critical of Anglo-Saxon appeasement. Ever since his conference with de Gaulle at Rambouillet in July 1960, Adenauer had seemed to be under the spell of the man the Americans irreverently called Big Charlie, and he now became increasingly insistent that German policy should be reoriented around a Franco-German axis.

Adenauer has often been compared with Bismarck, and the similarities are indeed striking, if not always flattering. Certainly in its complexity and deviousness Adenauer's policy in his last active years resembles Bismarck's conduct in the great Bulgarian crisis of 1887, of which a distinguished British historian once wrote that it was so complicated that it indicated "that the old gentleman had slightly lost his head."

Adenauer had always been in favor of a reconciliation with France; that idea had been as much a part of his political philosophy as NATO, EURATOM, the Common Market, and European unification. But, in turning toward de Gaulle in 1962, Adenauer was not merely celebrating, or reemphasizing, an old relationship; he was giving every indication of a willingness to accept ideas that contradicted the principles that had guided his policy since 1949. For de Gaulle did not believe in a genuinely European community, but a Europe of Fatherlands; he was not a supporter of NATO in its present form but wanted fundamental changes in its command structure; and he was opposed to British membership in the Common Market. Herbert Blankenhorn, Adenauer's long-time advisor on foreign politics, was appalled. De Gaulle, he warned, was seeking to bind Germany to an alliance that would split Europe into two camps, an English and a French one, that would destroy NATO and lead the Americans to withdraw their troops from Europe, that would not be accepted by the electorate in the long run, and that would destroy Adenauer's historical reputation. The suggested new course was simply not rational foreign policy.

Blankenhorn's argument was so obviously logical that one must wonder about Adenauer's motives. They were probably mixed and, from the policy point of view, irresponsible. He was certainly moved by a desire to lash out demonstratively against Anglo-American appeasement, but his radical change of front was also a malicious attempt to undercut the Atlanticist policy of Ludwig Erhard, his putative successor, and to saddle him with a policy he couldn't sustain, and it smacked also of a desire to revenge himself on his foreign minister, Gerhard Schrîder, who, he was convinced, was negotiating with the Americans behind his back. One could think of other motives, including a reversion to his old lack of faith in the German people, now that their faith in his judgment appeared to be waning. When Blankenhorn said to him that Germany had twice committed the sin of binding itself to weak allies, in 1914 and 1939, and that it must not make such a commitment again, Adenauer retorted that it was necessary to bind the Germans. Otherwise, they would suddenly go over to the Russians or try to dance between the blocs. The Germans were politically stupid; they were political dreamers. And they had become soft.

In any event, Blankenhorn was right. The suggested new course was unacceptable to Adenauer's own party, which suspected that it would have disastrous political consequences, and the party took advantage of the public outcry against Adenauer's behavior in the notorious *Spiegel* case of October 1962 (when he sought to prosecute the editors of the Hamburg news weekly for high treason because of a story they had printed about NATO maneuvers) to exact a promise from the old man that he would retire from office in 1963. Before that time came, he got his treaty with France, but it was a Treaty of Friendship without significant political conditions.

Konrad Adenauer stepped down in October 1963, an event that foreshadowed a significant change in West German foreign policy: on the one hand a reaffirmation of the tie with the West but on the other an end to the old inflexible Policy of Strength. Three months earlier, at the Political Academy in Tutzing, there was a symposium on German reunification, in the course of which Egon Bahr of the SPD argued for a new approach to the East, a "policy of small steps" that would bring about "change through rapprochement." Bahr's slogan, *Wandel durch Annäherung*, proved to have a wide public appeal and affected even members of Adenauer's own party. It was to become the principle that animated the *Ostpolitik*, or new Eastern policy, of Willy Brandt after 1969, but it is often forgotten that the first steps in Ostpolitik were taken by Gerhard Schröder of the CDU during the government of the Great Coalition in 1968.

When we think of Tutzing, therefore, we think of Bahr's speech, but Bahr was not the guest of honor at that symposium. Konrad Adenauer was, and in his remarks, after discussing the Soviet Union's internal problems, he pleaded against any accommodation with the Soviets until they had foresworn their policy of aggression. He believed, he said, that "only the next generation will see the verdict in this great struggle." Until that time, perhaps decades in the future, West Germany and her allies must remain "armed and ready for action." Adenauer remained until the end unpersuaded by Bahr's policy of Entspannung and did not believe it could advance the reunification of his country. Only if the government remained resolute, unyielding, and patient would that come to pass. In one of his last speeches, at the CDU party congress in March 1966, the former Chancellor said:

> We remain convinced that Germany must be reunited in peace ... I will not give up hope that one day the Soviet Union will realize that this division of Europe is not to its advantage. We must watch to see when that moment comes, and when a time nears or seems to near that presents a favorable opportunity, then we must not leave it unused.

In his audience on that March day was the 34-year-old chairman of the CDU in Rheinland-Pfalz, Helmut Kohl. Thirty-three years later, when the moment that Adenauer had foreseen arrived, Kohl followed his old leader's advice. Now that unification has come to Germany, a debate has begun over the question whether the greater credit for having brought it about belongs to Konrad Adenauer or to the proponents of *Wandel durch Annäherung*. Proponents of the former school argue that *Ostpolitik* did nothing but legitimize the governments of East Germany and the other satellite states and allowed them to hang on for another thirty years while doing nothing to alleviate the suffering of their peoples and that Adenauer policy would have united Germany much sooner. Advocates of the latter view argue that this overlooks the extreme danger of nuclear war during the late Adenauer years and insist that the great merit of *Ostpolitik* was that, as Willy Brandt once said, it stopped the peoples of the East from regarding West Germany as a revanchist power and a threat to peace and that this gradually encouraged a loosening of ties with Moscow that undermined the strength of the Soviet Empire. This is not a debate that is going to end soon, and the argument that both the Adenauer policy and Ostpolitik helped prepare the way for unification is not going to restrain politicians and publicists, and, alas!, even historians, from doing what they like to do best, indulging their prejudices. We can leave them to it, hoping that in their zeal they will not forget that Konrad Adenauer should be remembered not only for what he did for unification but for what he did for Europe.

Aside from that, it should be remembered, as we have been speaking of Adenauer's mounting suspicion of the United States and his predilection in 1962 for France, that in 1989, when it became apparent that unification was a real possibility, and when Helmut Kohl came forward with his Ten-Point Program, the British were shocked and the French incensed, and Mitterand went all the way to Kiev to try to persuade Gorbachev to do something to prevent it. Only the United States was genuinely supportive, and President Bush and Ambassador Vernon Walter did what they could to remove the difficulties in Helmut Kohl's way.

2. THE UNITED STATES AND THE ARMAMENT OF THE FEDERAL REPUBLIC OF GERMANY*

Reiner Pommerin

While the Allies were still fighting the armed forces of the "Third Reich," military and political leaders in the West paradoxically began to express concerns about the consequences of a victory over Germany. At the First Quebec Conference in August 1943, the American Chief of Staff, General George C. Marshall, "raised for only a moment the curtain on a question that was later to loom large in Western thinking."[1] Marshall told Sir Alan Brooke that "he would be interested to know the British Chief of Staff's view on the possible results of the situation in Russia with regard to the deployment of Allied Forces—for example, in the event of an overwhelming Russian success, would the Germans be likely to facilitate our entry into the country to repel the Russians?"[2]

Although Brooke did not share Marshall's view of the Russians,[3] the question of the American Chief of Staff was symptomatic of the deep distrust that characterized relations between the Western democracies and the Soviet Union despite the Grand Alliance. That history of differences reached back to 1917 on the part of the Western Allies. It began

---

*The Federal Republic of Germany could not have been *rearmed* because it did not exist before 1949. The term *remilitarization* is also completely misleading for a second reason: The citizens of the new state, which was based on the democratic Basic Law, had no interest in rebuilding a society dominated by the rules and values of a military class, as it had been in the Wilhelminien era. As a result, with the concept of the *Innere Führung* the Bundeswehr after 1956 trained its soldiers as "citizens in uniform."

with the suspicion of the Soviet Union's policy of worldwide revolution, while on the Soviet side it began with the Western intervention against the Bolsheviks. After Hitler's attack on the Soviet Union much of this history was seemingly reversed. Actually it was only "that war breeds strange bedfellows,"[4] and the new understanding would turn out to be only temporary.

Two years after Marshall's discussion with Brooke, at a time when Britain, the United States, and the USSR were in the last stages of fighting against an all-but-defeated Germany, the Yalta Conference took place, attended by Franklin D. Roosevelt, Sir Winston Churchill, and Josef Stalin. The West, and especially the president of the United States, still hoped that the war-time alliance could be transformed into a long lasting peacetime cooperation.

At Yalta, the Allies decided not to dismember Germany but laid the ground for its complete disarmament. The German military forces were to be disbanded and all arms destroyed. The terms were specified in the Treaty of Demilitarization of Germany:

(a) The German armed forces, including the Army, Navy, Luftwaffe and any auxiliaries, however designated, are and remain completely disarmed, demobilized and disbanded.
(b) The German General Staff is broken up for all time.
(c) No German military organization by whatever name or designation, or in whatever form or guise, is permitted to be established or operate in Germany or abroad.[5]

Despite the agreement on German demilitarization, anxiety about the future course of the Soviet Union now grew in Great Britain as well. This was clearly shown by the words of the "iron-curtain-telegram" that Churchill sent to President Harry S. Truman on 12 May 1945: "What will be the position in a year or two when the British and American armies have melted, and the French have not been formed on any major scale, and when Russia may choose to keep 200 or 300 divisions on active service?"[6]

Churchill was not yet able to convince the American government of the Soviet threat, but he took action on his own. He made a decision that for obvious reasons had to be kept absolutely secret. He some years later astounded an audience at his constituency at Woodford with the admission that "Even before the war had ended and while the Germans were surrendering by hundreds of thousands, and our streets were crowded with cheering people, I telegraphed to Lord Montgomery directing him to be careful in collecting the German arms to stack them so that they could easily be issued again to the German soldiers whom we should have to work with if the Soviet advance continued."[7]

Churchill's bold step was motivated by a number of considerations. Seeing National Socialist Germany as a variant of Prussian-German militarism,[8] he looked at Germany as a potential partner in his efforts to stop the Soviet armies from moving into northwestern Europe. The perception that the United States was about to leave the European continent, as it had announced before, and the fear that, in view of the decline of France, Britain would have to face the USSR alone, also prompted Churchill to take preliminary measures to be ready to stop the Communist advance before the war had ended.

Even after Churchill had turned over his office to the Labour leader Clement Attlee, attempts to maintain German forces in British hands continued for some time. This was not hidden from the Russians. Months after the war in Europe had ended, the Soviet Union continued to charge Britain with keeping a large German army in a state of preparedness. These charges, generally accompanied by details of names, places, and units in training in the British zone of occupation, were, as we know now, based on facts.

Still, the significance of these developments should not be exaggerated. After the German surrender, the Western democracies fulfilled their wartime pledges and quickly began to demobilize. Within weeks after Japan's surrender, American combat capability began eroding. Most American and British forces were withdrawn from the European continent and disbanded. American and British forces in Europe after demobilization in 1946 numbered only 391,000 and 488,000 respectively. In contrast, the Soviet Union, as Churchill had predicted, kept its war industries going and its armed forces on a war footing. In 1946 the strength of the forces of the Soviet Union amounted to some six million men.

By the spring of the same year, when the fusion of the Social Democratic and Communist parties had led to a serious deterioration in British-Soviet relations,[9] and the Cold War had started in earnest, the German wartime forces had been completely disbanded. But for the military planners in East and West there was no doubt about the value of the German soldier, and both sides soon started to think about the use of the military potential in their zones of occupation. "As prospects waned that East and West could agree on methods to deal with the Germans as a common danger, Germany increasingly assumed the aspect of a prize to be won."[10]

In January 1946 the Historical Division of the U.S. Army established an Operational History (German) Section. It was intended that high-ranking former officers of the Wehrmacht, led by *Generaloberst* a.D. Franz Halder, were to help write the official history of the U.S. Army in the second World War. But very quickly, the topics of their papers changed from historical reminiscences to concerns about the present and future. Plan of attack by the USSR on Western Europe, possible barriers to the East, options to defend the territory east of the Rhine, and the future of warfare itself were among the subjects considered. The German generals were of course flattered that the victor in the war asked for their experiences, especially because this time the generals seemed to be ideologically, politically, and militarily on the right side.[11]

The former generals of the Wehrmacht also thought about ways to defend Western Europe with the help of experienced German soldiers who had already fought against the Red Army. The former Lieutenant-General Wilhelm Schmalz, who had been commander of the "Hermann Göring" tank division, considered a European army without separate national contingents to be the best solution. This concept, which anticipated the Pleven Plan, according to Schmalz could also promote West European political integration. Others suggested German divisions under an Allied command or border troops staffed with German volunteers.[12]

As early as 1947 the U.S. Army began to think about the future place of Germany and Japan in the international strategic balance.[13] The Joint War Plans Branch, at that time still called the Operations and Plans Division of the U.S. Army, offered some highly tentative speculations, which some officers serving with the U.S. Army in Germany in the American occupation zone accepted as well.[14]

At this time, however, the United States had no general strategic plan and its nuclear capability was still very limited. At the end of 1947 the atomic bomb stockpile consisted of 13 bombs, and there were only 32 bombers capable of carrying such bombs.[15] But more important was the fact that in the United States and also in Britain the general staffs still counted on a long period of peace—some 10 to 15 years. The threat posed by the USSR therefore seemed to be much more psychological and economic than military in nature.[16] A future "total war" seemed far more likely in the Middle East or in Asia than in Europe. Colonel Charles E. Bonesteel, the United States Military Attaché in London, was more farsighted: he argued that a united Germany controlled by or allied with the USSR would be a bigger threat for the security of Western civilization than a divided Germany.[17] However, such thoughts, which were obviously in conflict with the official disarmament and demilitarization policy of the United States, remained isolated and by no means indicated a serious change of United States policy, which at the time was that Germany should be kept disarmed.

In 1947 the Joint Chiefs of Staff (JCS) began to realize that the security of the United States was closely connected with that of Western Europe. Moreover, Germany was considered to be the strongest military power of the region. "Without German aid the remaining countries of Western Europe could scarcely be expected to withstand the armies of our ideological opponents until the United States could mobilize and place in the field sufficient armed forces to achieve their defeat. With a revived Germany fighting on the side of the Western Allies this would be a possibility. ... The economic revival of Germany is therefore of primary importance from the viewpoint of United States security."[18] On a list ranking 16 countries in order of their importance to the national security of the United States, Germany was in third position, following Britain and France.

But in the war plan "HALFMOON," which was accepted as the basis for further planning by the JCS after the coup d'état in Czechoslovakia and the start of the blockade of Berlin, West German soldiers as yet had no place.[19] The American forces were still expected to leave Western Europe, and the United States' job was to have been done by the Strategic Air Command flying massive nuclear attacks on targets inside the Soviet Union. France intended to defend itself at the Rhine until support came from the United States and Britain. Britain hoped to be able to keep a war away from her islands, in part by involving the Germans.

As early as January 1948, in a paper submitted to the U.S. Department of State, British Foreign Secretary Ernest Bevin advocated a West German contribution to the defense of Western Europe: "As soon as circumstances permit we should, of course, wish also to include Spain and Germany without whom no Western system can be complete."[20] Field Marshal Viscount Montgomery argued at his WEU Headquarters that West Germany should be made part of the Western defense plans. Recognizing that without the West Germans a true "forward strategy" could not be established,[21] he favored West German association with NATO and the Western Union.

After the Brussels Treaty had been signed in April 1948, the JCS discussed the relations of the United States to the new grouping in Europe. Although the treaty did not mention German armament, the question of new German armed forces was a delicate one. Before the treaty was signed in Brussels, no state had officially suggested the armament of West Germany, now raised with increasing frequency.

As a meeting of the National Security Council in May 1948 showed, the Secretary of the Army and the JCS wanted to leave open the possibility of a later accession of Germany and Spain to the multilateral treaty arrangement. But the State Department's policy was to associate the United States and Europe as soon as possible. At the present time the department thought it inopportune to run the risk of political discord with France by suggesting West German armament.

In the meantime the Soviet Union began to organize a paramilitary police force, the *Kasernierte Volkspolizei*, in their zone of occupation in Germany. Officially this force was needed for the protection of the border, but in actuality it was training cadres for military units.

The blockade of Berlin, which began in June 1948 and lasted 323 days, led to the first, albeit short-lived, public discussion in the print media of defense and armament issues in West Germany. But soon the interest of the press went back to the work of the Parliamentary Council at Bonn which was discussing the Basic Law.

Military experts continued to work behind the scenes, however. Dr. Hans Speidel, a former Lieutenant-General of the Wehrmacht, at this time wrote a memorandum in which he rejected neutrality for West Germany. He believed that German security could be provided only by the military strength of the Western powers. He therefore asked for an American commitment to Europe and a unified military command. He did not advocate armament of West Germany, because he thought this matter was far less important than the protection of West Germany by the Western Allies.

The rumor that Montgomery had come out in favor of a defense at the Rhine prompted additional comments from Speidel in November and December 1948. He objected to a defense line on the Rhine, which to him meant nothing but giving the USSR control over Germany, Austria, and Switzerland. Although he still thought it important to convince the United States to participate in a defense of West Germany and West Europe along the Elbe river, Speidel now suddenly mentioned a West German contribution for the defense of West Germany and Europe. He suggested the formation of German security forces that would consist of armored brigades of 15 divisions under German command within a greater European army.[22]

In December 1948, Speidel met with Konrad Adenauer, at that time President of the Parliamentary Council at Bonn. Adenauer, who would soon be the first Chancellor of the new Federal Republic of Germany, was impressed by Speidel's analysis. In a public statement on 30 January 1949, Adenauer called for a guarantee of German security by the Western powers as well as a defense of Europe on the Elbe.[23] Somewhat later Adenauer also indicated that the FRG would demand "membership of Germany in the North Atlantic security alliance in terms of complete equality."[24]

But the official American policy to continue the disarmament of Germany remained unchanged. In April 1949, Acheson told the Senate Foreign Relations Committee during hearings on the North Atlantic Treaty that "the disarmament and demilitarization of Germany must be complete and absolute ... a discussion of including West Germany in the pact is not possible."[25]

By May 1949 the Berlin Airlift had proved to be an overwhelming success, bolstering Western confidence, but the announcement on 22 September 1949 that the Soviet Union had detonated an atomic device caused consternation in Western military circles and increased the fear in Europe of imminent war with the Soviet Union. The specialists in Washington were surprised the Soviets had developed the atomic bomb so quickly. But they also knew that at least in 1949 or 1950 the Soviets did not have the ability to deliver the atomic bomb effectively.

The birth of NATO was not unanimously welcomed by the Germans. Some former generals even advised against Federal Republic membership in the alliance. In sharp contrast, however, Speidel and Adolf Heusinger, also a former Lieutenant-General, published a paper, asking instead for full incorporation of the Federal Republic into the alliance as an equal partner. They wanted 25 mechanized or armored divisions to defend Europe, 15 of them from the Federal Republic. They also mentioned the need for a strong tactical air force, which they even said should be armed with nuclear weapons. To make it easier for the other West European nations to accept German soldiers, Heusinger and Speidel agreed to an American commander-in-chief; only the divisional commands should remain under national commanders.

In May 1949, a few days after the Parliamentary Council had adopted the Basic Law of the Federal Republic of Germany, General Lucius D. Clay, the American Military Governor, left his post. His newly appointed successor, the American High Commissioner for Germany, John J. McCloy, arrived in Berlin at the beginning of July. Earlier, during discussions with the Department of State about the contents of the "Policy Directive" for his new assignment, McCloy had asked for a statement concerning the future role of the Federal Republic in the West European defense system. But the Department of State, by referring to the well known French attitude toward this question, had declined to include such a statement in the "Policy Directive."[26] Instead, in his meetings with Chancellor Adenauer, McCloy's instructions were only that it still was the policy of the Truman administration "to keep Germany deprived of the means of waging war, so that the country will not be a threat to the independence of other nations or to the peace of the world. To this end the High Commission must maintain an effective system of disarmament control and inspection to be exercised through the Military Security Board."[27] Therefore Article 3 of the Petersberg Agreement stated clearly that the government of the Federal Republic committed itself to a firm intent to demilitarize its territory. A Military Security Office was to supervise this policy.[28]

A memorandum by Assistant Secretary of State George W. Perkins in October 1949 showed that the Department of State was not as prepared as the U.S. military to arm the Federal Republic of Germany. "It is true," wrote the State Department official, "that Pentagon thinking envisages use of German manpower in the defense of Western Europe at some time in the future and under very careful safeguard. It is also true that some lower-ranking officers in Germany may think and talk indiscreetly on this subject. It is not true that the U.S. military authorities favor the prompt rearmament of Germany, or are considering anything like 25 divisions, or favor inclusion of Germany in MAP or the Atlantic Treaty at this time, or that substantial numbers of young men in Germany are drilling in paramilitary organizations. We have no reason whatever to believe, and compelling reasons not to believe, that the military are acting in any way in this field without our knowledge or contrary to the above."[29]

When the retired General Clay, in agreement with the JCS, publicly recommended the formation of a "composite military force of Western European Nations at [to] which Germany could contribute with limited forces of a special type,"[30] the Secretary of State, Dean Acheson, and President Truman both made it quite clear that the United States was not contemplating the creation of a small German army. They both considered this to be a rumor and Truman replied emphatically that statements on this topic were made out of the whole cloth by newspapermen "and that there was not a word of truth in it."[31] But, as the records of the talks between Adenauer an the High Commissioners show,[32] exactly at this time the issue came up frequently during discussions on the Petersberg.

In December 1949 Chancellor Adenauer enlivened public discussion. A month earlier he had already started to give interviews on defense issues to the French newspapers *L'Est Républicain* and *L'Epoque*. He had suggested German soldiers taking part in a European defense system, in which the Federal Republic should be integrated. Surprisingly, at first there was hardly any reaction to his statements.

On 1 December the NATO Defense Council had met in Paris to discuss a strategic concept for Western Europe. Rumors that the council would endorse a defense at the Rhine obviously terrified Adenauer. Three days later he again gave an interview, this time to the *Cleveland Plain Dealer*, which he thought would be read frequently by President Truman. The Chancellor again offered soldiers for a European army. He also declared that if German troops were to be raised they should not serve as mercenaries but on an equal footing with other units. Although the Chancellor referred to such a development as "one for the remote future,"[33] his remarks now caught the attention of the U.S. and European press, which in turn led to discussions in the Federal Republic's Parliament. Polls quickly showed that 60.2 percent of the German population were not willing to join an armed force. Obviously the German government had to tread carefully in view of the opposition of much of its own populace to the idea of armament; still the Chancellor persisted. Adenauer wanted to use armament as a way of cementing the Federal Republic into Western Europe.

On 8 December Adenauer talked to the High Commissioners on the subject of his country's security. He asked for a guarantee that the three nations would defend the Federal Republic in case of a Soviet attack.[34] He would continue to ask for this guarantee every fortnight until May 1950; in February 1950 he even repeated this wish in public. Not untypical for the situation was that on the same day a law called *Beseitigung des Militarismus und Nazismus* was issued by the Allied High Commission.[35]

German armament was acknowledged to be a military necessity, because, without the economic and military power of the Federal Republic, the Western Union Defense Organization and even NATO had little, if any, chance of producing forces to match those of the Soviet Union. But no joint planning on the subject was initiated, as the arming of Germany remained a political problem, not a military one.

In France, almost as soon as the war had ended, high-ranking officers such as General Gaston Hervé Billotte and General Revers began to worry about the future defense of Europe. Motivated, as was true of most of the French officers, by traditional anti-Communist and anti-Soviet attitudes, they tried to develop concepts for a common defense of Europe. Without the support of the United States, such a defense seemed impossible to them. In this context, as General Matthew B. Ridgeway had stated, it soon became obvious that Soviet aggression could not be stopped "without the best infantry of Europe," the German infantry.[36]

After the Treaty of Brussels was signed, the French General Staff did not have to be convinced by the American observers that one could not fight against the Soviet Union east of the Rhine without the support of the Germans living there. The French General Staff itself thought it unreasonable not to take advantage of an unequivocally anti-Communist population, leaving the West Germans unarmed while the East Germans were armed by the Soviet Union. Another argument for armament of the Federal Republic was the suspicion that this country could grow economically much faster than the West European nations if it was not burdened by the costs of maintaining armed forces.

The French generals also began to realize that, due to the costs of the war in Indochina, France was unable to build up the number of forces it had promised for NATO. Therefore, the armament of the Federal Republic became an even more urgent matter for the French General Staff. But the view of the generals was not shared by the majority of the lower-ranking French officers or by most French politicians. Officers serving with the French occupation forces in Germany were especially fearful of German remilitarization. While most French generals supported the idea of an armament of West Germany and believed that the adoption of forward defense implied a German military contribution, French politicians hesitated or even opposed it.

The French National Assembly had approved France's membership in NATO only by adding an amendment that a French approval was necessary for a new member to join the alliance. With the help of this amendment, France had a de facto veto on any German membership. In July 1949 the French Foreign Minister, Robert Schuman, underlined the opinion of his government by stating: "Germany has no army and should not have one. It has no arms and will not have any. ... It was therefore unthinkable, for France and for all her allies, that Germany could be allowed to adhere to the Atlantic pact as a nation capable of defending itself or of aiding in the defense of other nations."[37] The official position of Britain and the United States remained equally plain.

The treatment of West Germany had already moved away from the punitive stage, but the question of armament only five years after the end of the second World War obviously involved some deep seated psychological factors. Some of the fears prevalent at that time in Britain, France, and the United States were expressed by John Foster Dulles, who wrote in early 1950: "Can Germany be held against the Soviet Union, except perhaps by German troops? Does that mean the rearmament of Germany? Will France consent, and what dependence can be placed on rearmed Germany? Can we be sure that they will shoot in what we think is the right direction?"[38]

In Washington in the course of talks between the Army, Air Force, Navy, the Department of State, and the Ministry of Defense, the JCS suggested to Secretary of Defense Louis Arthur Johnson that at the London Conference of the three Western Powers in May the question of an integration of West German military divisions into NATO should be raised.[39] But when the issue was brought up in the higher echelons of the administration, stressing that it was impossible to reach needed manpower and military production levels for the defense of Europe without the Federal Republic, both the State Department and the President objected strongly. As a result, in London, Bevin and Acheson declared that any move to arm the Federal Republic was premature.[40]

Adenauer's security concerns were not lessened in May 1950 when the United States, Britain, and France refused to guarantee the Federal Republic's territorial integrity in the event of war. This refusal forced the Chancellor and his government to think even more seriously about security. Adenauer convened a secret conference of military experts in the summer of 1950 to thrash out a German security policy. The result was the *Himmeroder-Denkschrift*.[41]

Politically, the report said, the Federal Republic required recognition of its equality with the members of NATO and the promise that its territory east of the Rhine would be actively defended. Militarily, the *Denkschrift* advocated a two-stage strategy of mobile defense. The first phase called for a force of 12 to 18 German armored divisions conducting an aggressive defense along the intra-German border. If this aggressive defense failed, a strong and more static defense line should be erected along the Rhine. This required 30 additional divisions taken from other NATO nations. An active German army of 12 divisions, which would be able to expand to 18 divisions and 6 corps headquarters, was planned, with a total of 500,000 men under arms. This report proved to be most influential during the first years of the new Federal Republic's armed forces, the *Bundeswehr*.[42] Adenauer adopted most of its recommendations, for example those concerning the size and composition of the German army. But he strongly rejected the idea that German units alone should guard the intra-German border.

The outbreak of the Korean War showed that the Soviet Union was willing to use armed force. It appeared that Western Europe could now become an additional easy target for the Red Army. The war in Korea became a political turning point and initiated a complete revolution in American foreign policy and in the attitude of the American people.[43] As the memorandum: "Establishment of a European Defense Force" showed, the State Department now suddenly shared the JCS's view that reliance on the Federal Republic was necessary for the defense of Western Europe. Still more important, the President, too, decided on 9 September, to support armament of the Federal Republic.

But France, however, still opposed the formation of national West German forces. Even before the Conference of the Foreign Ministers of the three Western Powers in New York on 12 September, Foreign Minister Schuman made it clear that France was not yet willing to accept German armament.[44] In New York, the United States directly linked the quest for West German soldiers with the offer of American assistance for the defense of West Europe. After considerable pressure by the United States and Britain, France approved the recruitment of West German soldiers in principle. Schuman was only able to delay the official French declaration of consent. Knowing the mood of the French Parliament and public and fearing a political crisis, Schuman, working together with Jean Monnet, proposed armament of the Federal Republic within a European framework, the so-called Pleven Plan. Prime Minister René Pleven proposed building a European army, merging troops and equipment completely and controlling this force with an integrated political and military authority. But the Federal Republic was not granted complete equality, and the discrimination against the Federal Republic became obvious when Pleven added a series of additional safeguards.

The JCS so far had opposed sending any new American forces to Europe until more military resources had been made available within Europe itself. The American price for reinforcing Europe was arming the Federal Republic and incorporating German forces into NATO. Now, as he later wrote, President Truman finally became convinced that "without Germany, the defense of Europe was a rear guard action on the shores of the Atlantic Ocean. With Germany, there could be a defense in depth, powerful enough to offer effective resistance to aggression from the East. The logic behind this situation is very plain. Any map will show it, and a little arithmetic will prove what the addition of German manpower means to the strength of the joint defense of Europe."[45]

The French proposal raised major doubts about its military viability, and the United States at first refused to support it. Constant British and American pressure on France—and American readiness for a compromise

—eventually led to the acceptance of the Spofford Plan, although its implementation was postponed. Under this plan, West German regimental combat teams, tactical air units, and a small naval force would be organized by a Federal minister of works under control of the High Commission. In December 1950 both NATO's Military Committee and the council agreed to the Spofford Plan and to the participation of the Federal Republic in the defense of Europe.[46] At the request of the council, Eisenhower was appointed as Supreme Allied Commander Europe (SACEUR). But the specific role that the Federal Republic should play in the defense remained unclear, and the Pleven Plan was never ratified by the parliaments of the member states.

For the United States the proposed European Defense Community (EDC) became more and more attractive. It seemed a way of achieving both the armament of the Federal Republic and the political integration of Europe. To this end the State Department, with the consent of the JCS, prepared a paper for the Truman-Pleven conference in January 1951. The President should "(1) declare emphatically that a unified neutralized Germany was unacceptable to the United States and (2) accentuate the importance of pressing negotiations to develop a new contractual relationship with Western Germany."[47]

A JCS review of the current world situation and the ability of the American forces currently under arms to meet United States commitments came to the following conclusion with respect to Germany: "The Soviets apparently realized much earlier than did the West that Germany is the key to the future of Europe. Accordingly, the Soviets now dominate East Germany and have created a large quasi-military East German police force. The visible military might and power of the USSR are affecting adversely the Western orientation of West Germany."[48] The JCS recognized that France was still afraid of a resurgent, militaristic Germany and the Germans would therefore be unlikely to be permitted to create defense forces in the context of NATO. If France would continue to vacillate and did not rapidly build up her military strength, the United States might be forced to review its strategic policy toward continental Europe. And the review's conclusion was: "A Germany oriented toward or dominated by the USSR increases enormously the chances of victory for the East in the event of general war."[49]

For the Central Intelligence Agency (CIA) Board of National Estimates it was unlikely that the USSR would use overt military action against armament of the Federal Republic. But "West German militarization will be used by the USSR as 'justification' for retaining and perhaps increasing its own forces in East Germany and in the other Satellites ... The Grotewohl letter is designed to encourage both East and West Germans to take some initiative towards the achievement of unification, and to submit a common proposal to the consideration of the four occupying powers."[50]

The U.S. Senate held hearings in February on the proposal to send additional troops to Europe. Eisenhower testified in favor, claiming that with 40 divisions (active and reserve) NATO could conduct an effective resistance to a Soviet assault. Defense Secretary Marshall echoed this optimistic view. Claiming that at that time morale was the greatest factor, Marshall argued that the American force would constitute a keystone for NATO's efforts. The JCS agreed, claiming that ground troops were necessary to repel an invasion of Western Europe. Even the Air Force Chief, General Hoyt S. Vandenberg, admitted that the Soviets could overrun Europe despite losses inflicted by strategic bombing if no delaying force existed on the ground. The Senate, on 4 April, approved both the dispatch of the troops and Eisenhower's appointment as NATO commander.

It had become obvious that the American military favored a mobile defense. But any delaying action in Europe was certain to unsettle France. In April 1951, de Gaulle claimed that Britain and the United States intended to abandon the continent to the Soviets. A defense based on delaying tactics meant to de Gaulle only another Dunkirk-style evacuation. He believed his two allies were in reality disposed to limit their effort to defense of a few points: England, Spain, and a Breton redoubt. Indeed, the American war plan OFFTACKLE envisioned a withdrawal from the continent, and, in November 1951, the JCS even approved a scheme that contemplated an American retreat to Spain and Britain. It was as a result of Montgomery's persistent work that Supreme Headquarters Allied Powers Europe (SHAPE) was ordered in May 1951 to draw up a plan for the overall defense of Europe and assumed the use of German forces in this effort.

Eisenhower successfully linked the political problem of German participation with the military problem of building an adequate NATO force. The general's review of the NATO defense plan in August 1951, according to the State Department, was, "the first plan based on the forward strategy," and, the assessment continued, "he hits the German problem head on. The report flatly states that the required force must contain a substantial German element ... Eisenhower has masterfully impaled our allies on the horns of a dilemma—military versus political.

They can assume an intolerable military burden or they can agree to accept Germany as a political equal."⁵¹

In July 1951, after the establishment of the EDC had been proposed in Paris, the JCS sent a memorandum to President Truman, who approved the course of action the document recommended on 2 August.

> It seems to us desirable that you should determine certain general principles which will guide U.S. policy in bringing about most effectively and most rapidly German participation in the defense of Western Europe without arousing European antagonisms which would militate against continued European co-operation in the defense effort. ...
> 1. Agreement on the creation of a European Defense Force which would serve under NATO.
> 2. A specific plan for raising German contingents at the earliest possible date; and
> 3. A political arrangement with Germany restoring substantial German sovereignty. ...
> In regard to the contractual arrangements with Germany ... , we must move broadly and decisively in creating a new status for Germany. ...⁵²

At the beginning of the talks on the EDC in London in February 1952, Adenauer had suggested that a sentence assuring equal supply of arms to German contingents should apply to arms "of all kinds." But he quickly accepted a U.S.-U.K. redraft limiting this assurance to arms of types "necessary to fulfill Ger[many's] assigned task to [the] def[ense] of Europe."⁵³ After intensive diplomatic maneuvering, the allies signed the EDC Treaty in Paris in May 1952.

The signing of the EDC treaty seemed to give additional assurance that all of Western Europe would be defended. The signatories, Italy, France, Britain, Belgium, the Netherlands, and the Federal Republic, pledged to form an army, composed of national units of division-size, under an integrated high command. The new force's equipment, training, and organization would be supervised by SACEUR, and the EDC army would be placed at NATO's disposal.

Most importantly, the treaty authorized the formation of a West German military composed of army, air force, and navy units in an active force. France, faced simultaneously with increasing colonial problems in Algeria and Indochina and with the need to build a European-based army, had softened its stance on German armament. However, by the end of 1952 the treaty had not been ratified by any of the signatories. Strong elements in the French government and parliament opposed to the formation of a German army blocked passage. And in Germany, the opposition party, the Social Democrats (SPD), warned that an armed

German State could provoke Soviet opposition and possible preemptive action. Confusion about France's position led to rumors in the summer of 1952 that the French would withdraw their forces from Germany if the Soviets attacked. Repeated denials from SHAPE convinced no one.

Any hope of arming the Germans under the auspices of the EDC soon evaporated. By the summer of 1954 only three nations had ratified the treaty: the Netherlands, Luxembourg, and the Federal Republic of Germany. In France, after months of negotiations and stalling, events finally came to a head on 30 August 1954, when the question was put to a vote in the French National Assembly. In the face of a weak government defense of the treaty, a resolution opposing ratification was passed by a margin of 319 to 264.[54] "The Adenauer government, with the backing of its main sponsor, the United States, had helped to replace the Pleven-Plan with the EDC treaty, but while the former was not acceptable to the FRG, the latter was not acceptable to France."[55]

Prior to NATO's adoption of a nuclear strategy, a German military contribution to NATO was considered by many to be militarily essential if a forward defense was to be successful. This opinion did not change with the onset of President Eisenhower's "New Look" and the strategy of "Massive retaliation" written down in the MC 48. Due to the reduced American force levels in Europe, a German army became even more important. Immediately after he received the news about the fate of the EDC from Paris, Eisenhower sent Secretary of State John Foster Dulles to Paris to organize a NATO meeting.

With the help of Britain's Foreign Secretary, Sir Anthony Eden, who promised to both the United States and France that Britain would keep forces in the Federal Republic as long as necessary, Adenauer, following conferences in London and Paris, accepted a limitation of the size of the Bundeswehr to 12 divisions and a total of 500,000 men. The Federal Republic pledged not to produce biological, chemical, and nuclear weapons; and the establishment of a general staff and a military role independent of NATO was not allowed. Italy and the Federal Republic were to become members of the WEU, and the Federal Republic would be brought into NATO as a sovereign member. The new agreement was reached easily, and the accord was signed in Paris on 23 October 1954. The Federal Republic of Germany became a member of NATO on 5 May 1955.

At the end of 1954 the National Assembly of France finally accepted the London and Paris accords. Indignation in Bonn and Washington soon gave way to what was almost a sense of satisfaction after the powers had decided to integrate the Federal Republic into the NATO framework. Most of the FRG's senior officials resented the waste of time, but "the NATO solution, of course, had been their preference all along."[56]

On the development of the strategic concepts of NATO—"Massive Retaliation" and "Flexible Response"—the Federal Republic had no influence at all.[57] Only after the Standing Group was dissolved and the Nuclear Planning Group began its work in 1968 did the Federal Republic begin to move in the direction Adenauer had indicated in September 1952, four years before the first soldier was wearing the uniform of the Bundeswehr. In a speech to the leaders of the CDU he claimed: "It is of eminent importance for Germany to gain more influence on the strategy of defense to get the chance to keep a nuclear war away from our country."[58]

Notes

1. Forrest C. Pogue, *George C. Marshall: Organizer of Victory, 1943–1945* (New York, 1973), 249.
2. "Meeting of the Combined Chiefs of Staff, 20 August 1943," *Foreign Relations of the United States* (hereafter cited as *FRUS*), The Conference at Washington and Quebec, 1943 (Washington, 1970), part B, 911.
3. See John Baylis, "British wartime thinking about a post-war European Security Group," *Review of International Studies* 9 (1983), 265–81.
4. Arthur L. Smith, *Churchill's German Army: Wartime Strategy and Cold War Politics, 1943–1947* (Beverly Hills, 1977), 22.
5. "Draft Treaty prepared by the Deputy Foreign Economic Administrator (Cox), 17 February 1945," *FRUS 1945* (Washington, 1968), 3: part A, 425.
6. *The North Atlantic Treaty Organization: Facts and Figures* (Brussels, 1989), 3.
7. Smith, 11–12.
8. Bundesministerium für Innerdeutsche Beziehungen (Hrsg.), *Dokumente zur Deutschlandpolitik*, I. Reihe/Band.1 (Frankfurt am Main, 1984), X–XLVII.
9. See Reiner Pommerin, "Die Zwangsvereinigung von KPD und SPD zur SED: Eine britische Analyse vom April 1946," *Vierteljahrshefte für Zeitgeschichte* 36 (no. 2, April 1988), 319–38.
10. Lawrence W. Martin, "The American Decision To Rearm Germany," Harold Stein, ed., *American Civil-Military Decisions: A Book of Case Studies* (Birmingham, Alabama, 1963), 645.
11. Christian Greiner, "Operational History (German) Section und Naval Historical Team. Deutsches militärstrategisches Denken im Dienst der amerikanischen Streitkräfte von 1946 bis 1950," *Militärgeschichte: Probleme- Thesen- Wege, im Auftrag des Militärgeschichtlichen Forschungsamtes aus Anlß seines 25jährigen Bestehens* ausgewählt und zusammengestellt von Manfred Messerschmidt, Klaus A. Maier, Werner Rahn und Bruno Thoß (Stuttgart, 1982), 409–35.
12. Ibid., 422–23.
13. Hermann-Josef Rupieper, *Der besetzte Verbündete: Die amerikanische Deutschlandpolitik 1949–1955* (Opladen, 1991), 100.

14. Robert McGeehan, *The German Rearmament Question: American Diplomacy and European Defense after World War II* (Chicago, 1971), 16.
15. Michael D. Yaffe, *A Higher Priority than the Korean War! The Crash Programs to Modify the Bombers for the Bomb*, paper presented at the Nuclear History Program's 4th Study and Review Conference, Sophia-Antipolis, France, 23–27 June 1993, 6.
16. James F. Schnabel, *The History of the Joint Chiefs of Staff: The Joint Chiefs of Staff and National Policy*, vol. 1: 1945–1947 (Wilmington, 1979), 131–32.
17. Wolfgang Krieger, *General Lucius D. Clay und die amerikanische Deutschlandpolitik 1945–1949* (Stuttgart, 1987), 269.
18. "Report by the Joint Strategic Survey Commission to the Joint Chiefs of Staff, 29 April 1947," *FRUS 1947*, 1: 740–41.
19. Christian Greiner, "The Defense of Western Europe and the Rearmament of West Germany, 1947–1950," Olaf Riste, ed., *Western Security: The Formative Years: European and Atlantic Defense 1947–1953* (Oslo, 1984), 150–77.
20. "Summary of a memorandum representing Mr. Bevin's views on the formation of a Western Union, 13 January 1948," *FRUS 1948* (Washington, 1976), 3: 5.
21. Bernhard L. Montgomery, *The Memoirs of Field Marshall Montgomery* (New York, 1958), 457–58.
22. Hans Speidel, *Aus unserer Zeit. Erinnerungen* (Berlin, 1977), 249–52.
23. Gerhard Wettig, *Politik im Rampenlicht: Aktionsweisen moderner Aussenpolitik* (Frankfurt am Main, 1967), 93.
24. *Die Welt*, 31 March 1949.
25. Martin, 646.
26. Rupieper, 35–36.
27. "Policy Directive for the United States High Commissioner for Germany (Mc Cloy), 17 November 1949," *FRUS 1949* (Washington, 1974), 3: 325.
28. *Keesings Archiv der Gegenwart*, 1948/49, 2143.
29. "Memorandum by the Assistant Secretary of State for European Affairs (Perkins) to the Secretary of State (Acheson), 11 October 1949," *FRUS 1949, 3:* 286.
30. "The Secretary of State to the United States High Commissioner for Germany (McCloy), 21 November 1949," ibid., 340.
31. Ibid., 341.
32. *Akten zur Auswärtigen Politik der Bundesrepublik Deutschland*, hrsg. von Hans-Peter Schwarz unter Mitarbeit von Reiner Pommerin, Band. 1: Adenauer und die Hohen Kommissare, 1949–1951. Bearbeitet von Frank-Lothar Kroll und Manfred Nebelin (München, 1989),(hereafter cited as Schwarz, *Adenauer, Bd.1*).
33. Wettig, 96.
34. Schwarz, *Adenauer, Bd.1*, 54–55.
35. *Keesings Archiv der Gegenwart*, 1949, 2170.
36. For the attitude of the French generals towards the armament of the FRG but against the EVG, see Pierre Guillen, "Die französische Generalität, die Aufrüstung der Bundesrepublik und die EVG (1950–1954)," *Die Europäische Verteidigungsgemeinschaft: Stand und Probleme der Forschung*, im *Auftrag des Militärgeschichtlichen Forschungsamtes* hrsg. von Hans-Erich Volkmann und Walter Schwengler (Boppard am Rhein, 1985), 125–57.
37. Zitat Schumann
38. John Foster Dulles, *War or Peace* (New York, 1950), 157.
39. Joseph Bernhard Egan, "The struggle for the soul of Faust: The American drive for German rearmament, 1950–1951" (Ph.D. Diss., University of Connecticut, 1985), 114–15.
40. The United States Delegation a the Tripartide Foreign Ministers Meeting to the Acting Secretary of State, 13 May 1950, *FRUS 1950* (Washington, 1977), 3: 1056.

41. Hans-Jürgen Rautenberg, "Die Himmeroder Denkschrift vom Oktober 1950: Politische und militärische Überlegungen für einen Beitrag der Bundesrepublik Deutschland zur westdeutschen Verteidigung," *Militärgeschichtliche Mitteilungen* 1 (1977), 135–206.
42. Speidel, 275.
43. Samuel F. Wells, "The First Cold War Buildup: Europe and the United States Strategy and Policy, 1950–1953," Olaf Riste, ed., *Western Security: The Formative Years: European and Atlantic Defense 1947–1953* (Oslo, 1984), 181–97.
44. *Stuttgarter Zeitung*, 7 September 1950.
45. Harry S. Truman, *Memoirs: Years of Trial and Hope* (Garden City, 1956), 2: 253.
46. "Report of the North Atlantic Council of Deputies on Military Committee Document MC 30, 9 December 1950," *FRUS 1950*, 3: 531–47.
47. Walter S. Poole, *The History of the Joint Chiefs of Staff. The Joint Chiefs of Staff and National Policy*, vol. 4: 1950–1952 (Wilmington, 1980), 256.
48. "Study by the Joint Chiefs of Staff, 15 January 1951," *FRUS 1951* (Washington, 1979), 1: 65.
49. Ibid., 66.
50. "Probable Soviet Reactions to a Remilitarization of Western Germany, 22. December 1950," Scott A. Koch, *Cold War Records, Selected Estimates on the Soviet Union, 1950–1959* (Washington, 1993), 116.
51. "Office Memorandum by J. Graham Parsons to George W. Perkins, 28 August 1951," Record of the Department of State, 740.5/8–2851, National Security Archives.
52. Poole, 262–63.
53. "United States Delegation to the Department of State, 21 February 1952," *FRUS 1952–1954* (Washington 1983), 5/1: 75.
54. Jaques Bariety, "La décision de réarmer l'Allemagne, l'échec de la Communauté Européenne de Défense et les accords de Paris du 23 octobre 1954 vus du coté francais," *Revue Belge de Philologie et d' Histoire, Fasc.2: Histoire Médiévale, Moderne et Contemporaine* 71 (1993), 354–83.
55. David Large, "Grand Illusions: The United States, the Federal Republic of Germany, and the European Defense Community, 1950–1954," Jeffrey M. Diefendorf/Axel Frohn/Hermann-Josef Rupieper, eds., *American Policy and the Reconstruction of Germany, 1945–1955* (Cambridge, 1993), 392.
56. Ibid., 393.
57. Johannes Steinhoff/Reiner Pommerin, *Strategiewechsel: Bundesrepublik und Nuklearstrategie in der Ära Adenauer-Kennedy* (Baden-Baden, 1992).
58. Rudolf Morsey, Hans-Peter Schwarz (Hrsg.), *Adenauer, Teegespräche 1950–1954*. Bearbeitet von Hanns Jürgen Küsters (Berlin, 1985), 357–58.

3. AMBIVALENCE AND ATTRACTION:
THE GERMAN SOCIAL DEMOCRATS AND THE UNITED STATES, 1945-1974

Dietrich Orlow

Much has been written recently about the need to define the new contours of the partnership between the reunited Germany and the United States. In the aftermath of German reunification and renewed concerns about German political and economic hegemony in Europe, it is useful to recall that for much of the second half of the twentieth century (West) German-American relations seemed decidedly less complicated. In fact, most accounts portray the Americans as the decisive agents in West German affairs, responsible for everything from creating the Federal Republic[1] to playing a decisive role in its subsequent elections.

But American political foreign aid was hardly evenhanded. Most scholars picture a *special relationship* between the Americans and the Christian Democrats, while portraying contacts between the United States and the Social Democrats as decidedly more strained. According to this view, especially in the 1950s American support helped Konrad Adenauer and the Christian Democrats to achieve impressive electoral victories.[2]

This *special relationship* has led many left-wing scholars of postwar German history to portray the Americans as the villains who prevented the establishment of democratic socialism in Germany after the second World War.[3] German left-wing criticism of the Americans in turn finds its counterpart in mistrust of the German Social Democrats by conservative American scholars. In a recent contribution Jeffrey Herf praised Kurt Schumacher, the leader of the Social Democrats after the second

World War (and hardly an American favorite while he was alive) for his fervent anti-Communism, while severely criticizing Schumacher's successors for weakening the barrier between Communism and Social Democracy.[4]

Perhaps it is time for a somewhat revisionist view of the relations between the U.S. and the West German Social Democrats. Neither the assumption of virtual American omnipotence in guiding the affairs of West Germany, nor the postulate of America's one-sided support for one of West Germany's political groupings is entirely correct. Dörte Winkler has already argued that for the occupation period, 1945 to 1949, the picture of American single-minded opposition to everything the Social Democrats stood for needs to be corrected. The Americans did not speak with one voice, nor did they pursue only one set of policies and priorities.[5] This conclusion is equally valid for the post-occupation years. Moreover, the other side of the equation, Social Democratic attitudes toward America and American policy-makers, were also more variegated than is generally believed. The SPD was not (and is not) a monolithic organization, and attitudes toward America within the party at all times covered a wide spectrum.

1945-1949

It is certainly true that during and immediately after the end of the second World War relations between the American occupation forces and the newly reorganized Social Democrats did not start out on the best of footings. In fact they labored under a number of handicaps. While a large number of Social Democrats who fled from Nazi Germany took up residence in France and later Great Britain, relatively few made their way to the United States. Moreover, most of those who did live in America either did not have close contacts with American decision-makers or, for a variety of reasons, were lost to the German party after the war. For example, Wilhelm Sollmann, a rising Reichstag deputy in the Weimar years, stayed in America after the war and played no further part in the life of the SPD. Albert Grzesinski, the long-time Prussian minister of the interior during the Weimar Republic, died as he was preparing to return to Germany. Some, of course, did return. Max Brauer, the mayor of Altona until 1933, became a much-respected Lord Mayor of Hamburg after the war, but his political power base remained in the British zone and he had little direct contact with the Americans after he returned to Germany.

In addition, during their stay in the U.S. the exiles were generally unable to do much to change the traditional prejudices of American officials against all Marxist groupings. Many of the wartime planners in Washington were traditional Republicans, for whom Marxism in any form was anathema. Under these circumstances it is not surprising that the influence of the exiled Social Democrats on American policy planning during the war was decidedly limited. True, Friedrich Stampfer, the editor of the party newspaper *Vorwärts* before 1933, and others cooperated with the OSS in planning propaganda activities against the Nazis, but the State Department quickly put an end to the OSS initiative.[6]

As the Americans established their military government in the U.S. zone (OMGUS) many of these prejudices lingered on. General Clay, the military commander in the U.S. zone, divided the German party spectrum into left-wing Marxist parties, which included the Communists and the Social Democrats, and parties of the center, which meant the Christian Democrats and the Free Democrats. Since most Americans instinctively favored centrist positions, it is hardly surprising that Clay had a better relationship with the German bourgeois parties than with the SPD.[7]

In addition, new factors emerged to block the emergence of a positive relationship between the American occupiers and the German Social Democrats. Both sides tended to act from ignorance of each other's institutional peculiarities. Some American decision-makers became fixated on Kurt Schumacher as the only personality that determined Social Democratic positions, ironically accepting Schumacher's own image of himself as the embodiment of the party. Unfortunately, such views ignored the early and growing significance of the party leader's critics, who were especially prominent among the SPD's regional leaders, the so-called *Landesfürsten*. And unlike many of his critics, Schumacher had no first-hand knowledge of America or the Americans. As a result, he (as well as his close associates in the *Büro Dr. Schumacher*) at first looked upon France and Great Britain as more important in shaping Germany's future than the United States. Later, after he recognized the Americans' significance, Schumacher became a bitter critic of American policies: he was convinced that OMGUS was deliberately sabotaging the SPD's and his own bid for power in the new democratic Germany.[8]

The decision-makers at OMGUS did not accept criticism lightly. In fact, Clay and his political advisor, Robert Murphy, came to look upon Schumacher and his party as the problem and not the solution for the rebirth of German democracy. For Clay Schumacher's political goals stood for everything that at least in American eyes had hindered German democracy in the past: a centralized Reich, a power monopoly for political parties, and, above all, unrepentant nationalism.[9]

The power struggle between Schumacher and Clay reached a climax in the battle over the Basic Law in April 1949. Ostensibly, the conflict concerned the financial powers of the federal government under the new West German constitution. Unlike several of the SPD's regional leaders, Schumacher insisted on assigning more financial prerogatives to the federal government than the Allied military commanders, including Clay, were initially willing to accept. But the conflict over constitutional principles quickly degenerated into a personal struggle between Clay and Schumacher. The American military commander accused the SPD leader of a variety of personal failings ranging from arrogance and dictatorial leadership of his party to failing to understand the principles of political democracy. Clay at one point threatened to resign if the Allies yielded to Schumacher, and the fact that the Social Democrats leader was eventually victorious in this battle of personalities certainly did not get the relationship between the Americans and the Social Democrats in the new Federal Republic off to a good start.[10]

If there were major divergences between the Americans and the Social Democrats on political issues, chasms seemed to divide the two sides on economic issues. An oft-repeated myth has it that there was widespread support among the German voters for the SPD's demand that Germany's economy be socialized, but that the plans for a radical restructuring of the German economy were systematically sabotaged by a series of American decisions designed to revitalize the free market system. At the end of the occupation years, so the argument goes, the SPD's dream of a democratic and socialist Germany in a democratic and socialist Europe was dead, while with American help German capitalism and German capitalists were alive and well.[11]

The cliché of Social Democrats and especially Schumacher personally frustrated in their political and economic ambitions by a solid phalanx of Americans acting as allies of restorationist and reactionary forces in Germany is a distortion in a number of ways. To begin with, *the* Americans never existed. Officials in the State and War Departments in Washington and at the various level of OMGUS represented a wide variety of views and personal preferences. Clay and Murphy may have equated Schumacher and German Social Democracy, but other officials were more far-sighted. Ludwig Bergsträsser's diary (in 1946 and 1947 Bergsträsser was the Social Democratic *Regierungspräsident* of Darmstadt) shows that there were almost daily and quite cordial contacts between

American officials and regional party leaders. Bergsträsser's experience can certainly be duplicated for *Landesfürsten* like Wilhelm Kaisen in Bremen and especially Ernst Reuter in Berlin.[12] The Americans were also constantly on the lookout for able Social Democrats to staff German government offices. When Carlo Schmid, the minister of justice in that part of Württemberg that was located in the French zone, achieved sudden prominence at the June, 1947 Munich meeting of Länder prime ministers, American officials immediately attempted to lure him to the Bizone with offers of a responsible position.[13]

On closer inspection the picture of persistent policy antagonisms between the Americans and the Social Democrats turns out to be equally simplistic. Here the McCarthy era in the United States did much to distort the historic record. In the immediate postwar period there was a sizable group of American officials, especially in the State Department, but also at OMGUS, who argued that the best guarantee for European political stability and economic recovery lay in the ideas and leaders represented by democratic socialism—the Labour Party in Great Britain, the SFIO in France, and the SPD in Germany. Their voices were soon muted, at OMGUS because they were opposed by Clay and his political advisor, and in the State Department because praising any form of Marxism did not seem the best way to get approval of the Marshall Plan from the Republican-dominated Congress. Later, with the advent of McCarthyism it became even more politic to bury whatever pro-socialist sentiments one might have had.[14]

Sophistication and nuanced attitudes were equally present on the other side of the equation. The thesis that the SPD and especially Kurt Schumacher were anti-American was a campaign-inspired slander by Konrad Adenauer and the Christian Democrats. In fact, irony of ironies, the French repeatedly worried that Schumacher was trying to "play the American card" against France.[15]

The French need not have worried. Schumacher went out of his way to avoid giving the impression that he was beholden to any of the Allies, but it is true that the party leader's relationship to America was considerably more positive than his battles with General Clay might suggest. Schumacher's conception of democratic socialism derived from a mixture of Marx, Lasalle, and the ideals of the French and the American Revolutions. His political ideas, that is to say, owed as much to Montesquieu and Thomas Jefferson as they did to the classic German thinkers. Moreover, his admiration for things American did not end with eighteenth century American history. The German party leader was also greatly impressed with the reforms brought about by Roosevelt's New Deal. According to Schumacher the New Deal had not brought socialism to America, but it had inaugurated a new era in the relations between capital and labor.[16]

Finally, although the Christian Democrats later succeeded in labelling the SPD as one of the "Marxist ways leading to Moscow,"[17] the Americans and the Social Democrats in some ways held remarkably parallel views on the Communist threat. In fact, at times no one sounded more like John Foster Dulles than Kurt Schumacher. Like some American decision-makers, Schumacher feared Eurasia swallowing Europe unless the West demonstrated strength, a concept that implied that Germany had to associate itself with the West to escape Communist domination. Schumacher's call for a Western *Offensivverteidigung* was Dulles' rollback of Communism under another name. SPD leaders also acknowledged that their first priority, the reunification of the country, could only be accomplished with the help of the Western powers, and that meant above all, the Americans.[18]

Ironically, anti-Communism was also a factor leading some American officials to support the "socialist" reconstruction of the German economy. It was not true that all Americans were hell-bent on reinstituting capitalism in Germany. On the contrary, many American officials agreed with Schumacher and the SPD that the best way of preventing the Communists from using the postwar economic problems for their own political purposes was not to sing the praises of American capitalism, but to support plans for a democratic socialist reconstruction—as opposed to the Stalinist variety—of the German and European economies.[19] (Incidentally, while most American officials rejected the contention by Schumacher and the SPD's economic expert in those days, Viktor Agartz, that democratic socialism was a more rational way of running an economy, some were remarkably sympathetic to the concept that a democratic *Planwirtschaft* was the most efficient way of structuring the economic rebuilding of Europe. In October 1946 Günter Markscheffel, the SPD's liaison to the French socialist party, had a long talk with Chip Bohlen, then Secretary of State James Byrnes' secretary. Bohlen was certainly sympathetic with the SPD's economic proposals. He specifically advised the party to stress the economic necessity of socialization measures in Germany rather than emphasize that the restructuring of the country's economy would help accomplish the party's political revolutionary goals.[20])

Within the American decision-making establishment, supporters of a democratic socialist reconstruction of the German economy lost out to the proponents of market economics. This is well-known, but the corollary development within the SPD has received less attention. Not only was there widespread criticism among the leadership cadres of the lack of concreteness in the party's socialization proposals, but, even more important, genuine and increasing lack of interest among the rank-and-file in the theory and practice of socialization. Fritz Henssler, the Social Democratic mayor of Dortmund, and in 1946 and 1947 the guiding force for attempts to put the coal mines and steel industry of the Ruhr under state control, a year later argued the party would do better concentrating on political rather than economic issues.[21] In the final analysis, socialization failed not because of American vetoes, but because Agartz and his supporters could not demonstrate to the Americans, the party's rank-and-file, or most German voters that a socialized economy was a quicker way to economic recovery than Erhard's model of the *soziale Marktwirtschaft*.[22]

1949–1961

During the Adenauer era relations between the SPD and American policy-makers seemed to reach a nadir. American goals and priorities appeared so closely aligned with the domestic and foreign policy goals of Konrad Adenauer and the CDU that the SPD's accusation of a virtual alliance between Washington and Bonn was not without foundation. In the Bundestag election of 1953 (the so-called Dulles election) high-ranking American officials, including the Secretary of State, all but endorsed the re-election of Konrad Adenauer.[23]

Embittered personal relations paralleled and compounded policy differences. Adenauer, a shrewd politician if ever there was one, used his close personal relationship with the American High Commissioner (and later ambassador in Bonn) John McCloy, to convince the Americans that he was the one truly pro-Western leader in the Federal Republic. Kurt Schumacher, increasingly embittered and frustrated in the last years of his life, railed against the McCloy-Adenauer coalition, but in official American circles he could not shake a reputation as "the one man menacing the unity of Western Europe." And the SPD leader certainly did not help matters with episodes such as accusing Adenauer of being the "chancellor of the Allies", or announcing that the SPD would not be bound by agreements, like the Schuman Plan, that integrated West Germany into the Western alliance.[24]

The picture of two entities communicating with each other mostly through invectives and epithets did have a basis in reality, then. During the 1950s American policy-makers and the official line of the SPD pursued diametrically opposed priorities. The Americans (and Adenauer) had as their first goal the integration of West Germany into the Western alliance. In contrast, the SPD insisted that German reunification, not Western integration, had to be the first priority of any German government, a position that led the Americans to keep their lingering suspicions that in the final analysis the SPD could not be trusted to reject Soviet siren calls that held out hope of reunification, albeit at the expense of Western integration.[25] Ironically, there was never any danger that the SPD would succumb to that temptation. Schumacher and his successors saw German national unification at all times as a consequence of the Soviets' yielding to the West's superior strength.[26]

In retrospect, it is clear that the SPD's official insistence on reunification as the first priority was a naive and illusionary position, but the bitterness that marked U.S.-SPD relations at this time resulted at least in part from the Americans' misunderstanding of Schumacher's and the SPD's position. Schumacher insisted that by placing unification ahead of Western integration he was actually serving the cause of the West. He argued, for example, that if the SPD had not spearheaded the opposition to the Schuman Plan and the European Defense Community in the name of German sovereignty and independence, that issue would have been preempted by the Communists or the neo-Nazis, both of which were not only anti-Western, but also anti-democratic.[27]

The party used the same argument during the controversy over the so-called Stalin notes of 1952. Although the SPD leaders had no real hope that the Soviet dictator would permit German reunification without unacceptable conditions, they insisted that rejecting the initiative out of hand as a propaganda ploy (which was Adenauer's and the Americans' position) would give the Communists additional political ammunition. In his last radio address a few weeks before his death Schumacher accused the Bonn government (and by implication the Americans) of reacting "in an overly casual manner" (*sehr lässig*) to the Soviet initiatives.[28]

If there had been hopes that the political divisions between the Americans and the SPD would become less stark after Schumacher's death, they were dashed by the emergence of a new issue in the mid-1950s: the debate over West German rearmament. For different reasons both the Americans and Adenauer felt West German rearmament was necessary. The Americans were convinced that without West German troops a creditable Western defense against Communist aggression could not be constructed. Adenauer accepted that argument, but he also used the issue to press for additional sovereignty for the fledgling Federal Republic. The SPD rejected both arguments by turning them on their heads. According to the official party position an eventual Bundeswehr, integrated into the Western military alliance, sealed the fact of Germany's division and, equally important, actually limited Germany's sovereignty by placing its armed forces under a multi-national command structure. The SPD's alternative proposal was a reunited Germany whose—very limited—armed forces would become part of an international system of agreements on security arrangements and armaments reduction by the Big Four.[29]

Despite clear evidence that its stand was politically counter-productive—the party made its security concept a major issue in its 1957 Bundestag election campaign, only to find that the issue aroused very little voter interest—the SPD appeared to continue its confrontation with the Christian Democrats and the Americans. The climax of this development was the publication in 1959 of the so-called Germany Plan (*Deutschlandplan*), a document that at first glance showed that like the Bourbons the party had forgotten nothing and learned nothing. This security concept, which called for a nuclear weapon-free zone in Central Europe and the reduction of military forces in the area, was diametrically opposed to such American ideas as deterrent forces and forward defenses. Its intellectual affinity to proposals advanced by the Polish Foreign Minister Adam Rapacki and the British Labour leader Hugh Gaitskell did not enlarge its credibility in Republican Washington. At the end of the decade, the SPD and the Americans seemed further apart than ever.[30]

Actually, that impression was thoroughly misleading. The Germany Plan was an intra-party public relations maneuver, not a serious political proposal. It was really a last homage by the Young Turks in the SPD to the old guard of the Schumacher generation. The document was drafted by a group of young leaders—including Fritz Erler, Herbert Wehner, and Helmut Schmidt—who had little sympathy (the latter two even less than the first) with its ideas, and who used the Plan to demonstrate to party leaders like Erich Ollenhauer that the SPD's hopes of linking reunification and agreements among the superpowers on disarmament were political illusions. The ideas presented in the Plan were, as Carlo Schmid said, obsolete as early as 1955 and dead on arrival in 1959. The proof lay in the public reception of the document in Germany, and the reaction of the Soviets. Although the Germany Plan appeared to have wide support among the party activists, it aroused little interest among the public at large. In addition, in another instance of historical irony, the Plan was officially announced one day after an SPD delegation (which included Fritz Erler, one of the Plan's principal authors) had returned from a visit to Moscow. Among other officials, they met with Nikita Krushchev, who left no doubt that the Soviet Union had no interest in German reunification under the terms outlined in the *Deutschlandplan*.[31]

In retrospect, even the intra-party support was exaggerated. Less than a year after its publication, the Germany Plan was formally abandoned by the SPD. This seemingly spectacular reversal, embodied in a famous Bundestag speech by Herbert Wehner, caused few repercussions in the life of the party. This was because the Plan represented the capstone of a developmental line that the SPD had been in the process of revising and abandoning for the last decade. This process, which began while Schumacher was still alive,[32] was important not only for the future of the SPD's position in German politics, but also played a major role in the relations between the Social Democrats and the United States in the 1950s and 1960s.

What in the 1960s came to be labeled as the pragmatization, de-ideologicization (*Entideologisierung*) or, more simply, the Americanization of the West European parties had a profound impact upon the SPD.[33] Alternately encouraged and criticized, but on the whole tolerated by Erich Ollenhauer, Schumacher's successor as party leader, in the 1950s a group of rejuvenators (*Erneuerer*) systematically moved the SPD toward the ideological revolution of the Bad Godesberg Program. With this new party platform the SPD abandoned all vestiges of Marxist determinism and became a reform-oriented, genuine *Volkspartei*, modelled, not incidentally, on the American catch-all parties.

The path that led to Bad Godesberg has often been described, but the role that the increasingly close relations between the Americans and the West German Social Democrats played in this process is often neglected. Throughout the 1950s SPD leaders traveled with increasing frequency to the United States. Men like Fritz Erler, who had numerous meetings with Walter Reuther, the president of the AFL-CIO at this time, came away deeply impressed with the transition from a secondary to a tertiary industrial economy that was taking place in America.[34]

A similar, long-term process of self-adjustment was taking place in the area of the party's ideas on foreign relations. The picture of an abrupt about-face in 1959/1960 is misleading. Evidence of divisions among the leadership—especially on the issue of West European integration—was not hard to find even during the Schumacher years. *Landesfürsten* such as Kaisen and Brauer severely criticized Schumacher's rejection of the *Ruhrstatut* (which had led to Schumacher's outburst that Adenauer was the "chancellor of the Allies"), the Schuman Plan, and the European Defense Community. In the case of the Schuman Plan, the EDC and even the Germany Treaty (*Deutschlandvertrag*) the Young Turks in the party left no doubt that the SPD would work within the framework of those treaties once they had been passed by a majority of the Bundestag.[35] The outbreak of the Korean War also brought the party closer to agreement with American positions; Schumacher, for example, immediately endorsed the concept of Western rearmament.

Even the SPD's reaction to the so-called Stalin notes of 1952 on closer examination demonstrated far more agreement than disagreement with the American position. True, old-guard leaders like Ollenhauer and Heine remained conspicuously silent, and, as we saw, publicly Schumacher accused the Americans and their German allies of failing to explore Stalin's intentions fully, but in private conversations with American officials other SPD leaders spoke another language. They insisted on attaching conditions to any further exploration of Stalin's initiatives that they (and the Americans) knew would be unacceptable to the Russians. In effect, then, the Social Democratic differences with the Americans concerned matters of tactics far more than matters of substance.[36]

In effect at the end of the decade, the SPD had undergone profound changes: the party had propelled itself to the threshold of a successful practitioner of the politics of the 1960s, a style of politics that until then had been regarded as typically American. Equally important, the SPD looked to the United States not just for inspiration in political tactics, but sought a genuine partnership with the Americans in the area of foreign and security policies.

1961–1966

It was not difficult to sense that major changes were in the air as the decade of the 1950s came to a close. The launching of Sputnik, the Sino-Soviet split, Nikita Krushchev's Berlin ultimatum all showed that the rigid contours of the postwar world were breaking up; multipolarism was about to replace bipolarism.[37]

New situations brought new leaders to the fore. In America the Kennedy generation took charge, and brought a brief sense of Camelot to the country. In Germany the change was no less dramatic, albeit not as romantic. Here, too (incidentally proving that there is no such thing as a new political slogan), there were increasing calls that it was "time for a change."[38] Leadership in the SPD and eventually West Germany fell to the Young Turks, men like Willy Brandt, Egon Bahr, Fritz Erler, Herbert Wehner, and Helmut Schmidt, who in the course of the 1960s replaced the Schumacher and Ollenhauer generation at the helm of the party.

As we shall see shortly, on the whole relations between the new group of Social Democratic leaders and the Americans were far better than had been true for the earlier generation, but even now the SPD remained something of an enigma for the Americans. Especially Willy Brandt and his intellectual mentor, Egon Bahr, evoked mixed feelings. Some American officials were deeply impressed with Brandt even before he achieved prominence as the SPD's chancellor candidate,[39] but others remained uneasy. In the 1970s Dean Acheson, no longer at the center of power and increasingly irascible in his old age, concluded Brandt was a virtual Communist. Henry Kissinger did not doubt Brandt's commitment to the West, but he did think that the Ostpolitik, the major foreign policy initiative associated with Brandt and Bahr, was wrong-headed and its authors lacked the sophistication required to carry it through.[40]

However, while ambivalence and mistrust remained (and remain), such sentiments were rapidly eclipsed by a sense of cooperation and mutual trust between the new SPD team and the American leaders. Part of the reason lay in personal and generational affinities. Brandt, the German Kennedy, meshed well with the new crowd at the White House. The American ambassador in Bonn, Joseph McGhee, developed a particularly close relationship to Fritz Erler; the SPD's spokesman on military and security affairs became the ambassador's major source of information about the SPD's evolving views on these issues. Even Egon Bahr, the man many American officials were least comfortable with, found open doors at the White House.[41]

In analyzing the much improved personal relations between the new Social Democratic leaders and the Americans, one factor is often overlooked. The Young Turks in the SPD were not unknown entities to the Americans, because most of them had long-standing contacts with the U.S. officials. Willy Brandt, for example, who became known to most Americans when he was elected mayor of West Berlin, had actually been a familiar face and name in American offices since the earliest days after the war. Since the beginning of 1946 he served as the *Büro Dr. Schumacher*'s liaison man in Berlin, and as his reports to Hannover, the so-called *Berlin-Berichte*, show Brandt was not only in almost daily contact with American officials, but he also agreed with much of their criticism of the Schumacher regime in the party.[42] There was also the more elusive factor of stylistic parallelism. Like the Kennedy generation, the *Erneuerer* in the SPD deliberately exploited the new medium of TV, and—again, American-style—attempted to involve interest groups outside the party in the decision-making process within the party.[43]

But good personal relations are one thing and agreements on domestic and foreign policy issues quite another. After 1966 the new Social Democratic leaders were in a position to make West German policy, not just to criticize it. There were few difficulties with the wave of domestic reforms, which the SPD-led coalitions initiated. In fact, the SPD's domestic reform program was often compared with contemporary American developments, like such as civil rights movement and later the Great Society.[44]

The situation was less clear-cut as far as new initiatives in the area of foreign policy, particularly the Ostpolitik, were concerned. The Americans welcomed the SPD's new emphasis on bipartisanship in foreign relations, but some critics voiced lingering doubts about the SPD's genuine commitment to Atlanticism, fearing that, even if the Ostpolitik did not result in a new Rapallo, it would make it more difficult for the West to confront the Soviets with a united front. Some scholars still contend that although this was not Brandt's and Bahr's intention, objectively the Ostpolitik actually served the Soviets' interests.[45]

However, the significance of such evidence of skepticism and pessimism should not be exaggerated. Far more important were the signs of parallelism in American and German foreign policies. With the "evil empire" confrontational policies of the early Reagan years in mind, we tend to forget that, like Brandt and Bahr, Kennedy and later Nixon, too, hoped to achieve detente with the Soviets. Brandt's and Bahr's Ostpolitik shared both goals and tactics with the Americans. The Ostpolitik was neither anti-American, nor was it conducted without American support. On the contrary, the German initiatives were pursued in close cooperation with the Americans. Egon Bahr remembered the tremendous support from the Kennedy administration for the *Politik der kleinen Schritte* of the Berlin government, and Willy Brandt later noted, *Im Großen: Gleichklang der Interessen* with Nixon's foreign policy.[46]

In fact, some authors in the 1970s felt the relationship had become all too close. They criticized the SPD's partial bracketing of the imperialist tendencies of American foreign policy, especially in Vietnam.[47] Nevertheless, the meshing of interests and personalities was not surprising.

Even before they took over the party, the Young Turks had made it very clear that their policy of *Gemeinsamkeiten in der Aussenpolitik* meant West European integration and consensual relations with the Americans.[48] To describe the Ostpolitik as a form of anti-Americanism is a serious distortion of the historic record. The new SPD and the new American leaders were able to cooperate much as Adenauer's CDU and an earlier generation of American officials had been able to, because in the meantime the Atlanticists in the SPD had won out, while the post-Adenauer CDU was having serious problems with its Gaullist wing.[49]

Conclusion

In retrospect, relations between the Americans and the West German Social Democrats were closest during the 1960s. The SPD leaders admired the Kennedy and Johnson style of domestic politics, and despite differences over the Vietnam War, in their conduct of foreign relations the SPD-led coalitions and the American governments pursued largely parallel goals. The success or failure of the Ostpolitik remains a topic of intense debate, but on the whole, I think the Ostpolitik served both German and American interests. *Wandel durch Annäherung* helped to undermine the Communist regime in former East Germany, and the Federal Republic's bilateral treaties with the Soviet Union and the states of Eastern Europe acted as one of the catalytic factors breaking up the post-Stalinist mold of the Soviet Bloc.[50]

Since then, of course, the world has changed profoundly. The conservatism of Reagan, Thatcher, and Kohl replaced the reformism of Brandt, Kennedy, and Johnson. As far as relations between the Americans and the Social Democrats are concerned, the pattern of ambivalence and attraction has returned. In the 1990s the SPD is in the midst of a serious structural and ideological crisis. Some in the party are advocating a new era of pragmatism as a way out of the crisis; their model is the reformed (and recently successful) American Democratic party. Others insist the problem is too much Americanism; the SPD needs to return to its roots as a true *Weltanschauungs* party. Among American conservatives there also remains ambivalence and some fear. They ask with Communism dead, will the SPD really stand up for Western democracy—as the conservatives see it—or yield to the siren calls of leftist statism?[51] History does not repeat itself, but it does appear that we have been at this juncture before.

NOTES

1. The accusation that the U.S. was instrumental in the process that led to the division of Germany was not limited to German or Communist accounts. See, for example, Vincent Auriol, *Journal du Septennat (version intégrale)*, ed. by Pierre Kerleroux (Paris, 1974), III:463 (30.12.1949) (hereafter cited as Auriol, *Journal*).
2. Hans-Jürgen Grabbe, *Unionsparteien, Sozialdemokratie und Vereinigte Staaten von Amerika 1945–1966* (Düsseldorf, 1983), 15 (hereafter cited as Grabbe, *SPD und USA*).
3. Reinhard Blum, *Soziale Marktwirtschaft: Wirtschaftspolitik zwischen Neoliberalismus und Ordoliberalismus* (Tübingen, 1969); and Hans-Hermann Hartwich, *Sozialstaatspostulat und Gesellschaftlicher Status Quo* (Cologne, 1970). Dörte Winkler, "Die amerikanische Sozialisierungspolitik in Deutschland 1945–1948," in: Heinrich August Winkler, ed., *Politische Weichenstellung im Nachkriegsdeutschland 1945–1953* (Göttingen, 1979) (hereafter cited as Winkler, Sozialisierungspolitik), 88–89, and 88 n. 1 provides a good overview of these theses for the occupation years, 1945–1949.
4. Jeffrey Herf, "Demokratie auf dem Prüfstand: Politische Kultur, Machtpolitik und die Nachrüstungskrise in Deutschland," *Vierteljahrshefte für Zeitgeschichte*, 40 (no. 1, January 1992), 22 (hereafter cited as Herf, "Demokratie").
5. Winkler, *Sozialisierungspolitik*, 90.
6. Grabbe, *SPD und USA*, 70; and Jan Foitzik, "Revolution und Demokratie: Zu den Sofort- und Übergangsplanungen des sozialdemokratischen Exils für Deutschland 1943–1945," in: *Internationale Wissenschaftliche Korrespondenz*, 24 (September, 1988), 317–20 and 341.
7. Grabbe, *SPD und USA*, 81 and 84.
8. Ibid., 51, 61, and 76; and Michael Fichter, "Der Wolf-Report und die gegensätzlichen gewerkschaftspolitischen Zielsetzungen der U.S. Militärregierung für Deutschland," *Internationale Wissenschaftliche Korrespondenz*, 14 (December, 1978), 444, 448, and 450–52.
9. Grabbe, *SPD und USA*, 63–64 and 99; and Grabbe, "Die deutsch-alliierte Kontroverse um den Grundgesetzentwurf im Frühjahr 1949," in: *Vierteljahrshefte für Zeitgeschichte*, 26 (no. 3, July, 1978), 416 (hereafter cited as Grabbe, *Kontroverse*).
10. Grabbe, *SPD und USA*, 171 and 174; and Grabbe, *Kontroverse*, 402–3, 411, and 413.
11. Grabbe, *SPD und USA*, 105ff and 135.
12. Ludwig Bergsträsser, *Befreiung, Besatzung, Neubeginn: Tagebuch des Darmstädter Regierungspräsidenten 1945–1948*, ed. by Walter Mühlhausen (Munich, 1987); and Grabbe, *SPD und USA*, 74–75.
13. Edgar Wolfrum, *Französische Besatzungspolitik und deutsche Sozialdemokratie* (Düsseldorf, 1991), 297 (hereafter cited as Wolfrum, *Besatzungspolitik*).
14. Helga Grebing, "Politische und soziale Probleme der Arbeiterklasse am Ende des Zweiten Weltkrieges und in der unmittelbaren Nachkriegszeit," in: *Internationale Wissenschaftliche Korrespondenz*, 22 (no. 1, 1986), 1–20; Winkler, *Sozialisierungspolitik*, pp. 101–02 and 109; and Grabbe, *SPD und USA*, 78.
15. Auriol, *Journal*, II:57–58 (30 January 1948).
16. Schumacher to C.A. Smith, 25 July 1946, Best. Schu. 31 (Archiv der Sozialdemokratie); Arnold Sywottek, "Tabuisierung und Anpassung in Ost und West: Bemerkungen zur deutschen Geschichte nach 1945," in: Thomas Koebner, et al., eds., *Deutschland nach Hitler: Zukunftspläne im Exil und aus der Besatzungszeit 1939–1949* (Cologne, 1987), 238; and Grabbe, *SPD und USA*, 53.
17. The allusion here, of course, is to the famous 1953 CDU election poster, *Alle Wege des Marxismus führen nach Moskau*.

18. See, Willy Brandt's report on a Referat by Ernst Reuter, "Die Politik der Partei," in: *Berlin Berichte*, 15 March 1948 (Archives of the SPD). See also, Wilfried Loth, "German Conceptions of Europe during the Escalation of the East-West Conflict, 1945–1949," in: Josef Becker and Franz Knipping, eds., *Power in Europe? Great Britain, France, Italy, and Germany in a Postwar World, 1945–1950* (Berlin, 1986), 524–27; Susanne Miller, *Die SPD vor und nach Godesberg* (Bonn, 1974), 18.
19. Winkler, *Sozialisierungspolitik*, 94–95 and 98; and Wolfrum, *Besatzungspolitik*, 223.
20. Markscheffel to SPD/PV, 8 October 1946, Best. Markscheffel, 7 (Archives of the SPD); Winkler, *Sozialisierungspolitik*, 99–103; and Grabbe, *SPD und USA*, 87ff.
21. See his remarks at a meeting of the SPD's executive committee (*Parteivorstand*), 28 and 29 May 1948, Best. *Parteivorstand* (Archives of the SPD).
22. *Berlin Berichte*, no. 14, 24 February 1948.
23. Harold Zink, *The United States and Germany* (New York, 1957), 338; Roger Morgan, *Washington und Bonn: Deutsch-amerikanische Beziehungen seit dem Zweiten Weltkrieg* (Munich, 1975), 29; Thomas A. Schwartz, *America's Germany: John J. McCloy and the Federal Republic of Germany* (Cambridge, MA, 1991), 284 (hereafter cited as Schwartz, *McCloy*); and Beatrix W. Bouvier, *Zwischen Godesberg und Grosser Koalition: Der Weg der SPD in die Regierungsverantwortung* (Bonn, 1990), 35 (hereafter cited as Bouvier, *SPD*).
24. Schwartz, *McCloy*, 53, 80–81, and 277; and Hermann-Josef Rupieper, *Der besetzte Verbündete: Die amerikanische Deutschlandpolitik 1949–1955* (Opladen, 1991), 312 (hereafter cited as Rupieper, *Verbündete*).
25. Hermann Graml, "Die Legende von der verpassten Gelegenheit: Zur sowjetischen Notenkampagne des Jahres 1952" *Vierteljahrshefte für Zeitgeschichte*, 29 (July, 1981), 311 (hereafter cited as Graml, *Legende*); and Dean Acheson, *Present at the Creation* (New York, 1970), 447.
26. Hartmut Soell, *Fritz Erler: Eine politische Biographie* (Berlin, 1976), I:362 (hereafter cited as Soell, *Erler*).
27. Kurt Schumacher, "Rede vor den Sozialen Arbeitsgemeinschaften," 24 May 1951, in: Schumacher, *Reden, Schriften, Korrespondenzen, 1945–1952*, ed. by Willy Albrecht (Bonn, 1985), 809 (hereafter cited as Schumacher, *Reden*); Schwartz, *McCloy*, p. 199; and Ulrich Buczylowski, *Kurt Schumacher und die deutsche Frage: Sicherheitspolitik und strategische Offensivkonzeption vom August 1950 bis September 1951* (Stuttgart-Degerloch, 1973), 149–50 (hereafter cited as Buszylowski, *Schumacher*).
28. See, Schumacher's speech, 15 July 1952, in: Schumacher, *Reden*, 192; Graml, *Legende*, 330–31; and Rupieper, *Verbündete*, 221 and 279.
29. Grabbe, "Kontroverse," 418; Wolfram F. Hanrieder, *Germany, America, Europe: Forty Years of German Foreign Policy* (New Haven, CT, 1989), 39; Winkler, *Sicherheit*, 27–31; Rupieper, *Verbündete*, 115–16; and Schwartz, *McCloy*, 186.
30. Lothar Wilker, *Die Sicherheitspolitik der SPD, 1955-1966* (Bonn-Bad Godesberg, 1977), pp. 41ff.
31. Wilker, *Sicherheit*, pp. 36–37 and 50ff.
32. Rupieper, *Verbündete*, 235–36.
33. For a review of the relevant literature see, Bouvier, *SPD*, 106ff.
34. Soell, *Erler*, I:267–72.
35. Graml, *Legende*, 314 and Buczylowski, *Schumacher*, 82, 88, and 136–38.
36. Graml, *Legende*, 313, 317–18, and 335.
37. Bouvier, *SPD*, 46–47, 122–24, and 286–88.
38. Reinhardt Lettau, "It's Time for a Change," in: Hans Werner Richter, ed., *Plädoyer für eine neue Regierung oder keine Alternative* (Reinbek b. Hamburg, 1965), 129–31. See also, Bouvier, *SPD*, 268.
39. Soell, *Erler*, I:413–14.

40. George McGhee, *At the Creation of a New Germany: From Adenauer to Brandt* (New Haven, CT, 1989), 141–42 (hereafter cited as McGhee, *Creation*); and Henry A. Kissinger, *Memoiren: 1973–1974* (Munich, 1982), 173. Acheson's views of Willy Brandt were reported in Martin Walker's review of Roy Jenkins' memoires, *New York Times Book Review*, 16 May 1993, 16.
41. McGhee, *Creation*, xx [sic] and 51; Diethelm Prowe, "Die Anfänge der Brandtschen Ostpolitik 1961–1963," in: Wolfgang Benz and Hermann Graml, eds., *Aspekte deutscher Außenpolitik im 20. Jahrhundert: Aufsätze Hans Rothfels zum Gedächtnis* (Stuttgart, 1976), 249–86; Bouvier, *SPD*, 76; and Soell, *Erler*, I:409ff and II:1044 n. 706.
42. See, for example, *Berlin Bericht*, no. 25, 14 March 1948.
43. Bouvier, *SPD*, 168–69.
44. Ibid., 84 and 168.
45. McGhee, *Creation*, 242; and Herf, "Demokratie," 19–20.
46. See, Brandt's handwritten comments on a speech concept, 21 Sept. 1969, Best. Markscheffel, 4 (Arch.d.SD). See also, Karsten Schröder, *Egon Bahr* (Rastatt, 1988), 106 and 110–11.
47. Soell, *Erler*, I:473.
48. Winkler, *Sicherheit*, 44, 136, and 218–19; Bouvier, *SPD*, 127, and 152.
49. Beatrix W. Bouvier, "Die SPD und Charles de Gaulle in den sechziger Jahren," in: Wilfred Loth, et al., eds., *Charles de Gaulle, Deutschland und Europa* (Opladen, 1991), 112–14; and Soell, *Erler*, I:466.
50. Helmut Kistler et al., *Bundesdeutsche Geschichte* (Stuttgart, 1986), 406.
51. See, Erhard Eppler's review of Gerhard Schröder's *Reifeprüfung*, "Mutiges Political Animal," in: *Der Spiegel*, 47 (no. 13, 29 March 1993), 44.

4. THE GENESIS OF AMERICAN POLICY TOWARD THE GDR:
SOME WORKING HYPOTHESES

Gerald R. Kleinfeld

"I met a man who was not there. He was not there again today. How I wish he would go away." *Hughes Mearns*

Describing American relations with the German Democratic Republic in its first decade is something of an exercise in futility. This was an entity with which the United States had no diplomatic relations, whose existence was not recognized, and that did not even have control over its own territory. More than 40 years later, on the eve of the fall of the Wall in Berlin, American scholars were debating whether the GDR was a permanent state, with its own "national" identity. Some earnestly argued that the German Democratic Republic was a successful entity, or that its population had a distinct national identity, and was not interested in unity with the West; but the debate never involved a large number of researchers. Before recognition of the GDR by the United States, a very small number of American scholars concentrated their research on the GDR, and after recognition the number increased only slightly, except among Germanists. The German Democratic Republic Studies Association in the United States, an association of university professors dedicated to research on the GDR, had, at its height, only 36 members, and it was officially affiliated with the American Association for the Advancement of Slavic Studies (AAASS), rather than with a group researching on Germany in general or with the American Political Science Association

(APSA). This was in spite of an active policy by the government of the German Democratic Republic, after recognition, courting American scholars. The GDR cultivated U.S. scholars through a concerted cultural policy, especially seeking out Germanists, who were invited to travel to Europe in order to participate in special seminars. In addition to discussions of literature, they were given glimpses of GDR society and could travel, although they were not encouraged to investigate beyond what they were shown. Some researchers were granted special interviews. Academic literature published by these American scholars reflected this narrow focus, the limited information available, and the constraints imposed by the GDR. A session on the German Democratic Republic at an annual conference of the APSA only a few years before unification contained papers that praised the social welfare system as being generous and adequate, concluding that it was better than that of the Federal Republic of Germany. The *Staatssicherheit* was rarely discussed in American books or articles on the GDR, and its influence was vastly underrated. Authors from the GDR were read and discussed in literary circles, but economic and social conditions were largely absent from news reporting and from most academic conferences as well. Thus, the GDR gained a modicum of respectability as a research field after recognition, but only at a distance. For the whole of its existence, including the period after unification, it was largely a *terra incognita* for the United States. The Hallstein Doctrine may have been replaced by recognition, but official relations were faintly formal. Still, even this was a substantial change from the time before recognition, when the GDR was something to be ignored whenever possible.

University courses in history and political science generally excluded the German Democratic Republic. Until the 1980s, when the German Studies Association encouraged the study of Germany since 1945, most history courses on Germany in the United States scarcely reached beyond 1945. Political science courses focused on Western European states, or tended to deal with the Soviet Union and the Soviet sphere, barely mentioning the GDR. It was even neglected in courses on Eastern Europe. West Germany, on the other hand, was studied extensively, often in comparison with other democracies. For example, in his widely used textbook, *The German Polity*, David Conradt deals exclusively with West Germany.[1] For years, the United States Department of State had a special research program on Eastern Europe. No research concentration on the German Democratic Republic was ever a feature of this program. After its collapse and the unification of Germany, the Department of

State rejected a suggestion to use program funds to sponsor research on the GDR. The GDR was generally not included in programs on Western Europe, and it was generally absent from those on Eastern Europe. Even in research, it did not exist.

Manfred Jonas, in his book *The United States and Germany*, published in 1984, writes simply "in 1974, John Sherman Cooper became the first American ambassador to ... the German Democratic Republic. His arrival there did nothing to alter the essential fact that, for the United States, the successor state to Hitler's Third Reich was the Federal Republic." He makes no other reference to the German Democratic Republic.[2] In the final chapter of his study, *Germany and the United States: A Special Relationship?*, Hans W. Gatzke offers: "I have said very little thus far about the German Democratic Republic. ... As far as America was concerned, East Germany was to remain in limbo until the two Germanies were reunited."[3] Such comments are typical.

Looking back, with Germany unified, the Soviet Union now dissolved, and Eastern Europe released from its grasp, it is difficult to imagine the way Americans felt in the immediate postwar years. More than four decades later, united Germany is a confirmed democracy with a large economy, thoroughly integrated into the West, tied to a secure friendship with France, embedded in the European Union, and strongly linked to the United States. But what were Western Europe and the United States thinking in 1945, or 1948, with cities destroyed all over Europe and economies ravaged during the World War begun by Hitler's Germany, then only recently ended? With Moscow today losing control even over its provinces within the Russian Federation, how are we to imagine the impact of the death of Jan Masaryk in 1948 and the fall of Czechoslovakia to a Communist dictatorship, or of the invasion of South Korea by North Korea in 1950? The apprehensions of the 1950s were real, whether they revolved around German militarism and remnants of Nazism or around Soviet Communist expansionism.

I would like to offer some working hypotheses for a study of the genesis of American relations with the German Democratic Republic during a time in which these relations were nil and the GDR was ignored. This is not, however, an examination of the German Question, nor of Allied negotiations on the German Question, nor the American position on the German Question. This chapter stems from a conference in which it was the responsibility of this author to discuss American policy towards the GDR. It is valid to reexamine the entire history of the GDR, based upon materials now available, but it is also important to understand the underlying assumptions of American policy in the early postwar years even if these assumptions held that the GDR should not be treated as a sovereign entity.

American policy officially ignored the GDR, to a considerable degree even after recognition and up to the end of the GDR as a state. The Federal Republic of Germany was important to the United States, and West German policy towards the GDR was important because West Germany was important, not because the GDR was perceived by the United States to be important in itself. A unified Germany would also be important. In the early postwar years, the GDR was a nonentity. The GDR was part of the German Question, of the Berlin Question, and of the wider issues of the Cold War, but it was not considered in Washington to be an independent policy source. The "realities" of the 1950s? Here, then, are my hypotheses:

First, the United States faced the Soviet Union as a major adversary, with the fault line running through the middle of Germany. A Soviet invasion of Western Europe was not excluded as a possibility. The United States intended to stay in Germany as a barrier to Soviet invasion.

Second, German unity, although considered by many Americans as potentially dangerous and destabilizing for Europe, was never totally dismissed as an American goal: no consensus existed in the United States for a permanent division of the country. For the entire history of divided Germany, even at this early stage when memories of the war were still fresh, the United States was readier than any of Germany's neighbors to see German unity.

Third, if German unity was an ultimate American goal, so was the integration of West Germany into the West. An economically strong and democratic West Germany was essential to American defense of Western Europe. The building of democracy there was crucial to Washington's European policy.

Fourth, the German Democratic Republic, as far as the foreign policy of the United States was concerned, was close to being totally meaningless. The Soviet zone of occupation had spawned a state that was not truly independent and whose existence was perceived to be ephemeral. Presumably, the German Democratic Republic would disappear within a united democratic Germany. The GDR was of concern only insofar as it might affect the German Question, the Berlin Question, military and strategic concerns, and relations with the Soviet Union. No steps could be taken in recognition of the German Democratic Republic that could weaken the democratic development of Western Germany and its integration in the West.

Fifth, the Berlin Question and the German Question diverged during this period. Defense of the Allied position in Berlin and freedom of West Berlin was a practical consideration that took precedence over solving the German Question.

A closer look at the hypotheses:

West Germany was on the fault line between the two power blocs in Europe. In the postwar period, the Soviet Union increasingly loomed as an adversary, and began by the time of the Kennedy Administration to achieve a level of nuclear capability that clearly made American concepts of massive retaliation outmoded, requiring that they be replaced with theories of flexible response. The German Democratic Republic was an excellent military jump-off pad for the Soviets but had no control over its own territory. It was heavily fortified, but the forces were either Soviet or under Soviet control. Thus, the GDR was not considered a state with which relations could affect the strategic balance, or the lessen the vulnerability of the West. All such decisions were in the hands of Moscow.

The fall of Czechoslovakia and the invasion of South Korea made Western vulnerability an issue and strengthened the American retreat from isolationism toward maintenance of a permanent military force in Europe and the creation of a defensive alliance. The fault line meant that Germany was a "front line state," which it remained until the end of Soviet control over Poland; but it also meant that the United States had experienced a revolution in foreign policy, and bipartisan internationalism was increasingly evident in Washington. This was the Truman Revolution. It was codified in the famous speech by Secretary of State Byrnes in Stuttgart on 6 September, 1946. Byrnes said:

> We have learned, whether we like it or not, that we live in one world, from which world we cannot isolate ourselves. ... We intend to continue our interest in the affairs of Europe and of the world. ... Security forces will probably have to remain in Germany for a long period. I want no misunderstanding. We are staying here. As long as there is an occupation army in Germany, American armed forces will be there as part of that occupation army.[4]

The defense of the West had become a primary goal of American policy. It remained the primary goal under Eisenhower and Dulles and was further cemented by two crucial developments: first, the death of Stalin and the arrival of a new leadership in the Soviet Union; and second, the gradual development of the USSR as a nuclear power. West German entrance into NATO solidified President Eisenhower's commitment to Bonn as the sole representative of the German people.

My second hypothesis suggests that unification was always a goal of American foreign policy, as long as the Germans themselves wanted it, when this seemed possible, and receded into the background only when other considerations made that expedient. Wolfgang-Uwe Friedrich describes American policy in regard to eventual German unification as "democratic Realpolitik."[5] For the Federal Republic of Germany, unification was a major public issue. As East Germans streamed across the border, it was an immediate crisis. For the United States, in a more global environment, German unification was only one of many problems. Nevertheless, it was an accepted element of American foreign policy in the immediate postwar years. Wolfram Hanrieder argues that Washington strove for a kind of "double containment," wherein both the Soviet Union and Germany would be contained by American policy.[6] This is too strong, and was more applicable to the immediate postwar years than later. American policy strove to change Germany, and to encourage its integration into the West. Never again would a kind of Germany be permitted to emerge that would challenge the peace of Europe. That kind of Germany would not arise. It would be replaced by a democratic Germany, firmly embracing Western principles, tied to Western European institutions, and not a risk to the peace of Europe.

What was not acceptable was a Germany floating between the blocs, in the *Schaukelpolitik* of old, nor one tied to the Soviet Union. Adenauer did not want this, and Dulles did not want it either. But, for both Adenauer and Dulles, integration of the Federal Republic of Germany into the West was a strong priority. Pragmatic realism ultimately made unification impossible during this period, but it continued to be alive in politics and could not be dismissed.[7] A democratic and economically strong and successful Federal Republic of Germany would be, in the American view, an attraction to the Germans in the GDR, and to all of Eastern Europe. Unification, therefore, would eventually come through this attraction and the weakness of the Soviet Union.[8]

The third hypothesis deals with the Federal Republic of Germany and its future role. Integration of the western part of Germany into the West was a major goal for Washington. It was the heart of American policy and was supported by both France and Britain, although each had its own idea of how that integration would be realized and what the role of West Germany would be. The United States encouraged the rearmament of the Federal Republic within a framework of mutual defense. At the same time, however, the Americans knew that the citizens of this brand new Bonn Republic were the same people who had been citizens of Hitler's Reich. Therefore, democratization was a major goal as well, and there was an understanding that it would take time until the constitutional practices had developed secure and accepted traditions. In other words, the adoption of a constitution called a provisional "Basic Law" did not immediately render West Germany a society of convinced democrats. Adenauer was himself cautious. Ambassador George McGhee, who served in Bonn during the chancellorships of Adenauer and Brandt, put it this way: "Long before I departed for Germany, the U.S. Government had recognized the Federal Republic of Germany as a key NATO ally. ... We also could not ignore the fact that Germany had recently lost a bitter war against the Western democracies and the Soviet Union."[9]

Because of its geography and rising economic importance, the Federal Republic was the cornerstone of Washington's European policy.[10] The new state had to be created, nurtured, encouraged in democratic development, and integrated into the West, and it had to produce a contribution to the mutual defense. It was the front line against Communism and the Soviets, and it would have to develop sufficient defensive capabilities while hosting large numbers of Allied forces. In its early years, its foreign activity would be limited. Afterwards, its foreign policy was expected to be closely tied to the global security policies of the West and to the European economic joint development that would ensure it prosperity and liberal government.

Complications began to emerge in the fifties. The growth of Soviet military and, especially, nuclear might made reconsiderations of defense strategy necessary. In 1957/58 the Rapacki Plan offered a nuclear-free zone for the Federal Republic of Germany, the German Democratic Republic, and Poland. The Berlin crisis during the Khrushchev period demonstrated the beginning of what some have called divergent security interests for the Federal Republic and the United States. This was prompted by the growth of Soviet nuclear power, reduction in the number of American forces in Germany, and the development of sea-based weapons, which gave the Americans an option of direct negotiations with the USSR. An American response in the direction of détente with the Soviet Union, better relations with East European states, or an American decision to seek a GDR signature on a nuclear test ban and nonproliferation agreements seemed possible.

Rising Soviet power led to a decoupling of the Berlin Question and the unification question. The search for conciliation with the Soviet

Union and a maintenance of the status quo anteceded Kennedy, and it was evident while Christian A. Herter was Secretary of State. The Dulles era was passing. As Nikita Khrushchev tried to boost the status of the GDR in the Berlin crisis of November 1958 when he proposed to transfer east Berlin to the GDR and recognize west Berlin as a separate entity, the German Question seemed to take a back seat. He followed this in January 1959 with a proposal for a peace treaty with the two German states as independent entities. The long crisis reached its end when Khrushchev failed to achieve his goal and the Allies refused to give up their rights for Berlin as a whole.

My fourth hypothesis argues that, within this context, the GDR as a state was meaningless. Perhaps it was even less than meaningless. It was considered a satellite regime, dominated by the Soviets, and the 17 June, 1953 rebellion demonstrated that its government would be blown away by popular revolt as soon as Moscow withdrew its troops. The GDR had negligible trading worth. It had no diplomatic weight in the world of the 1950s, and cultural contacts with the United States were virtually zero. There were only three areas in which Washington had any real concern about what the GDR was doing, and all three concerned the FRG as well. The first was the status of Berlin and everything that was in one way or another related to Berlin. Divided Berlin was the heart of divided Germany, the central emotional point. Western status in Berlin was both practically and symbolically representative of Western status in Germany as a whole. It was the nexus of the American European position, both strategically and as far as the future of West Germany was concerned. The second area was of German-German relations. The third, of course, was whether the GDR would ever acquire nuclear weapons.

As far as the first, the status of Berlin was concerned, this was a major matter for the GDR. The GDR had designated Berlin its capital. It was also an obvious sticking point because of the Four Power rights in the city. The United States was totally unwilling to grant the GDR any kind of status in Berlin that would compromise Four Power rights. American military vehicles patrolled the streets all through the city, including daily patrols into the Soviet zone. Air traffic was regulated by the four powers. Entrance into the zones was regulated by the Four Powers. The Western Powers insisted that the Soviet authority in their sector was equivalent to theirs in their sectors. The GDR claims in eastern Berlin would not diminish any of the Allied rights. Right up until 1990, the United States held with remarkable and obvious consistency to the agreements giving it authority in Berlin and over Germany as a whole.

During the Berlin blockade of 1948–49 and the second great Berlin crisis of 1958–61, when the Soviets tried to break Allied control over the city, they did attempt to secure some role for the East Germans. The Soviet Union did attempt to proclaim a version of GDR sovereignty, but this was not accepted by the Western Allies. For example, on 25 March, 1954, a Soviet declaration attributed full sovereignty to the German Democratic Republic. It was followed on 8 April, by a declaration of the Allied High Commission denying that sovereignty: "These governments do not recognize the sovereignty of the East German regime which is not based upon free elections, and do not intend to deal with it as a government."[11] On 17 July 1961, an American note to the Soviet Union on "Questions of Germany and Berlin" stated that the German Democratic Republic, referred to in quotation marks, "has been created by the Soviet Union as an instrument of Soviet foreign policy."[12]

A second area of importance in which the GDR was involved was German-German relations. The United States would not favor a neutral German state. By reviving the German Question, the Soviet Union could hope to thwart further integration of the Federal Republic into the West, including a military alliance; thus, the Stalin Note of 1952, and the various proposals for neutralization of a united Germany. Dulles would not accept such a possibility. A united and fully armed Germany bound to no alliance and free and loose in Europe, he told Willy Brandt in 1959, was simply unacceptable.

Maintaining Allied rights in Berlin was important to West Germany, because that meant maintaining the freedom of Berlin. The Hallstein Doctrine claimed that the Federal Republic was the sole democratic representative of Germany's people and asked other states not to recognize the GDR. Strictly speaking, even the Federal Republic did not follow this dictum completely, because there were many "technical contacts" with GDR officials in the Autobahn travel from the Federal Republic of Germany to Berlin and elsewhere. When Dulles in 1959 talked about GDR officials being "agents" of the USSR, the West Germans could not deny the Americans what they themselves were doing. Some sort of contact was necessary. Some have interpreted this American position as a softening; others—such as German Ambassador Grewe—viewed it as a tactical move.

This brings me to the fifth hypothesis, namely that the Berlin Question and the German Question began to diverge within this period. Berlin was both a part of the German Question, the ultimate reunification of Germany, and the Cold War. Should the Allies withdraw from Berlin, or the Allied position in Berlin be weakened, or anything happen that might subject West Berlin to East German influence, this would affect the struggle of the West with the Soviet Union. The Allied position in Berlin would be maintained, and West Germany would be integrated into the Western Alliance. Unification of Germany did not seem imminent. American policy was riveted upon Bonn, which should be integrated into the West, develop prosperity, and rear a new and democratic future generation. With respect to the German Question, Washington found no need to go beyond the policies of its German ally. Eventually, when diplomatic relations were finally established between the United States and the GDR, they were of the most limited kind, and concentrated upon certain set objectives. Never did a leader of the GDR visit the United States. Bonn had primacy, and this was to be known, to be emphasized, and to be underscored. There was no thought of playing one off against the other or developing relations with the GDR so as to create a legitimized, permanent, second German state. The United States treated the GDR as if it were a semi-autonomous Soviet province that owed its existence to Soviet troops and would disappear at some appropriate time.

On the other hand, and for precisely those reasons, the United States had a position of utmost importance for the GDR. This was the case for the entire 40-year history of the ill-fated state. During the time of the Cold War, the United States was the enemy incarnate. Textbooks, placards, propaganda through all of the media stressed how the United States was an imperialist power out to conquer the globe. RIAS, the American-sponsored radio station in Berlin, was singled out for special denunciation; cartoons depicted RIAS poison descending upon unsuspecting Eastern Germans. Dollar imperialism was another favorite theme. While criticizing the United States, it was equally important to gain recognition and legitimacy. This enemy image was continuous, projected by the regime throughout its existence. It was all the more necessary as the German Democratic Republic failed to prevent the flight of its own people to West Germany.

The success and freedom of the FRG contrasted only too obviously with the oppression and misery in the Soviet sphere. The German people in the East voted, as Lenin would have said, with their feet. They left. The GDR's own people denied it legitimacy. They went West, and the Wall was the result. With hundreds of thousands of American soldiers rotating in and out of West Germany, with students from American universities by the tens of thousands studying in the Federal Republic, and with untold numbers of American tourists, business people as well as politicians streaming past the Wall, it became for Americans the symbol not only of German division, but of the GDR as a giant prison. It may have served to help the economy and prevent the state from bleeding to death, but for Americans it robbed the state of any semblance of legitimacy.

America relied upon Germany as France and Britain assumed a different place. The Fourth French Republic was wounded in the quagmire of Vietnam and continued struggles with African territories that were striving for independence. Together with Britain, France pursued one last Middle Eastern gamble over the Suez Canal, then both retired to lick their wounds. Germany was the front line state in Europe, and the Western Powers relationship with the United States soon underwent a transformation. It took almost 40 years before George Bush could shock the Britons by speaking in Mainz in 1989 about a "partnership in leadership" with the FRG, but the new role of Germany after the Second World War, a role assumed by geography as well as by economic strength, clearly meant that the United States would base much of its security policy upon successful German membership in vital transatlantic institutions and in integrative Western European institutions. Even before West Germany achieved greater authority in foreign policy, Bonn had a level of importance that was crucial to U.S.-Soviet relations and to the future of Europe. Any American policy toward the GDR would have to take that into account. As Wolfram Hanrieder put it, "at least potentially, Germany replaced Britain in its traditional role as the arbiter of the European equilibrium, a role which neither superpower was ready to concede to the Germans. It was a role that France was also determined to deny to the Germans."[13]

The GDR was insignificant for the United States, but it was a *glacis*, a jumping off point for the Soviets, and could not be totally ignored. As it built the Wall in its quest for legitimacy and permanence, the GDR was a Soviet pawn in the struggle for Germany's future. The GDR administered sixteen million Germans, and was a satrapy that held its place in the Soviet economic sphere for a time. The United States might ultimately be forced to recognize it—but in the meantime need not deal with it. All legitimate bases of American rights in Germany were to be maintained, and the Soviet Union was the negotiating partner.

The questions revolving around Germany in the 1950s were vital to the United States. Nothing less than the future of Europe was at stake, and the future of the United States hung on the outcome of the Cold War. The German Democratic Republic was never considered an independent actor, which it was not. But more than that, more than other client states of the Soviet Union in Eastern Europe, Washington preferred to ignore it whenever possible. Its very existence was not accepted in American policy. It was, literally, a state which was not there.

Notes

1. David Conradt, *The German Polity* (New York, Longman, many editions).
2. Manfred Jonas, *The United States and Germany: A Diplomatic History* (Ithaca: Cornell University, 1984), 304.
3. Hans W. Gatzke, *Germany and the United States: A Special Relationship?* (Cambridge: Harvard University, 1980), 258.
4. "Address by Secretary of State Byrnes on United States Policy Regarding Germany," Stuttgart, 6 September, 1946, in United States Department of State, *Documents on Germany 1944–1985*, Department of State Publication 9446, 91.
5. Wolfgang-Uwe Friedrich, "Demokratische Realpolitik: Die Deutsche Frage als Problem der deutsch-amerikanischen Beziehungen 1949–1990" in Wolfgang-Uwe Friedrich, ed., *Die USA und die Deutsche Frage 1945–1990* (Frankfurt: Campus, 1991).
6. Wolfram Hanrieder, *Germany, America, Europe: Forty Years of German Foreign Policy* (New Haven: Yale University, 1989).
7. Wolf D. Gruner, *Die deutsche Frage: Ein Problem der europäischen Geschichte seit 1800* (Munich: C. H. Beck, 1985), 190–93.
8. See Klaus Schwabe, "Deutschlandpolitik als Integrationspolitik: Die USA und die Deutsche Frage, 1945–1954", in Friedrich, ed., 120.
9. George McGhee, *At the Creation of a New Germany* (New Haven: Yale University, 1989), 7.
10. See Hans-Jürgen Schröder, "Amerikanische Deutschlandpolitik im Kalten Krieg 1954–1961," in Friedrich, ed., 129.
11. See *Documents on Germany 1944–1985*, 418–19.
12. "Note from the United States to the Soviet Union on the Questions of Germany and Berlin, July 17, 1961," *Documents on Germany 1944–1985*, 756–57.
13. Hanrieder, *Germany, America, Europe*, 135.

5. WEST GERMAN RECONSTRUCTION AND AMERICAN INDUSTRIAL CULTURE, 1945–1960

Volker R. Berghahn

For many years after the second World War, political scientists and historians approached the reconstruction of the western parts of the defunct German Reich primarily from a political perspective. The same is true of the early history of the Federal Republic that emerged from the three western zones of occupation in 1949. Thus we have a large number of studies on the rebuilding of political parties and on the debates surrounding the drafting of the Bonn Basic Law.[1] A good deal of work has also been done on the de-Nazification and reeducation policies of the Allies and on the creation of a bureaucratic infrastructure to try to administer the chaos that the Nazi dictatorship and the war had left behind.[2] Books and articles have finally appeared on the situation of millions of refugees, displaced persons, and prisoners of war.[3] As for the 1950s, the workings of the West German parliamentary system, voting behavior, and federalism have received extensive attention.[4] Many studies have dealt with the thorny rearmament issue and with West Germany's political reintegration into Western Europe at the height of the Cold War.[5] In short, our knowledge of West German reconstruction from a political perspective, while by no means complete, is substantial.

As far as economic reconstruction is concerned, the state of research is far less satisfactory. Economic historians, it is true, have made good progress on the collection of quantitative material.[6] The origins and the impact of the Marshall Plan have inevitably provided a major focus in this respect,[7] and we have even had some controversy in this field in the wake of Werner Abelshauser's research, which has tended to downplay the significance of outside aid in the rise of the West German economy.[8] As for the 1950s, the "Economic Miracle" has been analyzed both from a quantitative and from an ideological perspective, with Ludwig Erhard's concept of *Soziale Marktwirtschaft* and the neo-liberal Freiburg School as focal points.[9] More recently, business historians have also entered the field to examine the development of individual firms or of branches of industry as they were subjected to Allied deconcentration and decartellization plans.[10] Finally, some work is now available on the reemergence of industrial pressure groups to complement the research that started quite early on the founding of trade unions and the construction of a new pattern of industrial relations, after the collapse of the peculiar system of labor organization and mobilization that the Nazis and the war had produced.[11]

Still, much work is left to be done, and it is to be hoped that the end of the Cold War will direct attention away from the political and security aspects of early West German history toward the economy; for, if one reads general histories of the period, which can, of course, do no more than reflect the state of research at a given time, the reader is rarely given the impression that West Germany rose to become one of the most powerful industrial nations of the postwar era.[12] The index of such histories tends to list many unknown politicians and generals; but one looks in vain for the names of leading industrialists and bankers, even though their contribution to the reconstruction process was much more important. This article cannot possibly fill all the gaps that continue to exist in our understanding of West Germany's economic reconstruction. Rather it aims to raise the question of the broader framework within which this process might most helpfully be analyzed. This is a framework that may also be useful for understanding the development of other Western European economies and societies after 1945 so that it may also open up opportunities for comparative historical research.

In introducing this framework, it seems best to begin with a debate that has been going on virtually since the end of the second World War about the meaning of the year 1945. The initial view was that the total defeat and collapse of the Third Reich represented a decisive rupture in modern German history. Contemporaries perceived 1945 as the "Zero Hour" when Germany, or at least the western zones of occupation, made a completely fresh start.[13] By the 1960s, this notion had come under vigorous attack. There was a growing impression, buttressed by elaborate research, that the postwar period had been one of restoration and that hence the continuities were more important to an understanding of the evolution of West German politics and society than the discontinuities.[14] This article argues that it is not possible to make such neat distinctions and that the country experienced both. In this sense, reconstruction has an ambiguous meaning that we should be clear about. On the one hand, it implies a rebuilding of what had existed before, and not just in a material sense. People, most of whom, after all, survived the war, do not change their attitudes, thought habits, and traditions overnight. Ideas, even if, objectively, they have become badly compromised, do live an "after-life."[15] This definitely applies to Germany's industrial elites, most of whom navigated the end of the Nazi regime quite well and soon found themselves in positions of power and influence once again. Not surprisingly perhaps, they tended to adhere to concepts of industrial organization that they had worked with before 1945.[16] At most they were prepared to shed only those that had been so thoroughly discredited as to have become unrespectable. In short, there was a good deal of conservatism and continuity that guided the reconstruction process in the industrial field.

On the other hand, it would be wrong to overlook that there was also change. Consequently, reconstruction is defined here also in the sense of recasting. It is argued that *Wiederaufbau* was more than rebuilding in the old style; it was also *Umbau*, not in a revolutionary sense, but in the sense that what ultimately emerged was a curious combination of old and new, with the balance tilted more toward the new in some issue areas and toward the old in others. In other words, there was no restoration in the strict meaning of the word; nor was there a rupture that turned German society and its economy upside down to give rise to something different. The challenge and difficult task is therefore to calibrate more precisely the mix of old and new and to identify the agents of change.

As regards West German industry, generational change was no doubt an important factor in the *Umbau* process.[17] With the gradual disappearance of an older generation of entrepreneurs that continued to cherish the traditional organizational forms and mindset of industry of the pre-1945 period, there emerged a younger generation whose socialization experience had been different and who found it easier to adapt to postwar ideas and conditions than their elders.

However, it is doubtful that change would have come so quickly after 1945, had it not been for the impact of an outside factor that had a profound influence on the development of the West German industrial system: the United States. This point will be plausible to all who accept the premise that America became the undisputed hegemonic power of the Western world after 1945. There is plenty of evidence, it seems, that Western Europe began to live under a Pax Americana, just as Eastern Europe came to exist under the Pax Sovietica.[18] But seeing the United States as an agent of change will be suspect to those "revisionists," particularly of the Williams School, who perceive America as a conservative power that tried, during the Cold War era, to restore and stabilize Western Europe and the Federal Republic as the most exposed region in its sphere of influence, right along the Iron Curtain.[19] However, it would seem unwise to underestimate the determination of Washington to do more than conserve Western Germany as an anti-Communist bastion and to affect something less than a tangible structural transformation of the German industrial system and, through it, of other Western European economies as well. American intervention in the Schuman Plan negotiations in 1950/51 is a telling case in point.[20]

Washington's determination to transform can be traced back to the beginning of the second World War, when the Allies found themselves locked in a life-and-death struggle with Hitler. Historians have interpreted the meaning of that war from a variety of angles. Again the power-political and military significance has been studied most intensively.[21] The war is also well understood as a struggle against the racist visions of Hitler's New Order.[22] But it was also a gigantic conflict between two ways of organizing a capitalist-industrial economy. This was certainly how it looked from the German side at the height of the war when victory seemed just around the corner. None of the various reordering concepts that were being debated in 1941/42, both within the Reich government and between the Nazi bureaucracy and the country's industrial and financial elites, found unanimous support.[23] However, there was a broad consensus that Germany would form a continental European bloc from the Atlantic coast to the Urals and beyond. The question of how open this bloc would be toward the rest of the world was never completely resolved, though the exigencies of the war helped strengthen the hand of the autarkists who expected the German-dominated bloc to be taken out of the world economy.

Basic agreement also existed about how this bloc was to be organized internally. German political leadership in the occupied territories was invariably taken for granted. The question was merely how far this leadership would extend to the reorganization of industry. Göring and some other top Nazis favored large-scale state intervention and direction. Others, an overwhelming majority of the captains of industry among them, supported the notion of guidance through private associations, on the model of the cartel system that they had perfected within the country during the 1930s. The literature published on this subject in Germany in the early 1940s is most revealing in this respect. [24] Probably one of the most detailed proposals to organize the economies of Europe on a cartel basis was produced by Arno Sölter, an economist close to the research centers set up by Werner Daitz, who in 1941 published his book *Grossraumkartell (Closed Space Cartel)*.[25] It is instructive reading for anyone interested in discovering what the New Economic Order might have looked like. No less importantly, like Hitler, all these experts saw the United States, rather than the Soviet Union, as the main antagonist and counter-model;[26] indeed, they viewed the Soviet model of socioeconomic organization with disdain, and its imminent defeat was taken for granted. Nor did they have much respect for the British Empire. Rather it was America that the Germans thought of when, in 1940, they read the following analysis of what was at stake in this global struggle: "And thus, in searching for the root cause of the quest for autarchy, we encounter two opposing modes of thought: the world-economic, cosmopolitan and the national-economic view. ... The notion of autarchy hence finds its basic root in the distinction between national economy and world economy, or, to be more precise: in the organizational principles that shape and regulate a national economy and its relations with other national economies." [27]

This is also how the contrast was seen in 1941/42 in Washington. Following the traumatic experiences of the Great Slump, influential American politicians and businessmen, especially on the East Coast, had begun by the late 1930s to move back to the idea of a peaceful, liberal-capitalist, Open Door multilateral world trading system to be established in the event of an Allied victory against the Axis powers.[28] The New Economic Order that they saw emerging in occupied Europe and in the Far East in the shape of Japan's Greater East Asian Co-Prosperity Sphere[29] was anathema to them, as, of course, were the Nazis' brutal policies of repression and "ethnic cleansing." The contrast was articulated in many articles and public declarations that appeared in the United States, particularly after 1941, among which Henry Luce's famous article in *Life* of February 1942, entitled "The American Century," was most frequently cited.[30] In this connection it is also worth re-reading the text of the Atlantic Charter, which encapsulated American peace aims so well.

Thenceforth these peace aims were refined by Washington, often in conjunction with a variety of think tanks where politicians met with academics and business leaders to discuss the shaping of the postwar world. Among these bodies, the Committee on Economic Development (CED) quickly began to play a leading role.[31] Central to its work in conferences and discussions during the early 1940s was the notion that, after this war, the second within a generation, the world economy had to be given a viable organizational and constitutional framework.[32] Once the rules of an Open Door capitalist order had been set, the players in industry would adjust their behavior and their national structures to comply with this new economic constitution. Nor is it surprising that it was the American industrial system that, in the view of the CED and of other leading associations, was to serve as the model for other countries. One of the key features of this model, enshrined in a voluminous body of anti-Trust legislation and jurisdiction, was the securing of the principle of market competition and the rejection of cartels and syndicates.[33] Other features will be discussed below.

The defeat of the Axis powers in 1945 implied that the American model of industrial organization had won out over those of Germany and Japan. To be sure, with the beginning of the Cold War, chances of establishing the kind of "One World" that the planners in the CED had been dreaming of during the war quickly diminished. What emerged was a Western "half world," [34] as Stalin set out to Sovietize the Eastern half that had fallen to him with the defeat of Hitler. But there were also differences of opinion in Washington over what to do with Germany and Japan. On the whole there was less dispute about whether the latter country should be reconstructed and reintegrated into the Western New Economic Order. As for Germany, it was above all the promotion of the Morgenthau Plan with its proposed deindustrialization of the Ruhr, the industrial heart and powerhouse of the Third Reich, that made its place within the emergent Pax Americana temporarily uncertain.[35] Although the Plan itself was shelved even before the end of the war, enough advocates both in Washington and in the U.S. occupation administration between 1944 and 1947 continued to call for a severe punishment of the Germans so that major interdepartmental struggles were unleashed between the Morgenthauians and those who believed early reconstruction and reintegration of Germany and its industrial potential to be indispensable to the success of postwar peace and prosperity at a level that had been achieved in the United States. By 1947 the Morgenthauians had been pushed into the background by the "reconstructionists," who now proceeded to reorganize West German industry along the lines of competitive liberal capitalism.[36] A key figure in this undertaking was a very interesting businessman: William Draper, a partner of Dillon, Read & Co. and head of the Economic Division in the Office of U.S. Military Government, who later moved to Japan to try out similar recipes of industrial transformation. Cartels and syndicates were outlawed; at the same time decartellization was not to be confounded with deconcentration. Only giant corporations such as IG Farben and Vereinigte Stahlwerke, which had enjoyed virtual monopoly positions under Nazism, were to be broken up into smaller units.[37] Yet these units were still to be large enough to be able to compete in the world market and, above all, to act as engines of growth during the reconstruction process.

It is important to bear these American goals in mind if one wants to understand why it was not a matter of restoring what had existed in Germany before 1933, but rather of transforming the highly structured and regimented capitalism that operated in Germany by the 1930s and that was deemed to have sustained the Third Reich and made its aggressive policies of conquest and exploitation possible. It must also be noted that Washington's industrial policies generated a good deal of resentment and resistance on the part of those West German entrepreneurs who, having reemerged in their companies and associations pretty much unscathed, continued to regard the German cartel system as fundamentally sound and worth retaining. This is an area where we can very neatly trace how powerful, older traditions and attitudes now came to enjoy an "after-life." To be sure, during the occupation period these traditions remained largely underground, as the Americans repeatedly threatened to prosecute relapses into the old pattern. But with the emergence of the Federal Republic and its gradual achievement of semi-sovereignty the question arose—as, by the way, it did in Japan, which was exposed to very similar pressures to adopt American-style anti-Trust measures—of how Allied decrees could be turned into permanent laws democratically ratified by the new Bonn Parliament.[38] Ludwig Erhard, the economics minister, became a determined advocate of a law "to secure competition."[39] As he put it in a speech in 1953, the bill he had presented to Parliament for this purpose constituted nothing less than the "Economic Basic Law" to complement the (political) Basic Law that had been introduced, also with American assistance, in 1949.[40] These Basic Laws were to set the framework and the ground rules by which West Germany would operate its parliamentary system, on the one the other. In the American view, a modern industrial society needed an open economic marketplace just as much as it required a free-wheeling political "market." These markets were complementary, and one could not exist without the other. In this sense, there were also two reeducation jobs to be done—one political and another of economic.

However, since many older businessmen found it so difficult to allow themselves to be "reeducated," Erhard met with vigorous opposition, especially from the conservative managers of heavy industry. Their enterprises had been among the most heavily cartellized in the past, and they now found it very difficult to come to terms with the different environment of the postwar Pax Americana. Their mobilizing efforts were so effective that Erhard's "Economic Basic Law" was delayed until 1957, when a compromise was finally struck: cartels and syndicates were outlawed in principle, as they had been in the United States by the Sherman Act since 1890; but a number of exceptions, to be granted by a supervisory Cartel Office, were permitted.[41] German industry has occasionally made use of this possibility. In the long term, however, it was wrenched away from its cartel tradition and developed, like its American counterpart, in an oligopolistic direction. Capitalist concentration resumed, promoting the emergence of multinationals such as Bayer, Siemens, and Volkswagen. Accordingly, Bayer, Hoechst, and BASF, which were forged from the breakup of IG Farben, today compete in the world market against giant American, Japanese, and British corporations, but also against each other. In this sense, German industry was not merely reconstructed but also recast. Its organizational structures look very different today from what they did before 1945.

The impact of the economic Pax Americana can be traced in spheres other than that of market organization. This larger influence is reflected in a revealing statement by R.M. Bissell Jr., the second-in-command in the Marshall Plan Administration in Europe. "Coca-Cola and Hollywood movies," he wrote, may be regarded in Europe "as two products of a shallow and crude civilization."[42] However, "American machinery, American management, and [American] engineering are everywhere respected." His hope was therefore that "a few European unions and entrepreneurs can be induced to try out the philosophy of higher productivity, higher wages, and higher profits from the lower prices and lower unit costs." He concluded: "It will not require enormous sums of money (even of European capital) to achieve vaster increases in production. But it will require a profound shift in social attitudes, attuning them to the mid-twentieth century."

Bissell here alluded to two interrelated factors that are perhaps even more relevant to the reconstruction question than the problem of decartellization and liberal-capitalist competition. The first factor is best discussed by reference to the work of American-trained Münster University sociologist Heinz Hartmann. In 1963 he published a book, entitled *Amerikanische Firmen in Deutschland (American Firms in Germany)*, in which he investigated the export of American industrial culture and its impact, primarily via American subsidiaries, on West Germany's industry.[43] Hartmann began by querying the then widespread view that technological exports pose fewer analytical problems than the export of organizations, attitudes, and ideologies, for example of the kind mentioned above with reference to market structures. Indeed, to him, he wrote, it is misleading to differentiate between so-called instrumental exports (machinery, etc.), on the one hand, and exports of a cultural kind, on the other. In his view, technology as such is never transferred from one country to another. There are always values behind technology that cannot be separated out. The adoption of foreign technology therefore inevitably involves acceptance of doctrines and attitudes, of which the technology is merely a tangible expression.

This means that when, during the period of reconstruction, West German companies introduced American technology, as many of them did, they imported more than machines, involving them in a complex process of interaction between the two industrial cultures. The case of Otto A. Friedrich, a member of the board of directors of Phoenix Gummiwaren A.G. in Harburg and later the company's director general, offers an illustration of this interaction and its complexities. As Friedrich recorded in his diary on 6 February 1948, his factory's equipment was lagging behind American technology by "many years."[44] Several months later, after inspecting a production hall for inner tubes, he noted that no "technological innovations and improvements" had been made, "except for a slightly more rational disposition of machinery."[45] However, some of this machinery, as Friedrich added, was so old that it could have been sent straight to the Museum of Technology at Munich. Meanwhile, news arrived from the United States that its rubber industry was undergoing a "revolutionary development" in blending technology. Given Phoenix's technological backwardness, it would take years, he wrote on 28 September 1948, to catch up.[46] He concluded that he would have to study the problem on location "as soon as possible."

But crossing the Atlantic and buying machinery was going to be very expensive. For example, a mold that Phoenix had ordered to be able to manufacture American-style "super cushion" tires cost some DM 20,000. Clearly, it was cheaper to sign cooperation agreements with American companies that were prepared to take a direct stake in Phoenix and share their technological secrets. And indeed this became the main purpose of Friedrich's trip to Akron, Ohio, in January 1949. There he visited B.F. Goodrich, whose management was showing an interest in a long-term licensing agreement and seemed prepared to put some capital into the German company. After Friedrich's return to Germany, negotations continued for many months and ultimately came to nought. Instead Phoenix linked up with Firestone Tire Company, which injected capital and technology and helped make Phoenix one of the leading tire manufacturers of West Germany. The relationship enabled the Harburg company to gain a head start in the development of tubeless tires when they came along in 1953.

However, Friedrich's relationship with America, where he had worked for several years as a young man in the 1920s, did not end there. He became one of the major voices in West German industry who were open to the import of the industrial-cultural goods that the United States offered to Europe after 1945. Thus, in 1949 he hired Paul Kura to improve employee relations in the company. Information and a company newsletter were distributed, and Kura was mandated to write a statement on "Ford's work methods." [47] As Friedrich noted in his diary on 18 Novembe, 1949: "I have left him the other materials that I collected on industrial relations in America. ..." Kura was also asked to organize a demonstration of American human-relations methods in the tire production shop. But Friedrich soon began to wonder whether the time was ripe for this step. He confessed he was very sympathetic toward American ideas; yet he was also aware of the reservations that his colleagues and the West German unions had about importing too many industrial practices from across the Atlantic. He therefore decided to engage in some vigorous proselytizing in the hope that West German industry, over time, would adopt at least some of the broader principles of American industrial culture. Accordingly he gave many public lectures on his impressions of the United States. He also promised, for example, Hans Rüger, the boss of Metzeler Tires, to send him his collection of "articles about Henry Ford II and the American system of shareholding by the workforce." [48] Meanwhile Otto's brother Carl Joachim, a well-known political science professor at Harvard University, urged that he study the curriculum of the Havard Business School and send one of his junior managers on the School's courses.

As this example shows, what must be studied is how the foreign imports are being offered by the country of origin. But we must also examine the assumptions and mentalities of the receiving industrial culture, because they are likely to act as filters. These filters will test how far the proposed imports are compatible with indigenous traditions. In other words, there are potentially very powerful impediments to the importation of foreign technologies and techniques, the analysis of which tells us something more generally about the character and evolution of the two interacting industrial systems and, in particular, the relationship between the hegemonic and the dependent power.

This is where the second factor comes into play. Few people in the late 1940s and early 1950s were more conscious of these difficulties of transfer than Bissell and his superior, Paul Hoffman, himself a former president of the Studebaker Corp. and a member of the CED. It is with the aim of easing the export of industrial culture that they used some of the Marshall Plan funds to promote visits by European managers and trade unionists to the United States to inspect at first hand the secrets of American mass production methods, but to see at the same time the fruits of low-cost, rationalized production as they benefited the mass consumption society that America had become. Henry Ford had been the first to make this link between mass production and mass consumption and had turned it into a powerful ideology.[49] More than this, Fordist ideology had yielded practical results; it had delivered the promised goods: his introduction of the assembly line had enabled him to reduce the price of the automobile so that by the 1920s it had become an affordable consumer good. As Bissell said, the hope was that the visitors would enthusiastically carry the Fordist message back to Europe and establish a similar link promising higher living standards and general prosperity. And for those who had to stay behind, Hoffman introduced a Training-Within-Industry program that would introduce participants to American industrial culture back in Europe.

Again, as in other spheres, there was opposition to the introduction of American methods of management and factory organization. Even the use of the word "manager" was frowned upon by some as unsuitable for the West German situation.[50] Insofar as these opponents believed in any management training at all, they would send their employees to Reinhard Hoehn's Harzburg Academy, where they would be taught an authoritarian model of leadership inspired by the Prussian General Staff.[51] So, here, too, there were obstacles, cultural and ideological "filters" that the hegemonic power of the West had to contend with in Germany and elsewhere. Other businessmen were more open to American ideas, and not only because they appreciated more quickly than their conservative colleagues that the by now massive hegemonic weight of the United States would decisively shape the structures and modes of operation of business in the Western world economy. They were willing to experiment and to integrate themselves in the genuine conviction that American, rather than traditional German, methods offered the best solution to the problems of modern industry. A man who represented this type of businessman well and who belonged to a younger generation of postwar managers was Ludwig Vaubel, soon to become director general of Vereinigte Glanzstoff, the chemicals trust in Wuppertal. In 1950, he had been the first German to complete the Advanced Management Course at the Harvard Business School.[52] His experiences there convinced him that West German industry was lagging far behind that of the United States. On his return, he therefore founded the "Wuppertal Circle," which organized seminars, modeled along American lines, designed to help fellow-industrialists catch up.[53] Later the group was expanded to become an umbrella organization for a network of institutes whose mission it was to spread knowledge about modern management through courses and publications and to promote contacts between academics in the universities and managers from various branches of industry.[54]

The revitalization of production was, therefore, never a goal in itself. The main aim of the "politics of productivity" [55] that became such a central part of the reconstruction effort, also in West Germany, was always to generate "prosperity for all," as Erhard typically proclaimed it,[56] and to raise consumption to levels already attained in the United States. Rationalized production of civilian goods on a mass basis with the latest industrial technology—complemented by full employment and low inflation, the other magic formulae of the postwar American boom—was to go hand in hand with mass consumption and widespread affluence.[57] The onset of the Cold War gave a fresh sense of urgency to these tasks, as material well-being and economic competition came to be used as Western antidotes to the specter of a Stalinist command economy and a policy of austerity adopted in Europe—just as a sharp contrast was drawn between the political "totalitarianism" of the Communists and the free "wheeling and dealing" of liberal parliamentary democracy.[58] Still, even if the Cold War had never started, the American model of mass production and mass consumption, as it has been presented here, would have been offered as part of reconstruction under the Pax Americana. Except for a very brief period in the mid-1920s and in only a few branches, German industry had never tried to make the link between mass production and mass consumption.[59] The Nazi economy, with its mass production for war and its adoption of an austerity program for the population, came to be the opposite of the Fordist dream, and the building of the Volkswagen Works in 1938 does not contradict this conclusion.[60]

The story does not end here. Bissell, it will be remembered, had been rather derogatory about "Coca-Cola and Hollywood movies." And yet, it seems, if one looks at West German reconstruction and the influence of American industrial culture, such consumer products, too, deserve our attention. At least a strong case can be made that it was not just West German market organizations and management methods that became "Americanized"; the West German consumer also fell under America's spell. Unfortunately this field is even more a *terra incognita* than the history of industrial reconstruction. And yet, looking around in Germany today, it is certainly striking to see how deep an inroad American consumer culture has made into that society.[61] The phenomenon is particularly striking in youth culture—its music, its dress, and its demeanor—as well as in the infusion of Americanisms into the German language.[62] But there are also the supermarkets, the fast-food restaurants, the television talk shows. There has been some debate whether this "Americanization of daily life" has been no more than an aspect of a wider modernization process affecting all advanced industrial and urban societies.[63] However, the term "modernization" would seem to be rather a catchall concept when more precise analytical categories are needed. Above all, it fails to deal with the fact that the ways and styles in which this "modern culture" expressed itself in Germany tended to appear in the United States first, before they traveled across the Atlantic, and this applies equally to both production and consumption.

At the same time it would be wrong to deny that the Germans, like other Europeans, have resisted American cultural imports. When Disney opened a theme park north of Paris, a prominent French politician spoke of a "cultural Chernobyl." Similar attitudes can be found in West Germany, often resulting in a reassertion of traditional German customs and values, both regional and national. This resistance was even stronger, at least in some quarters, during the early postwar period and found expression in a blatant anti-Americanism. On the other hand, just like German businessmen, the majority of Germans developed rather more ambiguous feelings toward cultural imports from across the Atlantic. At no point was the American model, the American way of doing things, adopted *in toto*, either in industry or in society at large. Instead, imports from America were tailored to fit the peculiarities of Germany's traditions. What emerged, therefore, was a blending of two industrial cultures, the results of which we can now study as we look at German society during the reconstruction period under the Pax Americana.

However, this article goes beyond an attempt to demonstrate the viability of an approach that looks at the reconstruction period in terms of a partial *Umbau*, a recasting, and a German-American industrial-cultural symbiosis and partial assimilation. It also offers, it seems to me, a way to undertake the comparative study of Western European societies, even if it is a comparison of a special kind; for, ultimately, this contribution deals with the history of an uneven relationship between two advanced industrial countries after World War II. There appears to be little doubt that America had a tangible influence on the development of West Germany's industry by virtue of its hegemonic weight. It can be assumed to have had a similar weight upon other Western European societies and upon Japan during the same period. The first task would therefore be to deepen our understanding of the American impact on these countries during the period of postwar reconstruction. In some cases this work has already begun, if one thinks of Richard Kuisel's work on France or Victoria de Grazia's on Italy.[64] Once further studies are available it will be possible to begin to extend the comparison between individual European societies, with the United States still serving as the *tertium comparationis* in the background that most comparative historians nowadays agree is the indispensable reference point for any viable comparison, because without this yardstick it will never be possible to know whether we are dealing with phenomena that are, in fact, comparable.

Notes

1. See, e.g., E.J. Davidson, *The Death and Life of Germany* (New York, 1959); A. Heidenheimer, *Adenauer and the CDU* (The Hague, 1960); G. Pridham, *Christian Democracy in Western Germany* (London, 1977); L. Herbst, ed., *Westdeutschland, 1945–1955* (Munich, 1986); K. Klotzbach, *Der Weg zur Staatspartei* (Berlin, 1982); J. Becker et al., eds., *Vorgeschichte der Bundesrepublik Deutschland* (Munich, 1979); K.P. Tauber, *Beyond Eagle and Swastika* (Middletown, Conn., 1962); P.H. Merkl, *The Origins of the West German Republic* (Oxford, 1963); W.-D. Narr, *CDU—SPD* (Stuttgart, 1966); H.-P. Schwarz, *Vom Reich zur Bundesrepublik* (Stuttgart, 1980); W. Benz, *Die Gründung der Bundesrepublik*, (Munich, 1984); A. Mintzel, *Die CSU* (Opladen, 1975); D. Buchhaas, *Die Volkspartei* (Düsseldorf, 1982); T. Eschenburg, *Jahre der Besatzung* (Stuttgart, 1983); J.F. Golay, *The Founding of the Federal Republic of*

Germany (Chicago, 1958); F.K. Fromme, *Von der Weimarer Verfassung zum Bonner Grundgesetz* (Tübingen, 1962).

2. See, e.g., L. Niethammer, *Entnazifizierung in Bayern* (Frankfurt, 1972); C. FitzGibbon, *Denazification* (London, 1969); M. Balfour, *Four-Power Control in Germany* (London,1956); H. Zink, *The United States in Germany* (Princeton, 1957); J. Tent, *Mission on the Rhine* (Chicago, 1982); M. Roseman, *Recasting the Ruhr, 1945–1958* (Oxford, 1992); J.E. Farquharson, *The Western Allies and the Politics of Food* (New York, 1985); J. Gimbel, *The American Occupation of Germany* (Stanford, 1968); H. Dollinger, *Deutschland unter den Besatzungsmächten* (Munich, 1967); E.N. Peterson, *The American Occupation of Germany* (Detroit, 1978).

3. See, e.g., E. Pfeil et al., *Eingliederunschancen und Eingliederungserfolge* (Tübingen, 1954); W. Benz, ed., *Die Vertreibung der Deutschen aus dem Osten* (Frankfurt, 1985).

4. See, e.g., G. Loewenberg, *Parlamentarismus im politischen System der Bundesrepublik* (Tübingen, 1969); U. Kitzinger, *German Electoral Politics* (Oxford, 1960); T. Ellwein, *Das Regierungssystem der Bundesrepublik Deutschland* (Opladen, 1983); R.H. Welles, *The States in the West German Federation* (New York, 1961).

5. See, e.g., W. Besson, *Die Aussenpolitik der Bundesrepublik* (Munich, 1970); W. Hanrieder, *West German Foreign Policy* (Stanford, 1967); F.R. Pfetsch, *Die Aussenpolitik der Bundesrepublik* (Munich, 198l); A. Baring, *Im Anfang war Adenauer* (Munich, 1982); Militärgeschichtliches Forschungsamt, ed., *Anfänge westdeutscher Sicherheitspolitik, 1945–1956*, 2 vols. (Munich, 1982/90); K. von Schubert, *Wiederbewaffnung und Westintegration* (Stuttgart, 1970); G. Wettig, *Entmilitarisierung und Wiederbewaffnung* (Munich, 1967). See also the contribution to the current volume by R. Pommerin.

6. See, e.g., W. Abelshauser, *Wirtschaftsgeschichte der Bundesrepublik* (Frankfurt, 1983); G. Ambrosius, *Die Durchsetzung der sozialen Marktwirtschaft in Westdeutschland* (Stuttgart, 1977); J. Backer, *Priming the German Economy* (Durham, N.C., 1971); N. Balabkins, *Germany under Direct Controls* (New Brunswick, 1964); C. Buchheim, *Die Wiedereingliederung Westdeutschlands in die Weltwirtschaft* (Munich, 1990); A. Kramer, *The West German Economy* (Oxford, 1990); J. Leaman, *The Political Economy of West Germany* (London, 1988).

7. See, e.g., L. Herbst et al., eds., *Vom Marshallplan zur EWG*, (Munich, 1990); C.S. Maier and G. Bischof, eds., *The Marshall Plan and Germany* (Oxford, 1991); J. Gimbel, *The Origins of the Marshall Plan* (Stanford, 1976); H.-J. Schröder, ed., *Marshallplan und deutscher Wiederaufstieg* (Wiesbaden, 1990).

8. W. Abelshauser, *Wirtschaft in Westdeutschland* (Stuttgart, 1975); A. Ritschl, "Die Währungsreform von 1948 und der Wiederaufstieg der deutschen Wirtschaft," in *Vierteljahrshefte für Zeitgeschichte* 33, 1985, 136–65. See also A. Milward, *The Reconstruction of Western Europe, 1945–1951* (London, 1984).

9. See, e.g., R. Blum, *Soziale Marktwirtschaft* (Tübingen, 1969); C. Heusgen, *Erhards Lehre von der Sozialen Marktwirtschaft* (Bern, 198l); H.F. Wünsche, *Ludwig Erhards Gesellschafts- und Wirtschaftskonzeption* (Landsberg, 1986). H. Adamsen, *Investitionshilfe für die Ruhr* (Wuppertal, 198l). See also the studies in note 6 above.

10. See, e.g., R.G. Stokes, *Divide and Prosper* (New York, 1988); R. Neebe, *Überseemärkte und Exportstrategien in der westdeutschen Wirtschaft* (Stuttgart, 1991); V.R. Berghahn, *The Americanisation of West German Industry, 1945–1973* (Oxford, 1987); J. Gillingham, *Coal, Steel and the Rebirth of Europe* (Cambridge, 1991).

11. See, e.g., T. Fichter, *Besatzungsmacht und Gewerkschaften* (Opladen, 1982); W. Hirsch-Weber, *Gewerkschaften in der Politik* (Cologne, 1959); W.M. Blumenthal, *Codetermination in the German Steel Industry* (Princeton, 1956); G. Braunthal, *The Federation of German Industry in Politics* (Ithaca, 1965); P. Laurence, *Managers and Management in West Germany* (London, 1980); A. Markovits, *The Politics of the West German Trade Unions* (Cambridge, 1986); H.J. Spiro, *The Politics of West German Codetermination*

(Cambridge, Mass., 1958); W. von Wangenheim, *Industrial Relations in West Germany* (London, 1984); H. Thum, *Mitbestimmung in der Montanindustrie* (Stuttgart, 1982); V. von Bethusy-Huc, *Demokratie und Interessenpolitik* (Wiesbaden, 1962).
12. Siehe H.-P. Schwarz, *Die Ära Adenauer*, 2 vols. (Stuttgart, 1981/83); K. Hildebrand, *Von Erhard zur Grossen Koalition* (Stuttgart, 1984).
13. See, e.g., J. Kocka, "1945: Neubeginn oder Restauration?" in C. Stern and H.-A. Winkler, eds., *Wendepunkte deutscher Geschichte* (Frankfurt, 1979), 141–68.
14. See, e.g., E. Schmidt, *Die verhinderte Neuordnung* (Frankfurt, 1981).
15. Term by R. König.
16. On Germany's industrial structure before 1945 see, e.g., H. Levy, *Industrial Germany* (London, 1935); V. Hentschel, *Wirtschaft und Wirtschaftspolitik im Wilhelminischen Deutschland* (Stuttgart, 1978); D. Abraham, *The Collapse of the Weimar Republic* (New York, 1986); P. Hayes, *Industry and Ideology* (Cambridge, 1987); A. Barkai, *Nazi Economics* (Oxford, 1990); A. Schweitzer, *Big Business in the Third Reich* (Bloomington, 1964); B. Weisbrod, *Schwerindustrie in der Weimarer Republik* (Wuppertal, 1978).
17. See Berghahn, *Americanisation*, esp. 10ff., 40ff., 230ff., 282ff.
18. See, e.g., W. Loth, *Die Teilung der Welt* (Munich, 1983); J.L. Gaddis, *The Long Peace* (Oxford, 1987).
19. See, e.g., G. Kolko, *The Politics of War* (New York, 1968).
20. See, e.g., Berghahn, *Americanisation*, 132ff.; Gillingham, *Coal*.
21. A. Hillgruber, *Hitlers Strategie* (Frankfurt, 1965); K. Hildebrand, *The Foreign Policy of the Third Reich* (London, 1973).
22. See, e.g., M. Broszat, *Nationalsozialistische Polenpolitik* (Stuttgart, 1961); K. Kwiet, *Das Reichskommissariat Niederlande* (Stuttgart, 1968); E. Thomsen, *Deutsche Besatzungspolitik in Dänemark* (Düsseldorf, 1971); A. Milward, *The New Order and the French Economy* (Oxford, 1970); L. Kettenacker, *Nationalsozialistische Volkstumspolitik im Elsass* (Stuttgart, 1973); A. Dallin, *German Rule in Russia* (London, 1957); U. Herbert, *Fremdarbeiter* (Berlin, 1985); R. Hilberg, *The Destruction of the European Jews* (London, 1961); L. Dawidowicz, *The War against the Jews* (Harmondsworth, 1976); G. Hirschfeld, ed., *The Politics of Genocide* (London, 1986); R.D. Müller, *Hitlers Ostkrieg und die deutsche Siedlungspolitik* (Frankfurt, 1991); C. Browning, *Fateful Years* (New York, 1986).
23. See, e.g., R.E. Hertzstein, *When Nazi Dreams Come True* (London, 1982); V.R. Berghahn, "German Big Business and the Quest for a European Economic Empire in the Twentieth Century," in Thomas J. Watson Jr. Institute for International Studies, ed., *Occasional Paper* #17, Providence, 1993, esp. 17ff.; R. Opitz, ed., *Europastrategien des deutschen Kapitals* (Cologne, 1977).
24. See, e.g., E. Teichert, *Autarkie und Grossraumwirtschaft in Deutschland* (Munich, 1984); L. Herbst, *Der totale Krieg und die Ordnung der Wirtschaft* (Stuttgart, 1982).
25. Dresden, 1941.
26. See, e.g., H.D. Schäfer, "Amerikanismus im Dritten Reich," in M. Prinz and R. Zitelmann, eds., *Nationalsozialismus und Modernisierung* (Darmstadt, 1991), 199–215. See also J. Dülffer et al., *Hitlers Städte* (Cologne, 1978).
27. H. Kemmler, *Autarkie in der organischen Wirtschaft* (Dresden, 1940), 13.
28. See, e.g., R.M. Collins, *The Business Response to Keynes* (New York, 1981); K. Rohe, ed., *Die Westmächte und das Dritte Reich* (Paderborn, 1982); C. Hull, *The Memoirs of Cordell Hull* (New York, 1948).
29. See, e.g., J. Lebra, *Japan's Greater East Asia Sphere in World War II* (Oxford, 1975); R.H. Myers and M.R. Peattie, eds., *The Japanese Colonial Empire* (Princeton, 1984).
30. See, e.g., L.S. Kaplan, "Western Europe in the American Century," in *Diplomatic History*, Spring 1982, 111–23.
31. See Collins, *Business Response*, passim; Berghahn, *Americanisation*, 86f.

32. Hence the initiation of the Havana Charter, GATT, the International Monetary Fund, and the World Bank.
33. See, e.g., E.H. Chamberlin, ed., *Monopoly and Competition and their Regulation* (London, 1954).
34. M. Balfour, *The Adversaries* (London, 1981).
35. See, e.g., J.M. Blum, *Roosevelt and Morgenthau* (Boston, 1970).
36. J.S. Martin, *All Honorable Men* (Boston 1950); C. Eisenberg, "U.S. Policy in Postwar Germany," in *Science and Society*, 1982, 24–38.
37. See, e.g., W. Bührer, *Ruhrstahl und Europa* (Munich, 1986); Stokes, *Divide*.
38. See Berghahn, *Americanisation*, 155ff.
39. Ibid., 159ff.
40. Ibid., 168.
41. Ibid., 181.
42. Quoted ibid., 247f.
43. Cologne, 1963.
44. Quoted in V.R. Berghahn and P.J. Friedrich, *Otto A. Friedrich* (Frankfurt, 1993), 39.
45. Ibid., 48.
46. Ibid., 39.
47. Ibid., 92.
48. Ibid., 93.
49. For a recent analysis of this exchange with respect to France see R.F. Kuisel, *Seducing the French* (Berkeley, 1993), 70ff.
50. See Berghahn, *Americanisation*, 250f.
51. See R. Guserl, *Das Harzburger Modell* (Wiesbaden, 1973).
52. See his very interesting diary of his time at Harvard. Photocopy in my possession.
53. See also L. Vaubel, *Unternehmer gehen zur Schule. Ein Erfahrungsbericht aus USA* (Düsseldorf, 1952).
54. See the statements issued by the Deutsche Vereinigung zur Förderung der Weiterbildung von Führungskräften (Wuppertaler Kreis) e.V.. Photocopies in my possession.
55. C.S. Maier, "The Politics of Productivity. The Foundations of American International Economic Policy after World War II," in P. Katzenstein, ed., *Between Power and Plenty* (Madison, 1978), 23–49.
56. L. Erhard, *Wohlstand für alle* (Düsseldorf, 1957).
57. See Collins, *Business Response*, passim.
58. On the importance of the totalitarianism paradigm for making this contrast, see A. Gleason, *Totalitarianism* (in press).
59. See above pp. 000. It is significant that this was also the peak period of America's industrial engagement in Germany.
60. See T. Mason, *Social Policy in the Third Reich* (Oxford, 1993).
61. See, e.g., R. Willett, *The Amerizanisation of Germany, 1945–1949* (New York, 1989); Kuisel, *Seducing*.
62. See K. Maase, *Bravo Amerika* (Hamburg, 1992); U. Poiger, *Taming the Wild West* (Brown University Ph.D. thesis).
63. See A. Sywottek, "The Americanization of Daily Life?" in M. Ermath, ed., *America and the Shaping of German Society, 1945–1955* (Oxford, 1993).
64. See Kuisel, *Seducing*; V. de Grazia, "Mass Culture and Sovereignty: The American Challenge to European Cinemas, 1920–1960," in *Journal of Modern History*, March 1989, 53–87. See also R. Wagnleitner, *Coca-Colonisation und Kalter Krieg* (Wien, 1991). Professor de Grazia has pioneered several workshops on American consumer culture and its impact abroad.

6. DAILY LIFE AND SOCIAL PATTERNS

Hermann Glaser

Let me first give a short numerical description of the terrible circumstances and conditions daily life was confronted with after the total war had ended in 1945:

> In Europe, 19.6 million soldiers either died or were reported missing in action. Of these, 3.7 million were German. Civilians killed numbered 4.7 million; 3.6 million of them were Germans. Of these some 540,000 were victims of bombing, and about 7 million died during deportation. Approximately 6 million Jews of various nationalities were murdered; a total of 9 million human beings were killed in concentration camps. Approximately 9.6 million people who had been forced into Germany tried to return home, while 12 million fled from former German territories. From 6 to 7 million German soldiers were prisoners of war. Nearly 4 million German soldiers and civilians were wounded. In Germany 3 million were left homeless, 2.25 million homes were completely destroyed, 2.5 million were damaged, and the war left 400 million cubic meters of debris. The Rubble Years had begun.[1]

On the other side, the survivors were marked by a cultural euphoria. One of the survivors was Hartmut von Hentig, who received his Ph.D. in the United States and was influenced by John Dewey's educational philosophy. He is now an outstanding education expert and philosopher in the Federal Republic of Germany. In 1945 he was a young officer who had emigrated into the army at the advice of his father. Like so many of his generation, he experienced the "zero hour" *(Stunde Null)* as the most liberating event of his life:

> Chaos and freedom, from that time on, will always be inseparable for me; in my mind they will remain associated with an overwhelmingly radiant summer in which I crossed the countryside on foot like a hundred thousand oth-

ers, sleeping behind bushes and barns, begging bread and gathering fruit from the side of the road, no one bothering anyone. The year 1945, now recorded in history books as the year of misery, of the last senseless act of destruction, of national humiliation and a feeling of having been personally violated or, more abstractly, as the year of the end of Nazi rule, the Thousand Year Reich, 1945 marks one of the most precious years of my life.[2]

On the other hand, those whose lives had been reduced to the bare minimum, who had perhaps vegetated in war prisons, had a different story to tell:

> This is my hat,
> this is my coat,
> in this linen pouch
> is my shaving equipment.
>
> Emergency supplies:
> my plate, my cup,
> I've scratched my name
> in the tin.
> Scratched it here with this
> precious nail
> which I keep hidden
> from greedy eyes. ... [3]

Günter Eich was one of the poets who founded a new lyric style. He took an inventory of the situation: direct, in a reductionist, stark and unadorned, bold and non-defensive way. "Inventory" was also the name of the poem. To overcome the material, spiritual, cultural, and moral breakdown, Thomas Mann (then living in exile in America) relayed this message over the BBC to German listeners on 1 May 1945:

> This hour may be difficult and painful, for Germany could not bring it about on its own. It may well be that monstrous and inexplicable damage has been done to the German name, and Germany has gambled away its power. But power isn't everything. It isn't even the main thing, and Germany's value has never come simply from its power. There was once, and there may come again, a time when to be German meant to be esteemed for the ability to relate power to dignity through the human contribution of the freedom of spirit.[4]

It is not my task to deal with the history of the German philosophy and culture in the forties and fifties, but I think one cannot neglect the relation between superstructure and foundation even when concentrating on daily life and social patterns. Therefore I might refer to spiritual motives. The most intense motive was the longing for a better life, more or less identical with the American dream, which also became a German dream. It is symptomatic that in the film *Liebe 47* (the film version of

Wolfgang Borcherts's drama *Draußen vor der Tür*) one of the protagonists feels encouraged, lifted out of her gray everyday existence, by looking at an American lifestyle magazine.

When Erich Kästner (at the time editor of the culture section of the *Neue Zeitung*, published by the American Military Government) returned to Zurich for the first time after the war in 1947, he marveled at the "metropolitan melody" that, it was believed, would never resound again in German cities. What a feeling to roll over asphalt, pulled by smooth, well-fed horses, and to see open carriages with rosy-cheeked brides and grooms. The coachmen wear shiny silk top hats, and fluttering strings on their coats. There are plates of almonds and coffee beans on the counters of bars, and guests serve themselves with indifference. There are well-stocked shoe shops with nylon stockings in the windows. English, American, Turkish, and Greek cigarettes are available everywhere. There are matches. Their boxes have two striking surfaces, which to Kästner seems almost a sin. The shop assistants are smooth like silk. The barber is concerned, asking whether the razor is indeed sharp enough. Baskets of strawberries stand in front of the shops stacked almost to the curb. Mounds of vegetables are piled behind the windows. Before dinner, a cart richly covered with hors d'oeuvres is brought in. There are glittering jewelry shops, plentiful confectioners' shops, book shops in which one may buy an unlimited number of books, travel agencies, department and clothing stores with Persian carpets, clocks, cameras; perfume shops, and full newsstands. "This was once also our world, and now we stare at it as if at a book of fairy tales like children who cannot read and look at the pictures with wonder."

Upon returning home to Schwabing, while standing at the window and reflecting on his days in Zurich, Kästner notices an old gentleman coming up the street with his dachshund. With measured steps they pass by the rubble heaps now overgrown with weeds. But the measuredness is not quite real. Suddenly, with a half-filled linen bag, the man climbs carefully and bashfully up on one of the overgrown heaps of debris, searching around in the green weeds. "What's he pulling out? What is he bringing into the barn? Dandelion and sorrel leaves! His wife had sent him out for some vegetables and lettuce. Hastily he pushes the nourishing weeds into his gray bag, climbs carefully down again, shakes the dust out of his trousers, and walks as elastically as a rheumatic attaché around the corner."[5]

Daily life in the Rubble Years: evoking daily dreams. When will there be peace?

When the world is filled with laughing children,
when corns piles up and kites soar high,
when doctors have to search for patients,
when houses sparkle with "fresh paint,"
when fraying hats are thrown away,
when "excuse me" is heard on subway cars.
Then, finally then, will there be peace.
When folk build silos and storage bins,
when a young girls asks,
"what are troops?"
When a pulled tooth gives the worst pain known,
and newspapers report obesity,
when the major heroes come from sports.
Then, finally then, will there be peace.
When joyful mothers rock their babes,
and uncles send their nephews watches,
when one can freely change address,
or drive a car that one has bought,
when worn out furniture gets replaced,
when one has meat and asks friends in.
But when, dear grandchild, will that be? [6]

This poem by Karl Schnog was published 1948 in *Ulenspiegel*, a magazine for literature, art, and satire, which was founded by Herbert Sandberg. Sandberg, while imprisoned in a concentration camp, planned that if he got out he would recreate something like the *Simplizissimus*. In 1945, in Berlin, he received an American license.

At about the same time that Schnog's poem appeared in the *Ulenspiegel*, the *Neue Zeitung* analyzed the pipe dreams of children and youths who participated in an essay contest for students from the elementary grades through senior high school. The main theme of the majority of the essays was food. "I could go to the bakery and get me some danishes, pretzels, and other sweets. And then I could go to the butcher and have some sausages." "I see mountains of chocolate, boiled sweets, dried fruits, and pudding." "I run to the baker's and fetch a sack of rolls. Then I run quickly to the dairy and pick up three pounds of butter. Then I sit down in front of the shop and eat my snack." In addition to fantasies of liberation, children dreamed of freeing their fathers and other relatives from prison and other emergency situations; another dominant motif involved fantasies of departure, interlocked with food fantasies. "If I were invisible I would never go to school. Then if I got hungry I could go into farmers' pantries and get something to eat. On Sundays I would always go to the movies. I would never have to stand in line. I could go to Africa in search of adventure. I could enter every circus and cinema."[7]

What I think these snapshots show is the power of longing that was to become an outstanding phenomenon of cultural and social anthropology in Germany. Its objective was flight from material misery.

Principle of hope: From that point of view it is necessary to reassess the fifties. They were not only a period of restoration, even a reactionary period, but also a departure into the colorful territory of modernism and modernization strongly influenced by Americanization (Westernization). Alexander and Margarete Mitscherlich observed and analyzed the phenomenon of the nonobservance of mourning. They pointed to the defense mechanisms that had been developed in relation to the entire period of the Third Reich: renunciation, isolation, changing the details, feigning attention and affection. In short, de-realization. Had these not been developed, a great many people in postwar Germany inevitably would have been overcome by an oppressive melancholy as a result of their narcissistic love for the Führer and the crimes committed in this service. "In narcissistic identification with the Führer, his failure became the failure of the 'I.' Although de-realization and the other defensive techniques hindered the outbreak of melancholy, they were not completely able to prevent a tremendous impoverishment of the 'I.'"[8]

I do not completely agree with Margarete and Alexander Mitscherlich when they state that the inability to mourn was the basis for the economic miracle. There has also been the chance to get rich and to share, to work efficiently and to show compassion. If your plate is full and your neighbor's plate empty, give him half of it. If not out of pity, then out of prudence (a saying by Marie von Ebner-Eschenbach). This was put into practice by the Law of Equalization of Burden in 1952. On the other hand, the fifties turned out to be a very egocentric and saturated period, yet pricked by cultural criticism, which was practiced in the feuilletons of the newspapers and in critical broadcasting (mainly in late-night shows): brilliantly witty, strikingly unsuccessful.

The quintessence of that mentality of the "economic miracle" was depicted by the very successful play *Der Besuch der alten Dame (The Visit)* by Friedrich Dürrenmatt, first staged in Munich in May 1956. In this play the unscrupulous, consciousless superficiality of the economic miracle was exposed: in Güllen, the merchant Alfred Ill abandoned his pregnant fiancée. Returning as one of the richest women in the world, she offers DM 500 million to the community if the residents kill her former lover. Should it be done or not—that is the question. The people of the town begin to haunt their victim. But then the problem is solved by accident. A heart attack kills Alfred Ill, and the people of Güllen get their reward. At the end, nobody seems to feel guilty: Alfred Ill "died of joy," as the mayor says, and the citizens rejoice and pray to God that their wealth will be eternal.

DIE FRAUEN: Ziemende Kleidung umschließt den zierlichen Leib nun

DER SOHN: Es steuert der Bursch den sportlichen Wagen

DIE MÄNNER: Die Limousine der Kaufmann

DIE TOCHTER: Das Mädchen jagt nach dem Ball auf roter Flache

DER ARZT: Im neuen, grüngekachelten Operationssaal operiert freudig der Arzt

ALLE: Das Abendessen
    Dampft im Haus. Zufrieden
    Wohlbeschuht
    Schmaucht ein jeglicher besseres Kraut

DER LEHRER: Lernbegierig lernen die Lernbegierigen

DE ZWEITE: Schatze auf Schatze turmt de emsige Industrielle

ALLE: Rembrandt auf Rubens

DE MALER: Die Kunst ernahret den Kunstler vollauf

DE PFARRER: Es berstet an Weihnachten, Ostern
    und Pfingsten
    vim Andrang de Christen das Munster

ALLE: Und die Zuge
    Die blitzenden hehren
    Eilend auf eisernen Gleisen
    Von Nachbarstadt zu Nachbarstadt, volkerverbindend
    Halten wieder.[9]

Brave new world: Daily life was sweet, abundant in dreams, and miserable in reality. *La Dolce Vita* (the title of a very well known film by Federico Fellini) was a compensatory emblem of the time.

An investigation of major importance for the new discipline of sociology stated five typical patterns of thinking among people who worked in industry (in 1950, the proportion of employees in agriculture was 23.2 percent, decreasing to 14.2 percent in 1960; the proportion in industry increased from 42.3 percent in 1950 to 47.8 percent in 1960; and the proportion in the service sector and government increased from 32.2 percent in 1950 to 37.1 percent in 1960):

- Only one percent still believed Marxist theory.
- One-third was resigned, not expecting any positive change.

- Twenty-five percent thought the trade unions should and could act more efficiently.
- Eight percent hoped, in accordance with social democratic thinking, that evolution towards a just society would take place.
- Only a small percentage was more or less satisfied with the achieved state of society.[10]

The very first cover of the mass-circulation magazine *Quick*, 1 January 1950, showed a much more optimistic picture of society. The brave new world of the Federal Republic is symbolized by a family photo: a young and neatly dressed mother holds up her well-fed child, while husband, grandma, and grandpa are happily watching the mother-child idyll. With a glass of champagne they are saying cheers to the child: "Now we have reached the happy fifties. Thou shalt experience the year 2000!" Slowly, hard work made sweet dreams possible: for example, nylon and perlon stockings which cost DM 200 at the time. Stocking manufacturer, Hans Thierfelder had left the Russian occupation zone in 1946 carrying with him only one suitcase. In 1951, he asked all German women to take part in a competition to determine the "Leg Queen." Hundreds of thousands of girls and women measured the length and extent of their thighs, calves, ankles, and feet. At the time, it was the biggest market analysis in the history of Germany.

To buy a new radio, recorder, television receiver was made possible by the entrepreneur Max Grundig. Grundig became a commercial myth because he had started to produce radios when doing so was still prohibited by the Allies. He did not sell radios, but a box of components that everyone could easily assemble into a radio set (*Heinzelmännchen*). In 1956, he produced a TV set that cost less than DM 1000.

Lucky were those who could buy a big new car similar to an American car. Manufacturer and entrepreneur Carl Friedrich Wilhelm Borgward produced such a car: with pontoon shape, white tires, and much chrome.

"Going south" was the motto: to experience Italy. (*Wenn bei Capri die rote Sonne. ...*) Between 1948 and 1955, half of the adults had already made one or more holiday trips. Hans Magnus Enzensberger, starting his career as a cultural critic in the fifties, stated that the flood of tourism meant a flight out of reality. If the reality were better, people would not flee.

German identity was finally stabilized when in 1954 one of the most popular dreams came true and the unbelievable happened: Germany won the world soccer championship. *Wir sind wieder wer!* Each champion of the team got DM 2500 as a reward, and a piece of upholstered furniture. (The highest income of an athlete at that time was not permitted to exceed DM 320.)

The fifties: *Das Land der großen Mitte (The land of the large center)* succeeded through hard labor. In 1950, an industrial worker had to work 11 hours and 16 minutes to be able to buy one pound of black coffee. In 1959, he had to work 3 hours and 7 minutes for one pound. Other comparisons: for one pound of good meat he had to work 2 hours and 18 minutes in 1950, and 1 hour and 12 minutes in 1959; for a VW beetle: 493 working days in 1950, 174 in 1959.

Although the monthly net income of the average workers did not exceed DM 234 the purchasing power was high. During the period of the black market, firms and merchants had piled up goods, and the Marshall Plan poured money into West Germany. With a growing number of millionaires, social injustice was considered less scandalous than the design of the new 5-Mark bill, showing Europe as a topless woman: it was regarded as a sign of the moral decay of the newly founded state. (The sexual revolution began during the sixties with Oswald Kolle as trendsetter. In 1951, the film *Die Sünderin [The Sinner]*, which contained some nudity, was still a scandal.)

Summing up the sweet, poor daily life of the time: "Had a dream: Not to marry too early, then a child, having a nice job and a car. Didn't imagine to have so little money; depends how many shifts he has in the mine. We can't afford much. The children want to eat, need clothes. I used to spend my money for myself ... no money to go to the hairdresser ... " Erika Runge, who published such realistic pieces of oral history with a strong socio-pedagogic intention, stated later in the sixties that her transcriptions were constructions because she used only fragments of talks, arranging them deliberately.[11]

The most important political event influencing the economic, social, and political situation in a fundamentally positive way was connected with the Law of the Equalization of Burden in 1951: distribution of burdens and financial equalization enabled the integration of 12 million people who had undergone extreme suffering during the war, were expelled to the East, or had fled from the Russian zone (later the GDR). This law, proof of anticipatory reasoning, put into practice the philosophy of the social market economy, the outstanding representative of which was Ludwig Erhard, whom Ralf Dahrendorf calls the most significant social revolutionary of postwar Germany. There was another revolution: not so much concerning social-economic conditions, but style, taste, and way of life. The Germans discovered the art of living. The term "new look" comprised all aspects of life: fashion, dwelling, clothes, furniture, meals, etiquette and so on. Everybody wanted to be beautiful, exquisite, and different, far from the average crowd.

The Beautiful was the title of a periodical (since 1955) that turned out to be one of the most successful publishing projects of the fifties and sixties. It addressed all people of taste and art, and encouraged all those who reflected on values and were not merely calculating prices. The magazine played a role similar to *Gartenlaube* in the 19th century, merging the strata and layers of society in an idealistic, affirmative way. The superstructure was shaped by "good taste." The products of good taste (furniture, curtains, lamps) were colorful, flamboyant, asymmetrical. The Germans were freed from the bonds of provincial, dull, and bourgeois attitudes.

In the sublime field of literature the ambivalent dreams of swinging West Germany were represented (mirrored, expressed, fostered, doubted, criticized, and emphasized) by Gottfried Benn. Aloof from daily life and yet in the very center of it, he articulated modern dreams and melancholy. Tristesse was the literary mood of the day.

Metropolitan modernity found itself localized in America. Cultural Westernization meant, to a large extent, Americanization. The new look of the Federal Republic from education to town planning (functionalism), from music to advertising aesthetics (Madison Avenue), from modern style and taste to automobile design, from kitchen devices to educational ideas, was highly influenced by American culture. The American dream shaped the German dream of the fifties; the disappointments followed in the sixties. What had been hailed was condemned. Because the illusions had been grand, the disappointments were strong.

When reflecting on the new departure of the Rubble Years and their continuation in the fifties, one should not forget to include the sentimental feelings for the swinging melody that inspired and encouraged the prewar, war, and postwar generations to engage in a democratic, federal, republican, and humane Germany, in constitutional patriotism—"Don't Fence Me In." (When Jimmy Jungermann produced one of Europe's hottest jazz programs for Radio Munich, one third of the 60,000 listener requests he received in a two-year period were for "Don't Fence Me In.") The melodious message should not be forgotten. In Germany or elsewhere.

Notes

1. Hermann Glaser, *The Rubble Years: The Cultural Roots of Postwar German, 1945–1948* (New York, 1986); Hermann Glaser, *Kulturgeschichte de Bundesrepublik Deutschland,* 3 volumes (Frankfurt am Main: S. Fischer, 1990).
2. Hartmut von Hentig, *Aufgeräumte Erfahrung: Texte zur eigenen Person* (München: Hauser, 1983), 8, 23.
3. Günter Eich, *Gesammelte Werke,* vol. 1 (Frankfurt am Main: Suhrkamp, 1973), 35.
4. Thomas Mann: "Deutsche Hörer! Fünfundzwanzig Radiosendungen nach Deutschland," in *Thomas Mann Werke: Das essayistische Werk. Taschenbuchausgabe in acht Bänden, Hrs. von Hans Bürgin. Politische Schriften und Reden.* vol. 3 (Frankfurt am Main: S. Fischer, 1986), 35.
5. Erich Kästner, "Reise in die Vergangenheit: Wiedersehen mit Dingen und Menschen," *Neue Zeitung,* 4 April 1948.
6. Karl Schnog, "Wann wird das sein?," *Ulenspiegel* 5 (1948), 2.
7. Walter Kolbenhoff, "Wenn ich unsichtbar wäre—Kinder schreiben über einen alten Wunschtraum," *Neue Zeitung,* 4 April 1948.
8. Alexander und Margarete Mitscherlich: *Die Unfähigkeit zu trauern: Grundlagen kollektiven Verhaltens* (München, 1967), 78f.
9. Friedrich Dürrenmatt, "De Besuch de alten Dame," *Komödien I* (Zurich: Peter Schifferli, 1957), 356.
10. Heinrich Popitz, Hans Paul Bahrdt, et al.: *Das Gesellschaftsbild des Arbeiters* (Tübingen, 1957).
11. *Bottroper Protokolle,* aufgezeichnet von Erika Runge (Frankfurt, am Main: Suhrenkamp 1958), 51f.

7. REBELS WITH A CAUSE?
AMERICAN POPULAR CULTURE, THE 1956 YOUTH RIOTS, AND NEW CONCEPTIONS OF MASCULINITY IN EAST AND WEST GERMANY

Uta G. Poiger

An apparently new social phenomenon preoccupied Germans in the mid-1950s: just ten years after the end of the second World War, a youth rebellion took place in East and West Germany, and the consumption of American popular culture was at its center. In September 1956, in a debate over the youth riots that had erupted in various West German cities, a member of the West Berlin parliament asserted that the instigators of riots in a West Berlin working-class neighborhood had modeled their behavior "word for word, picture for picture" after the American movie *The Wild One*, starring Marlon Brando.[1] A few weeks later, West German education expert Hans Muchow warned against "nihilists," whom he compared to the white gang leader in the American movie *Blackboard Jungle*. These nihilists, he explained, consciously regressed into a "wild state" that evoked memories of the National Socialist rise to power. East Germany, he added, had it easier in combatting these dangers.[2]

In this essay, I explore how, in the mid-1950s, young male "rebels" in East and West Germany resisted and disrupted gender-specific ideals for East and West German citizens that assigned the role of provider and soldier to men and that of caretaker to women.[3] Further, I investigate how both German states used attitudes about the United States, on the one hand, and the memory of National Socialism, on the other, as weapons to contain this adolescent behavior and fight the Cold War.

In postwar East and West Germany, American movies and music were central to discussions of rebellious youth and to the complicated relationships between masculinity and nationhood. By the early 1950s, East and West Germans were widely discussing the impact of American popular culture on young Germans. These debates focused mainly on American western and gangster movies, jazz music, and dances like the boogie. Throughout the 1950s American films made up the majority of movies released in West Germany, and many of them were widely discussed.[4] In East Germany, only six American movies were shown in the course of the 1950s, but East German authorities were well aware that every day thousands of East Germans, especially young people, crossed the borders to the Western sectors of Berlin in order to watch Western European and American movies.[5] East German papers even reviewed many American movies as soon as they opened in West Berlin. East and West Germans were convinced, and worried, that movies in general and American movies in particular played a significant role in shaping postwar German personalities.

In the mid-1950s the arrival of American "young rebel" movies, like *The Wild One* with Marlon Brando, *Rebel Without a Cause* with James Dean, and *Blackboard Jungle* with Sidney Poitier, along with the rock 'n' roll movie *Rock Around the Clock*, exacerbated parents' and officials' worries about American cultural influences.[6] When youth riots occurred with ever greater frequency in both West and East German cities after 1955, commentators in East and West quickly came to agree that these American movies served as models for German juvenile fashions, dances, and mannerisms, and even for the riots themselves. German commentators also extensively discussed the explanations for juvenile misbehavior suggested in American movies (which were themselves in a constant dialogue with the broader U.S. debates about American juvenile delinquency). Strongly believing in the direct effects of films on audience behavior, German officials did not want adolescents to see the allegedly realistic depictions of worrisome American conditions. They did, however, sometimes recommend them as warning examples to parents and educators. In both Germanys, the American productions *The Wild One*, *Blackboard Jungle*, *Rebel Without A Cause*, and *Rock Around the Clock* in many ways became stepping-stones for the evolving debates on young German rebels.[7]

East and West German observers and authorities focused their attention on young men, who made up the majority of rioters. Debates about male unruliness in East and West Germany were, in fact, debates about the role of the state and ideal citizens, and gender norms were at the core of these discussions. After 1945 the reconstruction of German national identities in East and West required careful attention to the reconstruction of German masculinity. Many Germans described the period from the rise of National Socialism to the postwar years in terms of emasculation, and in the aftermath of the second World War, Germans felt that their men had failed both physically and morally.[8] In reaction, East and West German authorities asserted that men's roles as productive breadwinners for their families were important to reconstructing postwar German identities.[9] Moreover, as became clear in the course of their respective rearmament efforts in the mid-1950s, East and West German officials tried to shape soldiers who were strong, but not overly militaristic.[10] Young males, with their American-influenced fashions and their rioting, raised fears about both unmanliness and male aggression, and thus challenged the fine line that authorities were walking.[11]

The fact that young German men imitated dress and behavior from American movies was especially frightening because commentators in postwar East and West Germany linked consumption, sexuality, and femininity. While these links had characterized discourses on consumer culture since the nineteenth century, connections between the consumption of mass culture and the feminization of men were particularly important to East and West Germans as they were trying to refurbish masculinity after the second World War.[12] For example, a West German education manual warned against the sexualizing and weakening effects, on boys, of shop windows, films, and Negro songs.[13] To commentators in East and West, the dress styles of German male young rebels therefore signaled an unmanly focus on consumption.

Indeed, East and West German reconstructions of ideal male citizens were always shaped by conceptions of femininity. While young men were undoubtedly at the center of debates about young rebels, American and German women were invoked as instigators of, victims of, and finally, solutions to the youth rebellion.[14]

In investigating the visions of German civilization that, in the mid-1950s, made young male rebels appear as extraordinary threats in both Germanys, I explore how gender norms were intertwined with concepts of class and racial difference.[15] In discussions of American young rebel movies that portrayed only white Americans, like *The Wild One* and *Rebel Without a Cause*, German authorities explicitly rejected styles they associated with working-class culture. I show how the reassertion of certain class-based gender norms shaped these indictments. Further, with *Blackboard Jungle* and the African-American-influenced music styles imported by movies like *Rock Around the Clock*, the racial assumptions behind critiques of German young rebels became explicit. Here asserting gender norms served to distinguish civilized Germanness from the threats of African-American culture, white American racism, and National Socialist barbarism. Taken together, these discussions of American influences on German youth show the complicated work of gender, class, and race in East and West German reconstructions of national identities.

Battles between adolescents and authorities over the consumption of American popular culture were contests over moral, cultural, and political authority; they offer the opportunity to explore how the politicization of culture in both states was interlinked with the reconstitution of gender and racial norms that were central to reconstructions of Germanness on both sides of the iron curtain.[16]

Americanization has in past years become a contested framework for the study of Western European, and specifically West German, postwar history. In some treatments, successful Americanization in Europe has been equated with the installation of liberal states and market economies.[17] On the other hand, studies of postwar Western European culture have often been quite critical of American influences, as is signified by the term "Coca-Colonization," which some scholars of Germany and Austria have used.[18] My focus on American influences on youth cultures in both East *and* West Germany moves beyond the alternatives of liberation and colonization. American popular culture, as imported into Germany, was commercial and mass mediated, and thus in some sense standardized. Yet East and West Germans, with their specific cultural and political baggage, assigned to American influences their own meanings, which remained continuously contested within and between the two German states.

Therefore, the behavior of East and West German young rebels and the ensuing debates raise important issues about the relationship of culture and politics. East and West German authorities struggled to ascertain what political motivations, if any, were at the root of unruly behavior. Their changing answers to this question determined whether they tried to repress or accommodate young rebels. These different responses were clearly informed by the memories of National Socialism and constitute an important part of the Cold War battles over German identities.

THE WILD ONE AND WEST GERMAN YOUTH RIOTS

In 1955, in reviews of the Marlon Brando movie *The Wild One*, West German commentators connected male unruliness to gender upheaval in the United States and identified it with working-class behavior. Since the early 1950s, reports had combined references to Brando's refusals to wear a suit—a symbolic rejection of bourgeois values—with treatments of his (sexual) success with American women. "His popularity is not astonishing," explained one article, for the American woman, "who is the most spoiled woman in the world—and who so often and with such pleasure stresses that she reigns over her man, does not hide anymore that her heart and her senses react most strongly to the brutal 'Gorilla sex appeal.'"[19] In *The Wild One*, which depicted a gang of white bikers terrorizing a small American town, Brando was a "hero with sex appeal, whom women allow to beat them up."[20] Thus, West German commentators portrayed American women as victims of men *and* saw female-induced brutality at the center of American male hyper-aggression. Most reviewers praised this allegedly realistic depiction of American conditions and used the movie as an opportunity to assert differences between West Germany and the United States.

One West German reviewer, however, warned in 1955 that *The Wild One* would become an ideal for many German adolescents.[21] Soon several incidents seemed to prove him correct. In June 1955 a West Berlin gang with heavy motorbikes, among them at least one young woman, frequently drove to a cafe called "Big Window" on the river Havel in the outskirts of West Berlin. They shocked patrons through "provocative skinnydipping" and noisiness. In clear allusion to the American example, they called themselves "The Wild Ones of the Big Window."[22]

The connections between American movies and adolescent misbehavior became more worrisome in the course of 1956. That summer, a gang that the media called *Totenkopfbande* (skull and crossbones gang, thus allegedly using a symbol from *The Wild One*) would regularly meet in the no-parking zone in front of a West Berlin bar on Thursday nights.[23] Disturbed by the noise of their motorbikes, people living in the neighborhood repeatedly called the police. Confrontations between the adolescents and the police usually followed and attracted a growing audience. On 12 July 1956, for example, about 200 adolescents gathered in front of the bar, and by 9 p.m. the numbers of spectators had swollen to about 5,000 adults and adolescents. Adolescents prevented cars from passing, and the police had some difficulties in reestablishing public order. When the same scenes repeated themselves a week later, the police turned to stronger means and used waterhoses to disperse the crowd.[24]

Disturbances recurred and spread to other cities. In the period from April to September, the West Berlin police alone counted 36 riots and arrested 309 male participants.[25] In the aftermath of these events, it became West German consensus that *The Wild One* had in fact started youth riots in West Germany, although earlier reviews had drawn parallels to biker gangs that had already existed. Yet, riots appeared to be the mere tip of an iceberg: it seemed that, rioting or not, more and more young men were hanging out in the streets, were wearing jeans, and were publicly listening to the latest American hits on their transistor radios.[26]

In reaction, West German observers combined pejorative references to American popular culture with an older German bourgeois attitude that associated male unrespectability with working-class men. In the 1950s, press and scholarship resurrected the term *Halbstarke* (literally, semistrong), which had been used for young male working-class delinquents since the 1910s, and discussed riots, as well as more widespread male adolescent mannerisms, as the *Halbstarkenproblem*.[27]

The fashions of *Halbstarke* particularly underlined the connection between American movies and German male unruliness. Standard dress for West German *Halbstarke* was jeans, T-shirts, and leather jackets, revealing clear similarities with the male heroes of *The Wild One*, *Rebel Without a Cause*, and *Blackboard Jungle*. Young males would go to great lengths in order to achieve the right look. Tight pants were a must, and it was important to wear the original Levis jeans "and not the imitations" from the German Woolworth stores. When T-shirts were not yet available in Germany, young men would wear the high backs of undershirts in the front, in order to achieve the high-cut neck. Their hair was greased back and combed into ducktail plumes.[28] Commentators increasingly identified *Halbstarke* by their fashions, and some simply referred to them as the "leather jackets."[29] In 1955 and early 1956, most West German observers believed that these styles were restricted to working-class male adolescents—and could be rejected as such.

In this context it is not surprising that West German officials were outraged at the American production *Rebel Without a Cause*, which reached Germany in 1956. For this movie portrayed white American middle-class youths behaving in ways that West Germans associated with unacceptable working-class styles: in the film young men from wealthy, white suburbia sported fashions like jeans and leather jackets, engaged in dangerous knife fights and deadly car races, and thus rebelled against parents and public order.[30] Many West German officials in the 1950s who recognized intense social conflict as one reason for the demise of the Weimar Republic did want to ameliorate class barriers in West Germany. But West German authorities, if they imagined a society devoid of class hierarchies, certainly did not want to see it symbolized by young middle-class men who, like the adolescents in *Rebel*, wore "working-class" jeans.[31] When it became obvious that not all West German *Halbstarke* were from working-class backgrounds, one West German commentator scoffed at the suggestion that West German *Halbstarke* were possibly prefiguring a classless society, as "respectability, moral behavior, and the educational influence of cultural values" were foreign to them, and their behavior and styles were clearly "at the bottom."[32] In 1956, when he urged that adolescents be offered better leisure-time activities, West German Minister of the Interior Gerhard Schrîder echoed such concerns and warned that "in the race with the enormous purchasing power of the mass taste, moral values are threatened."[33] West German officials rejected deviations from bourgeois female and male respectability and had special trouble coming to terms with middle-class adolescent rebels.

Border Disputes Over American Popular Culture

East German authorities successfully played on West German fears of American-led Western self-destruction. Indeed, they directed their own indictments of American popular culture as much at the West as at the East German consumer. "The fatherland of the youth is the German Democratic Republic," read one East German official statement, "because it is here that the best national traditions and the great cultural heritage of the German people are preserved, cultivated, and made accessible to the working people, and not where American non-culture, nationalist-supremacist race hatred, gangster movies, trash novels, boogie-woogie, etc., are supposed to prepare the adolescents for murder, killings, and war. ... We need healthy, courageous, skilled young people who are prepared to work and to defend the fatherland."[34] West Germany here was portrayed as inundated with American popular culture and therefore lacking an authentic national identity.

Frequently, East German officials accused West German and American authorities of manipulating West German male adolescents to commit American-led conspiracies against the East German state. For example, they blamed the June 1953 uprising in East Germany (commonly known as "June 17") on male adolescent provocateurs in "cowboy pants" and "Texas shirts" adorned with pictures of scantily clad girls in short skirts and cowboy hats. East German officials alleged that West German and American authorities had ordered these boys to wreak havoc in the East and to participate in a "fascist coup d'état." Like West German commentaries, East German critiques associated male adolescent rebels with sexually provocative women and unrespectable fashions. The East German officials implied that these male adolescents' focus on American fashions, and their desires to consume, led them politically astray. East Germans did not talk about these cultural expressions as working-class behavior, but by linking adolescent rebels to fascism, they used an indictment that was perhaps even more powerful in the postwar German context.[35]

In spite of frequent denials that adolescents could turn into delinquents under socialism, East German authorities clearly worried about American influences on East German youth as well. Movie theaters along the borders between the Western and the Soviet sectors were a special object of their scorn and concern. With low prices (supported by tax breaks from the West Berlin government), these theaters attracted young visitors from East Berlin. Internal East Berlin reports estimated in 1956 and 1957 that each day about 26,000 East Berliners went to the movies in so-called border theaters in West Berlin. In certain theaters, East Berlin adolescents made up 90 to 100 percent of the visitors.[36]

Both East and West German authorities were unhappy with the quality of movies shown in border theaters. The theaters ran mostly B movies, and West Berlin city officials repeatedly and unsuccessfully pressured theater owners to improve their programs. So too, East German officials often criticized the showings of American gangster movies, westerns, and juvenile-delinquency movies and periodically called for a "fight against the anti-humanist film in West Berlin."[37]

To the dismay of both East and West German authorities, the West Berlin border theaters were clearly exporting American styles, including dances and music rooted in African-American culture, into East Germany. In April 1956 the West Berlin youth magazine *Blickpunkt* described afternoon showings in the border theaters: young East Berliners came here straight from school to watch mostly American movies. "The speakers with the music, which was just as 'hot' as the atmosphere, were blaring the syncopated dixielands a little louder than in other movie theaters. That was necessary," commented the magazine, "because otherwise one would not hear the tune with all the audience's rhythmic stamping of their feet." *Blickpunkt* asked why these movie theaters, with their "cultural aid to the East," catered mainly to an audience of *Halbstarke* and why tax money was spent to "propagate" culture that was controversial even in West Germany?[38]

Indeed, young East German males also listened to American music, wore American fashions, and even rioted. When American jeans were prohibitively expensive, East Berliners, for example, would tighten domestic blue or black pants and outfit them with rivets.[39] In reaction, East German authorities either asserted that *Halbstarke* did not exist under socialism, or, if they acknowledged the presence of young rebels, preferred the English term "rowdies" over *Halbstarke*, thus suggesting that adolescent misbehavior was in fact a foreign import.[40] Like their West German counterparts, East German officials rejected a consumption-oriented masculinity that was apparently fashioned after American imports and that signaled lack of male restraint.

BLACKBOARD JUNGLE AND AMERICAN RACE RELATIONS

This East and West German consensus about what constituted proper masculinity (and femininity) had racial underpinnings, as became clear in debates over American movies and the American music they imported. Both German states were hostile toward the African-American-influenced music styles and dances, like boogie-woogie and rock 'n' roll, that East and West German adolescents copied from American films. These styles posed clear challenges to East and West German gender mores, and both sides labeled them "primitive." Yet, in seeming contradiction, both sides were at the same time critical of American racism. For example, one East German indictment of American popular culture had criticized boogie-woogie and race hatred in the same sentence. This contradiction also became apparent in East and West German reactions to rock 'n' roll and to *Blackboard Jungle*. This American juvenile-delinquency movie, which was released in West Germany in late 1955, depicted American race relations through the story of a white male teacher in an urban high school and introduced the rock 'n' roll hit "Rock Around the Clock."

West German reviewers compared *Rebel* and *Blackboard Jungle* and stressed that they were much more positively impressed with the latter.[41] Especially in its depictions of racial tensions and poverty, *Blackboard Jungle* seemed at once more convincing and safely distant to West German commentators. Some East and West Germans altogether ignored the issue of race relations in *Blackboard Jungle*, but others used the depictions of blacks, Puerto Ricans, and various white ethnic groups as an opportunity to distance themselves from American racism. Thus many West German papers emphasized the restraint and calmness of the unprejudiced white male teacher and of his hardworking African-American student, who together were able to isolate the white troublemaker.[42]

Blackboard Jungle gave a progressive view of race relations, for the movie undermined the stereotype of the black rapist and his white victim, when it showed young white men attacking a white female teacher.[43] Many West German papers illustrated reviews of *Blackboard Jungle* with a still photo in which the female teacher, swinging her hips and wearing high heels, walks by the crowd of male students; about half of these students, all whites, are shouting and whistling, while others, among them the black student, look on with some boredom.[44]

Some West German commentators made the visibly sexual woman, rather than her male attackers, into the sexual perpetrator. One paper commented on the "psychological failure ... especially of the female teacher who emphasized her sex appeal too much" and concluded that the movie depicted this as an excuse for the delinquents.[45] Another one found it "improbable and at least very reckless ... if a cute doll like the new female teacher is exposed to the *Halbstarke*."[46] Here again, West Germans tried to disassociate themselves from sexually expressive American women, while they portrayed these women as causes of working-class male adolescent upheaval across races. Similarly, a West German reviewer argued that West German single mothers, who sent their children to the movies in order to be undisturbed with their lovers at home, were responsible for German juvenile delinquency.[47] In these instances, sexually provocative American and German women served as a negative foil and obstacle to male self-restraint—whether in whites or blacks.

Other West German papers and the East German press saw the female teacher more as the innocent victim of the American delinquents.[48] One East German commentator extrapolated that the male delinquents in the movie were all potential murderers prone to violating even motherhood: American delinquents would allegedly murder their mothers.[49] Both takes on the movie—the teacher as sexual perpetrator and the teacher as innocent victim—reinforced gender ideals of female sexual passivity and male restraint. The film departed from racist American and European stereotypes when it pointed out that both white and black men could achieve this ideal masculinity.

One West German magazine, which did not recommend the movie for adolescents, even tried to "top" the racially liberal message. That this positive development occurs in one of the African-American students, the magazine commented in January 1956, "may seem to us in Germany symptomatic for the unused power of other races; as we know, Americans think differently and much less respectfully of the Negroes."[50] Such commentary positioned Germans as anti-racists who had overcome their racist, anti-Semitic past. In suggesting an alliance of sorts between Germans and African-Americans, however, it also helped Germans position *themselves* as victims; after displacements, reparations, and economic hardship in the aftermath of National Socialism and the second World War, many Germans felt victimized by the occupation forces.[51]

Both East and West German papers applauded *Blackboard Jungle* as a realistic depiction of conditions in America and gleefully reported attempts of the American ambassador in Italy, Clare Booth-Luce, to ban *Blackboard Jungle* from the Venice Film Festival.[52] Many West Germans expressed satisfaction when one of the West German rating boards recommended that movie as "especially valuable" (but only to people over 16), as this further confirmed that West Germany had indeed proven itself more liberal than the United States.[53]

Yet, reactions to *Blackboard Jungle* also pointed to the limits of racial liberalism in both Germanys: East and West German calls for racial equality proved to be compatible with rejections of African-American culture.[54] Thus East and West German reviewers of *Blackboard Jungle* revelled in the restrained, "cool" manliness of the hardworking African-American student, and yet some reviewers made the fast-paced jazz in the soundtracks of *Blackboard* and *The Wild One* into a symbol of juvenile delinquency. In late 1955 East and West German commentators did not know just what furor rock 'n' roll and *Blackboard Jungle*'s theme song, "Rock Around the Clock," would soon cause, but East German reviewers in particular criticized the "boogie-woogie" that male adolescents in *Blackboard Jungle* dance to during school breaks as an expression of juvenile delinquency.[55] West German reviewers felt that the fast-paced jazz in the soundtrack of *Blackboard* effectively symbolized and illustrated American male delinquency, and did not want German adolescents to adopt either the dances or the juvenile misbehavior associated with this music. East and West German commentators thus linked lack of male restraint to music like jazz and dances like boogie that they recognized as rooted in African-American culture.

At a public debate about *Blackboard* in West Berlin, participants found it "courageous" that the movie showed "the dark sides of freedom" and the "return to barbarism and a degeneration of mores."[56] One West German paper maintained in its review that juvenile delinquency was in fact an "expression of American civilization."[57] Historically both barbarism and degeneration were concepts that linked deviations from gender norms to racial inferiority, and in West Germany in the 1950s, the "dark side" of freedom was signified by lack of male restraint and women's exaggerated sexuality.

East German papers exploited such West German concerns when they hailed *Blackboard Jungle* as a realistic depiction of conditions in *both* the United States and West Germany. One East German reviewer maintained that juvenile delinquency did not occur in all countries: while *Halbstarke* were a special problem in West Berlin, Moscow did not know such a phenomenon.[58] At the same time, East German authorities, against better knowledge, asserted again that *Halbstarke* did not exist on their territory.

ROCK AROUND THE CLOCK AND EAST AND WEST GERMAN HOSTILITIES

East and West German visions of racial equality relied on an ideal of male restraint across classes and races. This very ideal allowed East and West German authorities to reject much of African-American culture, as became especially clear when Germans tried to come to terms with rock 'n' roll. From September 1956, the East and West German press reported about riots after screenings of the rock 'n' roll movie *Rock Around the Clock* and after rock concerts in the United States and Western European countries. Both sides further stressed connections between male unruliness and African-American culture.[59]

The West German magazine *Der Spiegel* portrayed rock 'n' roll fans as overly aggressive male delinquents and warned that American youths at Elvis Presley concerts were dancing by themselves "like haunted medicine men of a jungle tribe governed only by music—rock 'n' roll." *Der Spiegel* illustrated the article with pictures of two young white men: one of them with a nude upper body, another with a ducktail plume. Both "dancing rock 'n' roll fanatics" were swinging arms and hips in a fashion distinctly different from the European ballroom dances, where the restrained man led his female partner. The article added a punch at the American occupation in Germany when it asserted that American papers reported news from the "rock 'n' roll front" with the same steadiness that German papers "reported violent acts committed by American soldiers in Germany."[60]

In September 1956, the West German youth magazine *Bravo* announced the arrival of *Rock Around the Clock* in West Germany and explained that the "wild rhythm" of Bill Haley's music was rooted in the ritual music of "Africa's negroes." *Bravo* printed pictures of English male rock fans, explained that they had rioted during showings of the movie, and announced that, under the influence of rock 'n' roll, "cool Englishmen" had turned into "white negroes."[61] In the same article, the magazine urged its German audience not to behave like the English. Even as the magazine ostensibly admired rock 'n' roll, *Bravo*, in calling rioters "white negroes," labelled rioting a typically black behavior and thus warned against rock 'n' roll in racist terms.

As they had done earlier with boogie-woogie, East German officials assessed rock 'n' roll—in films and elsewhere—using racial undertones similar to West German reactions. East German officials described rock 'n' roll as "decadent" and "primitive" and as a threat to proper values. They used the emasculation of men by women to support these statements. For example, a 1956 cartoon in the *Berliner Zeitung* showed a small, thin Presley in front of a crowd of big girls and implied that rock 'n' roll turned proper gender roles upside down: American girls, who were throwing garterbelts, were sexual aggressors who emasculated men. The accompanying article put this reversal of gender roles in a racial context: it claimed that rock 'n' roll (described as American non-culture) appealed to primitive people. Thus in East and West German critiques of rock 'n' roll, allusions to gender disarray, and racial difference reinforced one another to render rock dangerous.

Therefore, in the mid-1950s an odd consensus emerged between East and West German authorities: both were critical of American racism, yet rejected cultural products they connected to African-American popular culture, because these posed threats to the gender mores both sides were establishing as central to their respective reconstructions of German identities. In fact, these fears gave East German officials a potent Cold War weapon.

East German Reevaluations of Young Rebels

In the course of 1956, two East German evaluations of West German *Halbstarke* emerged. Some East German officials continued to connect *Halbstarke* and their lack of male restraint to Western militarism and even fascism. Others, however, reevaluated their stance against American popular culture and juvenile behavior moving toward a new openness; they came to see *Halbstarke* as legitimate resisters against the West German political system and West German rearmament.

This greater tolerance on the part of some East German officials was partially due to the realization that, in the mid-1950s, East Germans were increasingly looking to West Germany for consumer goods. As interrogations of East Germans who were stopped by East German police on their way home from shopping in West Berlin indicated, shoppers described Western goods as more fashionable and cheaper—in spite of prohibitive exchange rates.[62] In the period after the 20th Party Congress of the Soviet CP, which had turned against Stalinism, the East German state youth organization Free German Youth (FDJ) confronted this problem without condemning every consumer of Western fashions.[63]

Indeed, the FDJ clearly tried to use consumption in order to attract young people in 1956. In public forums organized by the FDJ, young people asked why fashions in East Germany were not up to Western standards and complained especially that the new tighter pants were not available. The East German state tried to counter such complaints by announcing fashion shows and by opening special stores for teenager clothing.[64]

In May 1956, at a public forum organized by the East Berlin FDJ, adolescents and officials openly discussed why no American movies were shown in the GDR. Adolescents complained that East Germany produced no music films with "hits." They also asked why movies "like *Blackboard Jungle*" were not released in the GDR. Officials blamed this on the U.S. government, which prohibited the export to East Germany of any movie that found fault with American social conditions.[65] Here America, rather than East Germany, appeared repressive.

Issues of consumption were also at the center of the movie *Eine Berliner Romanze* (*Berlin Romance*), which the East German state film company produced in 1956. In this movie, two West Berlin boys, one called Hans and one called "Lord," pursue the East Berlin girl Uschi on one of her excursions to the Western part of the city. Both boys sport haircuts that resemble ducktail plumes, but the most striking attributes of Lord are his good clothes and his transistor radio, which he buys with money made from shady deals. One East German reviewer commented that both boys tended towards being *Halbstarke*, but he did not see this as a problem as "*Halbstarke* were unpleasant only if they appeared in groups." The reviewer went on to complain that it was too often forgotten that "on their own they were understanding, diligent, boyish, and funny."[66]

However, the East German program brochure for the movie made distinctions between Lord and the hardworking and exploited Hans. The movie sympathized with *Halbstarke*, but at the same time made clear that the desires that Western consumer culture and a capitalist economy raised could lead young men only in two directions: either into crime, as in the case of Lord—who was clearly more Americanized—or into poverty, as in the case of Hans. Uschi ultimately begins a relationship with Hans, and the movie ends with the hope that they will begin a stable life in the Eastern part of the city, where both will be able to find work. As the brochure stressed, Uschi, originally blinded by the glamor of the West, chooses Hans "not for his appearance."[67] With this focus on the taming stability of a heterosexual relationship, *Berliner Romanze* proposed a solution to male adolescent misbehavior that West Germans over the next years would also increasingly see as a remedy for their *Halbstarkenproblem*.

At the same time, however, East German indictments of *Halbstarke* continued. Some East German papers criticized the movie for not making clear distinctions between East and West, especially for not successfully countering Uschi's conviction that life in the East was boring.[68] Likewise, earlier accusations that had connected adolescent consumers of American popular culture to fascism (for example in the context of the June 1953 uprising) continued. Thus in September 1956, the East German press claimed that a West Berlin gang of adolescents, who had destroyed some public property and bathed in the nude, had displayed "cowboy movie posters" and "Nazi badges" in their headquarters.[69] The commentator clearly perceived nude bathing as a sexual transgression, which he linked to both American influences and National Socialism.

Yet that very month, in September of 1956, just as the West German *Halbstarken* riots reached a first peak and rock 'n' roll made it into the German consciousness, the FDJ effectively turned this East German logic around. Now, according to the FDJ, not the adolescent *Halbstarke* but their attackers used "old Nazi methods." The statement by the FDJ Central Council identified a so-called *Halbstarken* campaign directed at the West German youth by the "Hitler officers" from the defense ministry and other Bonn ministries. As the FDJ argued, West German authorities were attacking all of the West German and West Berlin youth "in order to force them into the barracks," that is, into the West German army. The FDJ claimed that the "appearance" of many West German adolescents—which of course drew heavily on American imports—signified that they preferred a life of "personal freedom" to "death on the battlefield."

Since *Halbstarken* behavior was heavily shaped by American examples, it was contradictory that the FDJ used this celebration of (male) resistance for a renewed indictment of American popular culture in West Germany. Whereas earlier statements had claimed that American popular culture directly militarized West German adolescents, East German officials now alleged that West German authorities first used American culture to corrupt youths into "lasciviousness" and "inhumanity" and then responded by disciplining these adolescents in the military.[70]

Several reports in East German papers hailed fights between West German adolescents and West German police or soldiers as resistance against conscription. In September 1956, the East Berlin paper *Der Morgen* analyzed the youth riots in West Germany as protest "against bad conditions in the workplace" and against "the threat of military drills." Even though the paper commented that their "drive to action" was often misdirected, it clearly evaluated *Halbstarken* behavior as an act of political resistance.[71] This constituted a departure from earlier East German official statements that had seen West German *Halbstarke* exclusively as importers of deviance and political unrest into East Germany.

Yet, this stance proved to be problematic for East German authorities. For in September of 1956, just as West Germany was experiencing a large number of riots, West German papers also reported riots in East Germany. In Rostock, for example, rioters had gathered in front of a movie theater and threatened policemen; it took the baton-wielding police more than an hour to regain control. Similar reports came out of Halle and East Berlin.[72]

East German officials saw such rioters within East German borders as a threat to state authority, and in October 1956 the FDJ ordered its East Berlin bureau to take special care to prevent "incidents by adolescent rowdies" at the anniversary of the founding of the GDR on October 7.[73] East German authorities used these official celebrations to display East Germany's might and unity. Perhaps ironically, this order was given at the very same meeting during which the FDJ Central Council suggested that West German *Halbstarke* were legitimately resisting West German authorities.

HALBSTARKE VERSUS WEST GERMAN CITIZEN/SOLDIERS

Despite the contradictions and hypocrisy of this stance, the East German reevaluation of *Halbstarken* behavior as an act of political resistance exacerbated fears over *Halbstarke* in West Germany. It put West German officials especially on the defensive, because East German authorities, while they had created a formal National People's Army in March of 1956, stressed that they were not introducing conscription. Although East German officials de facto pressured young men to join the army, especially if they wanted to get a university education, East

Germany did not introduce actual conscription until after the building of the Berlin Wall in August 1961. West Germany, on the other hand, introduced conscription in 1956, well aware that large parts of the population were wary of it.

The fact that riots occurred and American mannerisms spread just as West German politicians were busy convincing citizens of the necessity of both rearmament and conscription added to the political anxiety of West German observers. Male adolescent behavior raised fears about the lack of West German state authority and the power of American popular culture over young men. Through their fashions and mannerisms, *Halbstarke* ran counter to the new masculinity that West German authorities were constructing in the aftermath of National Socialism and in the face of the Cold War.

Although they were facing strong popular sentiment against rearmament, all West German mainstream political parties, including the governing Christian Democrats (CDU/CSU) and Free Democrats (FDP) and the opposition Social Democrats (SPD) had agreed since the early 1950s that the new democracy required a new male citizen and soldier who would undertake the military tasks with "sobriety" and "reliability."[74] With this new masculinity West German politicians sought to resurrect a positive German tradition of brave and obedient soldiers. On one hand, West German politicians tried to reject a militarist German history in which, as they put it, the military had escaped civilian control; on the other, they tried to overcome the immediate postwar period when the soldier allegedly had been "undervalued."[75]

One advertisement for the West German army suggested in 1956 that this soldier could assert his manly individuality in the process of defending "his people": "He who wants to remain master of his decisions and his time joins voluntarily."[76] The new West German soldier was thus part of a trend to reassert gender roles that National Socialism, war, and the postwar period had apparently turned upside down. West German officials defined this new German man in part by contrasting him with women's militarization under National Socialism. As the CSU politician Richard Jaeger put it in the West German parliament in 1955: "The BDM [the Nazi association of girls] marching in cadence, that was the triumph of militarism and the perversion of true soldiery."[77] The new West German citizen/soldier was to protect German families and homes, especially women and children. Officials thus were reasserting the role of the male protector and provider that women's labor in and out of the home during war and postwar emergencies had shattered—and that Marlon Brando and the other youth idols clearly continued to flout.

West German authorities resurrected old hostilities against mass behavior and mass culture in order to fight the danger of militarism, on the one hand, and to construct a restrained male "citizen in uniform," on the other. As Jaeger announced: "Against the mass technology and the mass army of the East, only the spiritually and intellectually educated individual fighter of the West can withstand and be superior."[78] This logic linked "mass," femininity, and over-aggression with both fascist militarism and the Cold War enemy. To counter these dangers, the moral education of the new citizen/soldier required the rejection of styles associated with the working class and with American mass culture that simultaneously feminized men *and* made them overly aggressive.

HALBSTARKE AND WEST GERMAN POLITICS

In this context, West German commentators and officials, like their East German counterparts, politicized American popular culture and the styles associated with it. At the same time, West Germans struggled over the East German suggestion that *Halbstarken* behavior was politically motivated.

Many West German commentators saw sinister political motivations behind *Halbstarke*. In their most outraged attacks on *Halbstarke*, West Germans employed the same logic as many East German indictments of American popular culture: they associated the behavior of *Halbstarke* and their consumption of American popular culture with alleged National Socialist and totalitarian threats. Thus, one West German commentator, discussing the effects of *Rock Around the Clock*, warned against the "craze" of film and jazz fans and excessive admiration of movie stars. He paralleled adolescents' "fanatic" behavior with that of Nazi followers and asked, "Who knows to what intricacy and audacity these mass highs, like the orgies of jazz fans, could grow, if at the critical moment certain motives were introduced?"[79] Further, the writer criticized "primitivism," the "loss of universal, humanistic education," "lack of true religious faith," and "superstitious belief in the healing power of psychoanalysis." In espousing a new masculine, yet non-militarist, ideal, West German commentators conflated Nazis and *Halbstarke*, even though there was no evidence that *Halbstarke* were espousing Nazi ideology.[80] Moreover, with their references to "primitivism," West Germans actually used vocabulary that had been part of Nazi racism. In reintroducing such terms in the context of criticizing youth consumption of jazz or rock, which were rooted in African-American culture, West German critics of the youth rebellion resurrected racial hierarchies even as they warned against a return to National Socialism.

Another West German commentator combined his critique of the high number of former SS officers who had been appointed to the West German army with a warning that *Halbstarke* on motorbikes, who were beating up soldiers, were a "motorbike-SA." In comparing *Halbstarke* to the SA (*Sturmabteilung*), which conjured up Nazism and homosexuality, he indicted young rebels as sexual deviants and also indicted homoeroticism. This link served to reject the notion brought forward by the GDR press that the actions of *Halbstarke* constituted legitimate resistance.[81]

In an influential 1956 West German treatment of *Halbstarke*, education expert Hans Muchow contrasted civilized (implicitly white) behavior with three stages of regression into a "wild form." Muchow, who was the first to formulate a comprehensive theory of *Halbstarken* behavior in the 1950s, in a curious way combined biology, genetics, psychology, and political analysis. Thus he argued that the biggest group of *Halbstarke* belonged to an ever-increasing group of "primitives," who could not achieve psychic maturity and, under the conditions of modern society, acted like "wild ones." They were biologically incapable of moving beyond menial labor, took joy in noise, and behaved rather cowardly, because they would flee as soon as the police arrived. Muchow clearly implied that they were unproductive and unmanly.

Muchow identified as a second group the "educationally frustrated" from "honorable circles" and "orderly families," and saw middle-class affluence as one root of *Halbstarken* behavior. As he explained, these adolescents oscillated between fear and aggression because their parents had fulfilled all their wishes—that is, had let them overconsume—or had not educated them at all. Muchow described both the primitives and the educationally frustrated as adolescents who "did not know what they were doing," in allusion to the German title of *Rebel Without a Cause*.

While Muchow claimed that the "primitives" and the "frustrated" made up the majority of *Halbstarke*, he alleged that a dangerous "avant garde" of "nihilists" led this majority. Muchow maintained that the "nihilists," "like the blonde gang leader in *Blackboard Jungle*," shaped the style of *Halbstarken* behavior, *consciously* regressed into the "wild state," took pleasure in dismantling values, and led other adolescents against the police and law and order.

Muchow's analysis affirmed the notion that German *Halbstarke* were modelling their styles and behavior on American movies and especially on *The Wild One, Blackboard Jungle,* and *Rebel Without A Cause*. American movies provided a vocabulary for Muchow's description of youthful misbehavior as a German and international phenomenon. At the same time Muchow's theory of *Halbstarke* drew on all existing fears that had shaped the German public debate: fears of working-class upheaval, the adoption of working-class styles by male middle-class youths, and conscious political actions against the state. Muchow stressed that these transgressions were not harmless and warned of parallels between the National Socialist rise to power and *Halbstarken* behavior. While Muchow rejected the notion that youth riots were directed by "political circles," he identified them as a danger to the state. The state had to counter them with strong action, such as using water hoses or (because mandatory military service had become "problematic") introducing mandatory social service of half a year. Further, Muchow recommended more state-directed cultural offerings for adolescents. As he concluded, "totalitarian systems" (like National Socialism and socialist states), with their state youth organizations, more easily tamed such adolescent rebellions.[82]

Thus *Halbstarke* worried West German commentators and officials in the context of the German Cold War. Another educator pointed to the dangerous implications of their behavior: he warned that a critique of "the Eastern dictatorship was vain hypocrisy or worse if we do not stop the process of regression into barbarism and brutalization, which is rooted in the abuse of democratic freedom."[83] In all of these debates an ideal West German citizen in uniform emerged who would have to defend Western families and Western culture on three fronts: against the National Socialist past, against the Cold War enemy in the East, and against the allegedly self-destructive exaggeration of freedom associated with American culture.

In this climate it was politically shrewd that, in September 1956, Chancellor Konrad Adenauer called attacks and defamations against the West German army shameful and announced that they were the work of *Halbstarke*. The Chancellor skillfully associated all opponents of the West German army with unmanly cultural expressions that all political parties rejected in 1956. Like so many other commentators, Adenauer at once delegitimized *and* politicized *Halbstarken* behavior. Dutifully, both the governing CDU and the opposition party SPD released statements in support of the West German army, and the SPD even warned against a return to the "rowdiness of the 1930s," which had led to the demise of the Weimar Republic.[84] Adenauer's and the SPD's stance further fostered the West German need to search for political motivations behind *Halbstarken* behavior.

WEST GERMAN DEPOLITICIZATION ATTEMPTS

Yet many West Germans tried to counter the notion that *Halbstarke* were engaging in political activities. Thus the West German press hardly reported on incidents that might confirm the East German suggestion that *Halbstarke* were legitimate resisters against conscription. In spite of Adenauer's accusations, West German papers hardly mentioned rioters who used the streets as a forum to express anger over Adenauer's policies and to protest the new conscription laws. One adolescent, for example, distributed leaflets stating: "*Halbstarke* are against conscription."[85] The West German press also ignored statements by the West Berlin chapter of the SPD youth organization *Die Falken*, which most clearly formulated a political vision that connected the consumption of American popular culture and styles associated with *Halbstarken* behavior to resistance against conscription. In advertisements to draw in new members in the mid-1950s, *Die Falken* stressed "that life did not just entail work" and that their leisure-time cultural offerings included folk dances as well as boogie-woogie, classical music as well as cool jazz. Significantly, they declared that for them "all of these questions ... were deeply political questions." Their indictment of conscription culminated in the announcement that, "We find it more useful to practice jazz than to march in a new uniform," and they offered assistance to everyone from East and West who resisted conscription.[86] This stance, which turned the consumption of unrespectable American popular culture like the boogie into a vehicle for political resistance, contrasted with the position of the main body of the SPD, as well as virtually all other public youth organizations, who were careful to distance themselves from *Halbstarke*.[87] And even within the West Berlin *Falken*, rifts existed between "rock 'n' roll" groups and those who wanted what they saw as intellectual and disciplined political work—and who were increasingly headed by middle- and upper-class male youths.[88]

Male *Halbstarke*, with their spontaneous gatherings and riots as well as with their public displays of unrespectable dances and fashions, certainly ran counter to proper political involvement, which all mainstream parties defined as voting, organized involvement in political parties, and service to the state. Because most of the riots indeed had no clear leadership but happened spontaneously when youths (mostly boys) took theaters apart or rampaged through the streets, one magazine commented somewhat condescendingly that these adolescents had no political agenda. Yet the very same article talked of the "evil power" of *Halbstarke*.[89]

When the West Berlin city parliament debated the youth riots in September 1956, Mayor Amrehn countered assertions that youth riots were politically directed. Instead he described the riots as an international phenomenon and stressed that they also had occurred in the United States and even in East Germany and the Soviet Union. Amrehn emphasized that West Berlin was no "Wild West," and as the main causes for riots he cited the scarcity of housing and the conditions of the war and postwar periods "that had loosened morality." Although Amrehn implied that poverty in the postwar period was one root of unruly youth behavior, he also acknowledged that many youths from "good homes" had been taking part in the riots.[90]

Amrehn and most members of the West Berlin parliament agreed that the police had to step in to guarantee public safety and to preserve the authority of the state. West Berlin officials decided to use more undercover agents, because adolescents were so hostile toward officers in uniform. At the same time Amrehn and his government, like the Bonn government, urged the press not to report on gangs and riots in detail.[91] Moreover, Amrehn and many speakers from various parties also agreed that "positive" youth social work and cultural programs were needed. Clearly they imagined programs that would counter the effects of American consumer culture. The speaker from the SPD who described West Berlin youth riots as modeled on American examples, especially on *The Wild One*, urged, with applause from both the SPD and CDU, that libraries be used to educate the youth into "valuable and worthy members of our community."[92]

An earlier attempt by the West Berlin government to cooperate with a commercial movie producer on a film (*Die Halbstarken*) that would speak to the problems of German young rebels had failed. In the spring of 1956, West Berlin city officials, actors, and producers had participated in public meetings in an effort to assure an authentic depiction of adolescents. The movie, a self-conscious German answer to *The Wild One* and *Blackboard Jungle*, took place in a working-class setting and depicted a gang of juveniles who committed robberies. It portrayed a young, sensual woman as the evil force behind the male delinquents in the film, and thus took up a phenomenon that West German reviewers of American young rebel movies had identified as a typically American problem. At the end of the movie she even shot her lover, the gang leader. The West Berlin government withdrew funding for the movie, because it did not show "any positive solutions" to the juvenile upheaval. When *Die Halbstarken* came out in October 1956 it certainly helped spread the term *Halbstarke*. Many critics, however, felt that it misrepresented young rebels as criminals.[93]

At the same time the movie furthered the notion that *Halbstarken* behavior was not politically motivated. Increasingly, West German commentators agreed with this evaluation. One paper even suggested that many actions by West German adolescents against the West German military were probably nonpolitical and sought to explain them as mere fights over the attention of girls. Nonetheless, the commentator saw a connection with politics: he identified the devaluation of everything military by the occupation forces as the political root of the adolescents' rejection of the West German army. At the same time he criticized East German authorities who interpreted "any bad word directed against a soldier" as protest against the Adenauer government.[94]

Conclusion

The significance of East and West German struggles over the influence of American popular culture goes beyond changes in adolescent dress and behavior. With the gender norms that East and West Germans formulated in the *Halbstarken* debates of the mid-1950s, both sides constructed the ideal of a new, self-restrained, post-fascist German man not taken over by consumer culture. At the same time, these gender mores were central to linking fascism and American popular culture, and to rejecting both. Distinguishing themselves from fascism was certainly a worthy project for East and West Germans, but we need to look carefully at these attempts to leave the past behind. In connecting deviations from gender norms—lack of male restraint and sexually provocative, emasculating women—to lower-class and African-American culture, East and West German officials reinscribed class and racial hierarchies even as they criticized poverty and American racism. Perhaps ironically, even though both Germanys were ethnically homogenous as never before, authorities relied on gender norms and negative racial stereotypes to contain rebellious youth behavior and to fight the Cold War battles.

Thus the debates about *Halbstarke* and American influences were not simply about Germany becoming more American; they were a crucial part in the complicated processes of reconstructing Germanness in East and West. East German authorities conflated the consumption of American popular culture with fascism and capitalist militarism, while West Germany conflated it with fascism and Eastern totalitarianism.[95] These moves served related political functions: in their quest for a Germanness untainted by National Socialism, both Germanys connected the threat of fascism to American cultural influences. East and West German fascination with America may have been part of what Michael Geyer has recently described as "forgetting the violent origins of society and the desperate effort to disguise its present appearance in foreign images."[96]

In East and West Germany, authorities translated these visions into public policy: they urged youngsters to read good books, to go to concerts to hear classical music, to watch only movies recommended by state agencies, or to take ballroom dance classes. Thus both states politicized culture and pushed cultural forms that did not pose challenges to the gender norms that were central to the reconstructions of German national identities in East and West.[97]

Yet, this logic clearly put West German authorities, who were struggling to build a military and political alliance with the United States, into a more vulnerable position. And to make things worse, West Germans felt quite threatened by FDJ efforts that, for a time in 1956, seemed to give *Halbstarke* cultural and political legitimacy. In this context many West Germans sought to assure themselves that *Halbstarke* were only a tiny minority, and at the same time rejected *Halbstarken* fashions and mannerisms. In October 1956 the polling institute EMNID published a study of West German and West Berlin adolescents with the rather timely title "How strong are the *Halbstarke*?" EMNID asserted that only few *Halbstarke* existed. Reports about EMNID's findings in the West German press revealed that many West Germans saw adolescents' American-influenced cultural styles as closely linked to a dangerous lack of political commitment to the West German state. In this atmosphere traditional European dances, with their compatibility with "bourgeois" gender mores, became a symbol of West German political stability. Newspapers distilled the EMNID study as follows: German adolescents respected authority, were satisfied with their work, had no illusions—and liked to dance the waltz.[98]

However, as the 1950s wore on, and as consumption assumed growing importance as a Western weapon in the Cold War, West Germans would have to develop new answers, and a different, consumption-oriented masculinity, in their efforts to find a new, German, way between Eastern totalitarianism and American-led alleged Western self-destruction.[99] As East German officials retreated from their 1956 stance that promised an accommodation of *Halbstarken* styles and reverted to earlier attacks on both young German rebels and American popular culture as fascist, West Germans would increasingly depoliticize both American imports and *Halbstarken* styles.

Notes

1. Research for this essay was supported by grants from the Universität Kiel, Brown University, and the German Historical Institute, Washington. For their helpful criticisms of earlier drafts, I would like to thank Lucy Barber, Omer Bartov, Marion Berghahn, Volker Berghahn, Mari Jo Buhle, Carolyn Dean, Jane Gerhard, Ruth Feldstein, Melani McAlister, Donna Penn, and Jessica Shubow. *Abgeordnetenhaus von Berlin: Stenographische Berichte: 2. Wahlperiode* (Berlin, 1956), 42nd Session, September 20, 1956, 522, (hereafter cited as *Abgh. Berlin*). Throughout, translations from the German are the author's.
2. Hans Heinrich Muchow, "Zur Psychologie und Pädagogik der 'Halbstarken,'" *Unsere Jugend* 8, part I, September 1956, 388–94; part II, October 1956, 442–49; part III, November 1956, 486–91.
3. On gendered notions of citizenship, see Nancy Fraser, "What's Critical About Critical Theory? The Case of Habermas and Gender," in Fraser, *Unruly Practices: Power, Discourse and Gender in Contemporary Social Theory* (Minneapolis: University of Minnesota Press, 1989), 113–43.
4. See statistics in Thomas Guback, *The International Film Industry: Western Europe and America Since 1945* (Bloomington: Indiana University Press, 1969), 47. American films were important, although they did not constitute the majority of top-grossing productions. For lists of top-grossing productions in West Germany, see Klaus Sigl, Werner Schneider, and Ingo Tornow, *Jede Menge Kohle? Kunst und Kommerz auf dem deutschen Filmmarkt der Nachkriegszeit: Filmpreise und Kassenerfolge 1949–1985* (Munich: Filmland Presse, 1986). On American movies in Germany, see also Victoria DeGrazia, "Mass Culture and Sovereignty: The American Challenge to European Cinemas, 1920–1960," *Journal of Modern History* 61, March 1989, 53–87.
5. For a list of the number of foreign productions shown per year in the GDR from 1945 to 1961 see Heinz Kersten, *Das Filmwesen in der Sowjetischen Besatzungszone*, part 1 (Bonn: Bundes-Verlag, 1963), 360–61.
6. *The Wild One* (U.S.A., 1954; German: *Der Wilde*); *Rebel Without a Cause* (U.S.A., 1955; German: ... *denn sie wissen nicht, was sie tun*); *Blackboard Jungle* (U.S.A., 1955; German: *Saat der Gewalt*); *Rock Around the Clock* (U.S.A., 1956; German: *Außer Rand und Band*).
7. See Heide Fehrenbach, "The Fight for the 'Christian West': German Film Control, the Churches and the Reconstruction of Civil Society in the Early Bonn Republic," *German Studies Review* 14, February 1991, 39–63; for East Germany, see Kersten, *Das Filmwesen*. On American juvenile delinquency debates, see Thomas Doherty,

Teenagers and Teenpics: The Juvenilization of American Movies in the 1950s (Boston: Unwin Hyman, 1988); James Gilbert, *A Cycle of Outrage: America's Reaction to the Juvenile Delinquent in the 1950s* (New York: Oxford University Press, 1986). For a polemic treatment of American teenage culture, see Jon Lewis, *The Road to Romance and Ruin: Teen Films and Youth Culture* (New York: Routledge, 1992).

8. See Heide Fehrenbach, "*Die Sünderin* or Who Killed the German Male? Early Postwar Cinema and the Betrayal of the Fatherland," in Sandra Frieden, Richard McCormick, et al., eds., *Gender and German Cinema*, vol. 2 (Providence: Berg, 1993); Ute Frevert, "Frauen auf dem Weg zur Gleichberechtigung—Hindernisse, Umleitungen, Einbahnstraßen," in Martin Broszat, ed., *Zäsuren nach 1945. Essays zur Periodisierung der deutschen Nachkriegsgeschichte* (Munich: R. Oldenbourg, 1990), 113–30. On German men hiding behind women in the early days of occupation, see Annemarie Troeger, "Between Rape and Prostitution," in Judith Friedlaender et al., eds., *Women in Culture and Politics: A Century of Change* (Bloomington: Indiana University Press, 1986), 97–117.

9. For West Germany, see Robert G. Moeller, *Protecting Motherhood: Women and the Family in the Politics of West Germany* (Berkeley: University of California Press, 1993); for East Germany, Ina Merkel, *... und Du, Frau an der Werkbank: Die DDR in den 50er Jahren* (Berlin: Elefanten Press, 1990) has pointed to the reproduction of a gender division of labor in spite of Socialist claims for women's equality and policies that urged women to join the work force.

10. On the political battles over West German rearmament, see Ulrich Albrecht, *Die Wiederaufrüstung der Bundesrepublik: Analyse und Dokumentation* (Cologne: Pahl-Rugenstein, 1980); Marc Cioc, *Pax Atomica: The Nuclear Defense Debate in West Germany During the Adenauer Era* (New York: Columbia University Press, 1988); Roger Morgan, *The United States and West Germany 1945–1973: A Study in Alliance Politics* (New York: Oxford University Press, 1974). On masculinity and the Wehrmacht in the Third Reich, see Omer Bartov, *Hitler's Army: Soldiers, Nazis and War in the Third Reich* (New York: Oxford University Press, 1991).

11. On West German youth cultures and American cultural influences in the 1950s, see the excellent study by Kaspar Maase, *Bravo Amerika: Erkundigungen zur Jugendkultur der Bundesrepublik in den fünfziger Jahren* (Hamburg: Junius, 1992); see also Heinz-Hermann Krüger, ed., *"Die Elvistolle, die hatte ich mir unauffällig wachsen lassen": Lebensgeschichte und jugendliche Alltagskultur in den fünfziger Jahren* (Opladen: Leske und Budrich, 1985). On the reception of American influences in East Germany, see Michael Rauhut, *Beat in der Grauzone: DDR-Rock, 1964–1972—Politik und Alltag* (Berlin: Basisdruck, 1993).

12. This logic had appeared with the rise of consumer culture in the nineteenth century. See especially Andreas Huyssen, *After the Great Divide: Modernism, Mass Culture, Postmodernism* (Bloomington: Indiana University Press, 1986).

13. See, for example, A. Gügler, *Euer Sohn in der Entwicklungskrise* (Stuttgart, 1952) excerpts reprinted in Peter Kuhnert and Ute Ackermann, "Jenseits von Lust und Liebe? Jugendsexualität in den 50er Jahren," in Krüger, ed., *"Die Elvistolle"*, 43–83, 50.

14. Scholarship has mostly repeated this focus on young men. For exceptions, see Christine Bertram und Heinz-Hermann Krüger, "Vom Backfisch zum Teenager—Mädchensozialisation in den 50er Jahren," in Krüger, ed., *"Die Elvistolle"*, 84–101; Angela Delille and Andrea Grohn, eds., *Perlonzeit: Wie die Frauen ihr Wirtschaftswunder erlebten* (Berlin: Elefanten Press, 1985). Maase, *Bravo Amerika*, mentions girls but does not make them central to his analysis.

15. Scholars of racism and colonialism are pointing to the complicated intersections of gender, race, and class in nineteenth- and twentieth-century discourses about civilization. See Gail Bederman, "Civilization, The Decline of Middle-Class Manliness,

and Ida B. Wells's Anti-Lynching Campaign," in Barbara Melosh, ed., *Gender and American History Since 1890* (New York: Routledge, 1994), 207–33; Hazel Carby, *Reconstructing Womanhood: The Emergence of the Afro-American Woman Novelist* (New York: Oxford University Press, 1987); Sander Gilman, *Difference and Pathology: Stereotypes of Sexuality, Race and Madness* (Ithaca: Cornell University Press, 1985); Paul Gilroy, *There Ain't No Black in the Union Jack: The Cultural Politics of Race and Nation* (London: Hutchinson, 1987); Vron Ware, *Beyond the Pale: White Women, Racism and History* (New York: Verso, 1992).
16. On postwar German hostility towards "difference," see Michael Geyer, "The Stigma of Violence, Nationalism, and War in 20th-Century Germany," *German Studies Review* 15, Winter 1992, 75–110.
17. For a treatment celebrating the stabilizing American impact (stable families, revived democracies, improved national sentiments) in postwar Europe, see Peter Duignan and L.H. Gann, *The Rebirth of the West: The Americanization of the Democratic World, 1945–1958* (Cambridge: Blackwell, 1992). For a much more nuanced study that focuses on American economic hegemony, see Volker R. Berghahn, *The Americanization of West German Industry, 1945–1973* (New York: Cambridge University Press, 1986).
18. Ralph Willet, *The Americanization of Germany, 1945–1949* (New York: Routledge, 1989), ix; Reinhold Wagnleitner, *Coca-Colonisation und Kalter Krieg—Die Kulturmission der USA in Oesterreich nach dem Zweiten Weltkrieg* (Wien: Verlag für Gesellschaftskritik, 1991); and Wagnleitner, "The Irony of American Culture Abroad: Austria and the Cold War," in Lary May, ed., *Recasting America: Culture and Politics in the Cold War* (Chicago: University of Chicago Press, 1989), 285–301. For useful critiques of "Americanization" as an analytical concept in the West German context, see Maase, *Bravo Amerika*, 21–40; and Arnold Sywottek, "The Americanization of Everyday Life? Early Trends in Consumer and Leisure-Time Behavior," in Michael Ermath, ed., *America and the Shaping of German Society 1945–1955* (Providence: Berg, 1993), 132–52.

Recently scholars are paying more attention to the baggage Europeans have brought to their encounter with the United States. See Richard Kuisel, *Seducing the French: The Dilemma of Americanization* (Berkeley, 1993), who has asserted that France's encounter with American influences in the postwar era is primarily about Frenchness. On West German hostilities toward America, see Dan Diner, *Verkehrte Welten: Antiamerikanismus in Deutschland: Ein historischer Essay* (Frankfurt am Main: Eichborn, 1993).
19. This indictment appeared in a review of *A Streetcar Named Desire* in West Germany: "Der 'Gorilla-Typ' triumphiert," *B.Z.*, 8 January 1954. The article used the American term "sex appeal."
20. "'Der Wilde' mit Pferdestärken," *Montagsecho*, April 12, 1955.
21. "Der Wilde," *Kurier*, 13 April 1955. Other reviews drew parallels to German biker gangs: "Der Wilde," *Abend*, 21 January 1955; "Das ist 'Der Wilde,'" *Montagsecho*, 7 March 1955.
22. In addition, a government report claimed that they had terrorized the bar owner by blackmailing him. "Die Berliner Jugendgerichtshilfe im Jahre 1955," *Der Rundbrief* 6, no. 4/5, 1956, Rep.13 Acc.1022 Nr.7, Landesarchiv Berlin (hereafter cited as LAB). A newspaper report referred to the group as "Marlon Brandos," "Hoher Anteil der Verkehrsdelikte an der Jugendkriminalität," *Tagesspiegel*, 19 August 1956. See also Curt Bondy, et al., *Jugendliche stören die Ordnung: Bericht und Stellungnahme zu den Halbstarkenkrawallen* (Munich: Juventa, 1957), 9, who described this incident as the beginning of youth riots.
23. "Skulls and Crossbones" is actually a symbol used by an infamous SS unit, but also by oppositional youth groups of the late 1930s known as *Edelweiß-Piraten*. See Detlev

Peukert, *Inside Nazi Germany: Conformity, Opposition and Racism in Everyday Life* (New Haven: Yale University Press, 1987), 154. It is not clear whether the Wedding youths themselves adopted it from the American movie (or from the SS), or whether the West German press assigned it to them. In any case, the member of the West Berlin parliament, who discussed the influence of *The Wild One* on the gang, Dr. Stein, (*Abgh. Berlin*, 42nd Session, 20 September 1956, 522) referred to the American example and did not mention any possible connections to the SS.

24. See "Neue Krawalle am Wedding," *Telegraf*, 13 July 1956; *Berlin. Chronik der Jahre 1955–1956* (Berlin: Heinz Spitzing, 1971), 552–3.
25. See minutes of the West Berlin Ausschuss für Jugend, 5 October 1956, LAB Rep.2 Acc.1949 Nr.2508.
26. See Maase, *Bravo Amerika*. Perhaps not surprisingly, reports mostly ignored the German women present even though they had focused so heavily on American women as instigators of male rebellion.
27. See Detlev Peukert, "Die 'Halbstarken'," *Zeitschrift für Pädagogik* 30, April 1984, 533–84. The closest American equivalent to this term was juvenile delinquency, which greatly obsessed Americans in the 1950s.
28. See Winfried Sträter, "'Das konnte ein Erwachsener nicht mit ruhigen Augen beobachten:' Die Halbstarken," in Berliner Geschichtswerkstatt e.V., ed., *Vom Lagerfeuer zur Musikbox. Jugendkulturen 1900–1960*, (Berlin: Elefanten Press, 1985), 137–70, 152; Maase, *Bravo Amerika*.
29. Others criticized their "rivet-jeans-dressed" (*nietenbehostes*) "inner life." See *7 Uhr Blatt*, 7 October 1956. Bondy et al., *Jugendliche stören die Ordnung*, 28, defined "Halbstarke" as male adolescents "who dress conspicuously and are interested in a loose, casual, and unproductive togetherness with companions of their age and sex."
30. See Karena Niehoff, "... denn sie wissen nicht, was sie tun," *Tagesspiegel*, April 1, 1956; Martin Rupert, "... denn sie wissen nicht, was sie tun," *Frankfurter Allgemeine Zeitung (FAZ)*, 31 March 1956; Arbeitsausschuss der FSK (Freiwillige Selbstkontrolle der Filmwirtschaft), "Jugendprotokoll: 'Denn sie wissen nicht, was sie tun...'," 19 January 1956, Landesbildstelle Berlin. For similar statements, see "... denn sie wissen nicht, was sie tun," *Beratungsdienst Jugend und Film*, August 1956. For readings of *Rebel* in the American context, see Peter Biskind, *Seeing is Believing: How Hollywood Taught Us to Stop Worrying and Love the Fifties* (New York: Pantheon, 1983), 200–217; Doherty, *Teenagers and Teenpics*; Gilbert, *A Cycle of Outrage*.
31. For a critique of the effacement of class differences in *Rebel* see "... denn sie wissen nicht, was sie tun," *FAZ*, 31 March 1956.
32. Stephan Roth, "Die ratlosen Ganzschwachen," *Die Zeit*, 11 April 1957.
33. *Verhandlungen des deutschen Bundestages: 2. Wahlperiode: Stenographische Berichte* (Bonn, 1956), vol. 32, 166th Session, 25 October 1956, 9175, (hereafter cited as *VDBT*).
34. *An Euch alle, die Ihr jung seid! Material der 12. Tagung des Zentralrats der Freien Deutschen Jugend vom 3. und 4. Februar 1956*, (Berlin, no date), 5.
35. For accusations after the June 1953 uprising, see "So sieht die faschistische Brut der Adenauer, Ollenhauer, Kaiser und Reuter aus!" *Neues Deutschland*, 21 June 1953. "So hausten sie—die Provokateure," *Junge Welt*, 23 June 1956; Ausschuß für Deutsche Einheit, ed. *Wer zog die Drähte? Der Juni-Putsch 1953 und seine Hintergründe* (Berlin: Junge Welt, 1954). My thanks to Herr Czihak of the Landesarchiv Berlin (Außenstelle Breite Straße) for lending me the latter. For another expression of this logic, see also the movie *Alarm im Zirkus* (GDR; 1954).
36. Abteilung Geldumlauf, Berliner Zahlungsverein, "Analyse des Besuches von Westberliner Kinos durch Bewohner unseres Wirtschaftsgebietes," 16 April 1956; "Analyse des Besuches von westberliner Lichtspieltheatern durch Bewohner unseres Währungsgebietes," 17 May 1957, both Rep.121 Nr.156, Landesarchiv Berlin,

Außenstelle Breite Straße (hereafter cited as LAB [STA]). Both reports also expressed concerns about the economic impact of these numbers.
37. For exchanges between West Berlin government officials and West Berlin theater owners, see especially the memo to Mayor Amrehn, 5 December 1955, LAB Rep.2 Acc.1636 Nr.2163. For East Germany, see Referat Film, "Plan 1956," Berlin, 12 December 1955, LAB (STA) Rep.121 Nr.225; *An Euch Alle.*
38. Werner Berger, "Schmarren für die Freiheit," *Blickpunkt,* April 1956.
39. Interviews with Peter Dannemann, January 1993, and with Dietmar Iser, July 1993. All interviews were conducted by the author. The names of those interviewed have been changed, and recordings and notes are in the author's possession. For an account on East German young rebels, see "Protokoll über einen Erfahrungsaustausch über die Arbeit der Jugendklubs in der DDR," 1960, A6724, Jugendarchiv beim Institut für zeitgeschichtliche Jugendforschung, Berlin (hereafter cited as JA-IzJ).
40. For such denials, see review of *Blackboard Jungle,* "Die kühne Attacke derer vom Telegraf," *B.Z. am Abend,* 21 November 1955. On East German rowdies, see "Protokoll der Sitzung des Zentralrats der FDJ," 19 September 1956, JA-IzJ 2608.
41. See, for example, "... denn sie wissen nicht, was sie tun," *FAZ,* 31 March 1956; "... denn sie wissen nicht, was sie tun," *Beratungsdienst Jugend und Film,* August 1956.
42. Fried Maximilian, "Die Saat der Gewalt," *Film, Bild, Ton* 5, 1955/56. The author of "Die Saat der Gewalt," *Abend,* 2 December 1955, saw the presence of many races in the United States as the root of juvenile misbehavior yet agreed with others who endorsed the progressive view of American race relations.
43. On the cultural and political impact of the stereotypes of the black rapist and his white female victim in both the United States and Europe, see, for example, Vron Ware, "Moments of Danger: Race, Gender, and Memories of Empire," *History and Theory,* Supplement 31, 1992, 116–37.
44. "Die Saat der Diplomatie," *Telegraf,* 5 November 1955; "Diskussion um die Zensur—vorerst platonisch," *Mannheimer Morgen,* 12 November 1955; "Die Saat der Gewalt," *Abend,* 3 November 1955.
45. "Saat der Gewalt," *Tagesspiegel,* 4 December 1955.
46. Werner Fiedler, "Brutalität—besonders wertvoll?" *Der Tag,* 2 December 1955. See also "Der Dompteur der Klasse," *Telegraf,* 2 December 1955; "Verfälschte Erziehungsprobleme," *Film, Bild, Ton* 5, 1955/1956.
47. Erich Richter, "Wenn die Umwelt versagt," *Blickpunkt,* March 1956.
48. See "Halbstarke und Spiesser in den USA," *Berliner Zeitung,* 12 December 1955; "Ein richtiger Direks fehlt," *Depesche,* 8 December 1955; "Die Saat der Gewalt," *Abend,* 3 November 1955.
49. "Wen verwirrte *Saat der Gewalt*?" *National-Zeitung,* 19 January 1956.
50. "Wir und der Film: 'Saat der Gewalt,'" *Jugendruf,* January 1956, 20.
51. On West German attempts to come to terms with the legacy of Nazi racism, especially of anti-Semitism, see Frank Stern, *The Whitewashing of the Yellow Badge: Antisemitism and Philosemitism in Postwar Germany* (New York: Pergamon, 1992).
52. "Die Saat der Diplomatie," *Telegraf,* 5 November 1955; "Amerikanische Schultragödie," *Wirtschaftszeitung,* 5 November 1955; "Wen verwirrte *Saat der Gewalt*?" *National-Zeitung,* 19 January 1956; "Halbstarke und Spiesser in den USA," *Berliner Zeitung,* 12 December 1955.
53. "Die Saat der Diplomatie," *Telegraf,* 5 November 1955. "'Besonders wertvoll,'" *Der Tag,* 28 October 1955.
54. For the connections between "racial liberalism" and "sexual conservatism" in the 1950s in the United States, see Ruth S. Feldstein, "'I Wanted the Whole World to See': Race, Gender and Constructions of Motherhood in the Death of Emmett Till," in Joanne Meyerowitz, ed., *Not June Cleaver: Women and Gender in Postwar America,*

1945–1960 (Philadelphia: Temple, 1994), 263–303; Melani McAlister, "Staging the American Century: Race, Gender, and Nation in U.S. Representations of the Middle East, 1945–1992," Ph.D. dissertation in progress, Brown University.
55. On *The Wild One* soundtrack, see "Das ist 'Der Wilde'," *Montagsecho*, 7 March 1955; "'Der Wilde' mit Pferdestärken," *Montagsecho*, 12 April 1955. For West German reactions to the *Blackboard Jungle* soundtrack, see "Die Saat der Gewalt," *Abend*, 2 December 1956; *Spandauer Volksblatt*, 4 December 1955; for East German reactions see "Halbstarke und Spiesser in den USA," *Berliner Zeitung*, 12 December 1955; "Wen verwirrte Saat der Gewalt?" *National-Zeitung*, 19 January 1956.
56. "Schattenseiten der Freiheit," *Kurier*, 3 December 1955.
57. "Amerikanische Schultragödie," *Wirtschaftszeitung*, 5 November 1955.
58. "Die kühne Attacke derer vom Telegraf," *B.Z. am Abend*, 21 November 1955.
59. See for example, "Die Königin greift ein," *Spandauer Volksblatt*, 19 September 1956; report about riots abroad in *National-Zeitung*, 28 September 1956.
60. "Der Über-Rhythmus," *Der Spiegel*, 26 September 1956.
61. "Die ganze Welt rockt und rollt," *Bravo*, 30 September 1956.
62. Jörg Roesler, "Privater Konsum in Ostdeutschland 1950–1960," in Axel Schildt and Arnold Sywottek, eds., *Modernisierung und Wiederaufbau: Die westdeutsche Gesellschaft der 50er Jahre* (Bonn: J.H.W. Dietz Nachf., 1993), 290–303.
63. Historians have asserted that, in contrast to other socialist states (such as Poland and Hungary) where various social groups, including workers, tried to transform socialism in 1956, only East German intellectuals used the greater space for maneuver. See Dietrich Staritz, *Geschichte der DDR 1949–85* (Frankfurt am Main: edition suhrkamp, 1985), 109. In light of the rising youth rebellion in East Germany and the tactics that the state and FDJ developed to deal with it, this view deserves re-evaluation.
64. On complaints, see FDJ-Kreisleitung Prenzlauer Berg, "Wocheneinschätzung," 25 February 1956, and 12 June 1956, JA-IzJ AB338.
65. "Warum laufen in der DDR keine amerikanischen Filme?" *Neues Deutschland*, 26 May 1956.
66. "Berlin—aus der Nähe gesehen," *Berliner Zeitung*, 20 May 1956.
67. Program brochure for *Eine Berliner Romanze*, *Progress Film-Illustrierte*, no.66, 1956.
68. See Martin Schulz, "Eine Berliner Romanze," *B.Z. am Abend*, 23 May 1956; Günter Stahnke, "Eine Berliner Romanze," *Junge Welt*, 18 May 1956.
69. "Gangsterliteratur und Naziorden," *Berliner Zeitung*, 16 September 1956.
70. Sekretariat des Zentralrats der FDJ, "Stellungnahme," supplement 1 to "Protokoll," Berlin, 19 September 1956, JA-IzJ 2608. This statement on "the events among parts of the youth in West Germany and West Berlin" was to be published in the FDJ newspaper *Junge Welt* and to be distributed to youth organizations in the West.
71. "Bonner Vergehen an der Jugend," *Der Morgen*, 14 September 1956. See also "Nato-Soldaten unbeliebt," *Neues Deutschland*, 19 September 1956.
72. "Halbstarke prügeln Volkspolizisten," *Nachtdepesche*, 2 October 1956; "Jugendkrawalle in der Zone," *Telegraf*, 3 October 1956.
73. See "Protokoll der Sitzung des Zentralrats," 19 September 1956, JA-IzJ 2608. These anniversaries would remain occasions for protest. In the fall of 1989 the East German opposition staged demonstrations around that date.
74. See *VDBT*, vol. 26, 92nd and 93rd Session, 27 and 28 June 1955, 5213–20, 5223–302; especially statements by defense minister Theodor Blank and by Erich Ollenhauer (SPD), Fritz Erler (SPD), Hasso von Manteuffel (FDP). For further statements by West German politicians against German militarism and for rearmament, see Hans-Joachim Harder und Norbert Wiggershaus, *Tradition und Reform in den Aufbaujahren der Bundeswehr* (Herford: E.S. Mittler & Sohn, 1985), 11–39. On consensus and disagreements over the terms of rearmament, see also Albrecht, *Wieder-*

bewaffnung; Anselm Doering-Manteuffel, *Die Bundesrepublik Deutschland in der Ära Adenauer: Außenpolitik und innere Entwicklung* (Darmstadt: Wissenschaftliche Buchgesellschaft, 1988), 73–77.
75. See *VDBT*, 93rd Session, 28 June 1955. Some West German politicians also warned against an army that was "too democratic." On the search for a positive German military tradition and the construction of the citizen in uniform, see Donald Abenheim, *Reforging the Iron Cross: The Search for Tradition in the West German Armed Forces* (Princeton: Princeton University Press, 1988); Harder and Wiggershaus, *Tradition und Reform*. None of the studies has treated rearmament specifically as a problem of masculinity.
76. Advertisements for the *Bundeswehr* in *Der Spiegel*, no. 30 and 31, 1956.
77. *VDBT*, 93rd Session, 28 June 1955, 5228.
78. *VDBT*, 93rd Session, 28 June 1955, 5230.
79. Walter Abendroth, "Das große Kopfschütteln über die Jugend," *Die Zeit*, 27 September 1956.
80. This certainly distinguishes *Halbstarke* of the 1950s from right-wing German skinheads of the 1980s and 1990s.
81. "Geprügelte Soldaten," *Rheinischer Merkur*, 12 October 1956.
82. Muchow, "Zur Psychologie und Pädagogik." Many German researchers of youth would use Muchow's thesis as a starting point. See for example Bondy et al., *Jugendliche stören die Ordnung*; Helmut Schelsky, *Die skeptische Generation: Eine Soziologie der deutschen Jugend* (Cologne, Eugen Diederichs, 1957); Günther Kaiser, *Randalierende Jugend: Eine soziologische und kriminologische Studie über die sogenannten "Halbstarken"* (Heidelberg: Quelle und Meyer, 1959).
83. Adolf Busemann, "Verwilderung und Verrohung," *Unsere Jugend* 8 April 1956, 159–68, 168.
84. See "Ausrüstung für sechs deutsche Divisionen," *Tagesspiegel*, 12 September 1956; Hans-Georg Hermann, "Die 'Lümmels' des Herrn Bundeskanzler," *Die andere Zeitung*, 27 September 1956. On the SPD stance, see Dietrich Schwarzkopf, "Der Bürger und die Bundeswehr," *Tagesspiegel*, 12 September 1956.
85. Kaiser, *Randalierende Jugend*, 197–98.
86. See the brochures distributed by the West Berlin Senator für Jugend und Sport, *Du und Deine Freizeit* (Berlin, no year, ca. 1956); and *Wohin? Freizeitfibel für die Schulabgänger 1957* (Berlin, 1957).
87. See Max Jäger, "Es ging nicht nur um Pin-up-Girls," *Blickpunkt*, March 1956; "Kein Allheilmittel," *Blickpunkt*, August 1956; "'Rock 'n' Roll' und Krawalle," *Blickpunkt*, December 1956.
88. On *Falken* ambivalence toward consumption, see Rolf Lindemann and Werner Schultz, *Die Falken in Berlin: Geschichte und Erinnerung—Jugendopposition in den fünfziger Jahren* (Berlin, Elefanten Press, 1987).
89. W. Born, "Die böse Macht der Halbstarken," *Wochenend*, no. 13, 1956.
90. *Abgh. Berlin*, 42nd Session, 20 September 1956, 517–523; "Parlaments-Debatte über Jugendkrawalle," *Tagesspiegel*, 21 September 1956; minutes of the West Berlin Ausschuß für Jugend, 28 September 1956, LAB Rep.2 Acc.1949 Nr.2508.
91. See minutes of the West Berlin Ausschuß für Jugend, 28 September 1956, LAB Rep.2 Acc.1949 Nr.2508.
92. *Abgh. Berlin*, 42nd Session, 20 September 1956, 522.
93. *Die Halbstarken* (FRG; 1956) For reports, see "Man nennt sie 'Halbstarke,'" *Tagesspiegel*, 17 April 1956; "Die Halbstarken," *Beratungsdienst Jugend und Film*, October 1956.
94. Dietrich Schwarzkopf, "Der Bürger und die Bundeswehr," *Tagesspiegel*, 12 September 1956.

95. This West German analysis was, of course, in tune with the Western totalitarianism paradigm that conflated fascism and Stalinism.
96. Geyer, "The Stigma of Violence," 102–3, has recently pointed to what he sees as a German inability, in the aftermath of National Socialism and the Weimar Republic, to conceive of "difference" in positive terms.
97. For West Germany, see brochures *Du und Deine Freizeit*; *Wohin?*; for East Germany, see *An Euch alle*.
98. Rolf Fröhner, *Wie stark sind die Halbstarken?* (Bielefeld: Maria von Stackelberg, 1956). For reviews, see "Wie ist die deutsche Jugend?" *Die Zeit*, 18 October 1956; "Die Eltern und Bismarck sind ihr Vorbild," *Der Tag*, 13 October 1956.
99. Theorists and historians have asserted that in the 1950s a new, masculine, subject of consumption was conceived. See Fraser, "What's Critical about Critical Theory?" For West Germany, see Maase, *Bravo Amerika*, who overstates the positive impact of this development. For the United States, see Barbara Ehrenreich, *The Hearts of Men: American Dreams and the Flight from Commitment* (New York: Anchor, 1983).

8. CULTURE AS AUTHORITY:
AMERICAN AND GERMAN TRANSACTIONS

Peter K. Breit

INTRODUCTION

The United States' cultural influence on Germany, 1945–1965, often thought to be transformational, was primarily transactional[1], in many instances paradoxical, and its long-term effects can only now be examined.[2] After 1952, it was not necessary that American culture be authoritative to be effective. It ultimately gained its authority through the interplay of factors in American and German cultures, through the nature of the multiple engagements between America and West Germany, and through events outside the ability of either to control.

These include: (1) the ethical and physical destruction wrought by Nazism and war; (2) the slow reemergence of a private, depoliticized, sector; (3) the thoroughness with which *external aspects* (symbols, music, art, etc.) of Nazi culture disappeared; (4) the initial absence of a stable social status; (5) uncertainty about Nazism's roots and pervasiveness; (6) the massive population shifts; (7) the daring of American culture which stressed spontaneity, consumability, and finally disposability; (8) the influence of emigre intellectuals; (9) the persistence of a public culture, fostered by the war's physical destruction; (10) the emergence of a cultural competitor in East Germany; (11) a culture increasingly identified with luxury; (12) an American cultural disposition eventually to regard its postwar activities not so much as a *trans*formation, but rather as a *re*formation, but which, in reaction to conditions, ended being a series of transactions; (13) the personality of American culture; (14) the consequences of the Nazi period, including division, the substitution of economic for political power, and the absence of Jews; (15) the confidence that unification would never come; (16) the frequent castaway quality of American popular culture, as this is considered below.

Even assuming the tractability of these phenomena, as Americans were inclined to do, there remained something for which they were unprepared. For the state of nearly complete destruction and American cultural endeavors coexisted with memories of a recent political order that had been a moral, intellectual, cultural code. In addition, the rapid deterioration of Allied relations helped determine that American cultural influences would derive whatever authority they might have from pursuing a policy of transaction rather than one of transformation.

AUTHORITY AND THE CULTURES

Authority involves political actors' relative ability to hold opinions, convert them into decisions, and have the decisions accepted.[3] *Popular* culture is the contemporary mode, its representation, its means of delivery, and its disposability. It is by definition largely ephemeral and competitive. *Pure* culture involves purposeful efforts to elevate intellectual, emotional, and preferential sensitivities via expressive as well as impressive cultivation. It aspires to permanence. *Political* culture is the system of values, goals, and means of achieving them that a polity sets for itself. It takes the elements included under *pure* culture and uses them, often through a popular medium, for political purposes.[4] To achieve broader authority than that produced by victory, the United States' German policy early combined the three as part of its military occupation.[5] Occupation regulations had and intended cultural effects. Joint Chiefs of Staff Directive 1779 (1945) explicitly fused the three. The U.S. Government took the position that

> there should be no forcible break in the cultural unity of Germany...; the manner and purposes of the reconstruction of the national German culture have a vital significance for the future of Germany.
>
> [The US must] make every effort to secure maximum coordination between the occupying powers of cultural objectives designed to serve the cause of peace.[6]

The "pure" cultural components were addressed in five additional sections, all of which reflected the political imperatives and sensibilities of the moment. Compelled to improvise, the political culture itself threatened to become a disposable improvisation.[7]

The Third Reich had unified popular, pure and political culture. Now two tendencies fought each other. First, because Nazis and communists used terms like "duty," "good citizenship," "responsibility for others," and "patriotism," and even "democracy," they seemed to be propaganda.[8] Second, there was "resistance to the ideas of the occupiers and to the programs of a new country about whose culture and civilization the Germans [were] very poorly informed."[9]

America used the occupation and gradually less direct methods to revive cultural components whose excellence was believed affirmed by Nazi efforts to eliminate them. Nazi standards were often used to decide with which cultural antecedents American reacculturation would attempt to fuse.[10]

The occupation demonstrated that one could, largely coincidentally, transport American culture to Germany. More purposeful examples of its movability came in the form of the "Freedom Train" which made its way across Europe displaying documents of an American political culture unabashedly regarded as "pure" culture. American pure culture was bound to a democracy measured horizontally in terms of how many countries adopt it. Democracy's depth, however, would remain another matter.

Traditionally, an aristocracy of specialists transcending frontiers constituted a transactional class, whose interactions would permeate domestic politics and culture. Diplomats, industrialists, spiritual leaders, military men, scientists, and intellectuals were ineffective with borders. The war just concluded had sundered this collaboration, but the now temporarily riddled frontiers and the needs of the hour gave rise to new relationships. As orchestrated in the U.S. zone of occupation, these relations reflected a United States cultural preference for industrialists over intellectuals, military personnel over diplomats, and spiritual leaders over scientists.

Europe's recent history and geopolitics fostered these relations. The permeability of the frontiers, the culture of the death camps, the political amnesia of people for whom Europe now lay in Germany, the opportunity, perceived as an imperative, which the immediate postwar world gave for a new start, perhaps with a primarily American cultural stamp, all joined with some more distinctly German qualities to produce a transactional culture.

Soldiers and their dependents are not jobbers of culture; lacking consciousness of what is going on, they are the often naive consorts of culture. In democracies, governments are neither culture mavens nor culture traffickers, and attempting to make them either simply ends up being very messy. This is especially the case where a militarily successful democratic army attempts to supplant a defeated authoritarian culture.

Long-term cultural effects in Germany were collateral and were sustained for two reasons: they could relate to something already in Germany, which survived Nazism, the war, and the occupation, and beginning as political expediencies, they were absorbed and rendered native German. "Pure" cultural objectives involved a blending of German and American impulses. Emigre, American, and eventually German political, intellectual, ethical, technical, scientific, and valuative specialists balanced one another. From the specific German perspective, the effort involved reclaiming and nurturing that which was peculiarly German, cleansed of its fascism, racism, nationalism, militarism, and romanticism. Perhaps the best examples of this was the deNazification of the Wagnerian opera.

Under the typically German expression *Kulturpolitik*, one understands "all measures taken to influence culture through the state and municipality, through churches and parties, through unions and industrial plants, through clubs and associations."[11] All of these, however, had been compromised, and some would remain bunkers of opposition. Still, efforts were made to shape the new *Kulturpolitik*. In 1951 a conference under the auspices of the High Commissioner for Germany at Weilburg asked questions now still being raised about German education. The ephemeral quality of U.S. influence can be found by comparing the summary of the discussions held then with contemporary, post-Cold War, concerns, spurred no doubt by unification.

Distinctive "[communities] of fate" separate Americans and Germans,[12] whether one calls such a community "character," a "cultural pattern,"[13] or "a particular—indeed, a unique kind—of historical experience",[14] Much as corporations have personalities, so have states.[15] That is to say, they have repetitive qualities that distinguish them from others.[16] This means that Germany has a personality.[17]

For Americans, the assumption that a "perversion" of this personality inheres in German culture produced brief efforts to transform Germany after the war.[18] The difference between a transformation and destruction, was quickly acknowledged, if only for practical, rather than ethical, reasons.[19] Every destruction is a transformation; not every transformation is a destruction. The American cultural emphasis shifted from being transformational to being frankly transactional, and, while striving for authority, did not intend elevating loser *and winner*.

Political, ethical, and didactic reasons abounded not to attempt eradicating all vestiges of the immediate past. Unless Americans wished to reduce success to mere logistic superiority, they needed a record of the discredited system. This imperative would have long-term political, intellectual, ethical, and cultural consequences. But the United States needed also to cull those elements that might have kept alive some of the values the victors wished to nurture.

While the impulse to deracinate may be politically and even psychologically satisfying, there are reasons the United States did not follow it. To the extent there was a conscious cultural thrust to American policy, one quickly realized that one could not leave in the European heart an organized people[20] without memory.[21] The discussion of a people without a memory did not occur until unification.[22]

Culture, "however inadequately defined, always presupposes human society."[23] But was it possible to speak of a society? What Xenophon called the "ambulatory polity" and Toynbee "cities on the move," may only with difficulty be called a society.

> Mass economic upheaval ... lack of attention to the human problems of an industrial civilization, the impersonality of the social organization of cities, the melting pot; transitory geographical residence; social mobility; weakening of supernatural sanctions—all these trends have contributed to make individuals feel unattached, adrift upon a meaning less voyage.[24]

If one views the two world wars as a continuity, the period since 1914, possibly excluding only Weimar, had been a "catastrophe."[25]

"Calamity molds an entire culture in its own image." [26] Prospects of prolonging the calamity were strong as Americans confronted numerous tasks requiring discernment, including allocation of personnel and money for "cultural" purposes as compared to other occupational tasks.

Culture may be the intellectuals' primary weapon. But it is a weapon shared by others, and in postwar Germany's first years "the absorption of working-class people and peasants [had] been easier than that of intellectuals. Not only was there more demand for the services of the former, but their economic development [was] much simpler."[27] It is an open question whether German recovery was significantly affected by the intellectual impoverishment caused by the exodus or deaths of intellectuals between 1933 and 1945.[28] In any case, emigrant intellectuals played only a minor role in the implementation of policy, although many served in advisory positions throughout Washington during the war.

For some years after 1945, a condition of war continued. Recent wars decreased the numbers and energies of those best equipped to deal with modern armaments. This war had consumed (where prewar regimes had not already banished them) many of the very people needed to reconstruct the continent and, most critically, Germany. In the end, more than any conscious American cultural policy, the resilience of indigenous survivors and their readiness to transact in the process of rebuilding combined with the United States' transactional approach to produce Germany's economic and social transformation.[29] Cultural factors followed collaterally.

Americans revived sources onto which to graft a new political culture. This meant recognizing that there is no "political without cultural democracy [and that one pays for one's] freedom of opinion by [permitting others to] have freedom of choice in cultural matters."[30] This was all done largely naively. West Germany would have been different had no effort been made to resuscitate "positive" indigenous cultural elements. But Germany's recent culture offered only contradictory points of contact, and America's most recent experiences with Germany had been ambiguous at best. Through a combination of balancing factors, not all of which were conscious, culture encouraged stability.

These factors include limitations on reimportation of German cultural elements nurtured in exile. Disagreement among emigres was often so deep that American authorities could choose among contradictory interpretations or ignore them, concluding that the discord was not about Germany at all, but personal, disingenuous, and really an effort of individuals adhering to competing value schemes to justify themselves after the trauma of Weimar.[31]

With heightened asperity, emigres accused one another of having contributed to Weimar's collapse.[32] Thus, probably largely by chance, certain cultural approaches were not used to achieve democracy. A parallel situation today involves citizens of the former German Democratic Republic and other Germans. Some emigres rejected a political role in postwar Germany. Carl Zuckmayer represented this *neu-unpolitische* position. His argument was clear: he questioned the possibility and the utility of immigrant "political activity"[33] and "adhered to the non-partisan and independent position of artistic creativity."[34]

But there was another development: assimilation diluted the effectiveness of many emigres.[35] Few returned to Germany. Those who did were often suspected by Americans of being somehow irredeemable and were accepted by Germans as proof that, after all was said and done, their culture, including simple *Sehnsucht*, still prevailed. For those who returned under the auspices of the U.S. military, the reception was often cool, as the experiences of Klaus Mann suggest, those of Henry Kissinger notwithstanding. Occasionally a lachrymose attitude prevailed long into the post-war era among intellectuals who were not invited to return.

America's loyalty oaths affected emigres' influence on culture in Germany. For a time, without this political *permissu superiorum*, one could not travel; with one, one was suspected of having succumbed to "the provincialism of national loyalty."³⁶ When America cast its net the widest, its vertical insecurity became the most striking.

Americans never fully realized the truth of the attitude of many German emigres that "it was not so much [Hitler's] tyranny and brutality which shocked [them], but the unimaginably low level of his cultural expressions."³⁷ For Americans, only the former mattered. What shaped the environment in which Americans attempted to acculturate West Germans? Total collapse of the system that had, *mutatis mutandis*, governed Germany for three-quarters of a century was thought essential. So, too, was a limited and "provisional" administrative division, but not the destruction of its people, sought mainly for the period of Germany's reformation.

Also important were homeless Germans, the expellees and the refugees, in addition to millions of non-Germans, including GIs, composing the vortex of the new republic. Veterans, injured and whole, as well as POW's and MIA's were another environmental factor. As an institution, the American military, even with its constant changes, was often the only stable center of authority.

The *Marktwirtschaft* and its *embourgeoisement* gradually produced social mobility. But a more random one in search of domicile and employment came first. The stages of demographic development, beginning with the displaced persons in Germany, the presence of homeless Germans, expellees and refugees, in addition to millions of non-German occupation and then NATO troops and dependents, became the new republic's moving center.

Demographic problems were increased by older people, housing shortages, uncertain employment, and inflation.³⁸ The cultural task was to encourage "a returning awareness of genuine inner values, of religion, of family, and the need for communal organizations."³⁹ The vital term in all of this is *genuine*.⁴⁰

Germany's systemic collapse continued the pattern of intertwining public and intellectual values. Culture is not subject to laws of physics prohibiting the simultaneous presence of two objects in the same place. It is one of culture's idiosyncrasies that one can hear or see, or see and hear, two cultural messages simultaneously. Politically, one can hear a democratic speech on the radio and thumb through one's albums of authoritarianism. Physically one may be in an authoritarian polity, while intellectually one may dream of freedom.[41]

A conqueror has the limited right to attempt cultural change in a defeated state. But in the American case, more was involved: the buoyancy of American culture, its irrepressibility, indeed its vital amorphousness was an antidote to structured, measured, and ultimately not simply Nazi, but traditional, German culture. Germany's initial postwar shapelessness, caused largely by the coincidence of physical and emotional destruction, and the vitality of American culture, which dominated even that of the other Western allies, had significant social consequences, including regarding juvenile delinquency as a healthy rejection of authority.

American culture's sheer quantity and inescapability initially produced a form of authority.[42] American culture was a combination of insolence and daring, toted, as though it were simply a physical "thing," by soldiers who rarely took themselves as seriously as the situation warranted. They carried with them America's congenital and cultural necessity to be liked.

Much of the war was simply "business," which, by definition, is transactional and involves the ability to arrange, exchange, and ultimately to discard. In distant America the war reflected the chronological sense of a "duration" rather than a scriptural struggle between ethical systems. Americans regarded the war as a transaction. Therein we have another basis for the contention that the cultural influence would be episodic.

Also at work in frustrating any likelihood that, officially, American culture would act as authority was the "cognitive dissonance" of American occupants who "expected to find a nation of monsters ... [but] rather quickly noticed that the people who had cheered Hitler and participated in the war to its bitter end now behaved correctly and unobtrusively, showed themselves to be compliant, and caused no great difficulties."[43] Americans concluded that Germans alternated between strutting and groveling. Germans detected something, too, and it was more accurate. Beneath the apparent ease with which Americans comported themselves lay a tension reflecting America's diverse cultural backgrounds. Its racial and religious strains were prominently reported in the German press. This aspect of American public culture was displayed in segregated bars and dance halls. For their part, German women who befriended blacks were ostracized.

At war's end approximately 370,000 German prisoners of war were in the United States.[44] Reflecting America's cultural disposition and personality, a program was designed to develop "practical means of bringing the German quest for power and the German tendency toward aggression under control."[45] Twenty-five thousand participated in programs to provide "intellectual diversion ... before returning them to Europe and permitting them again to become members of their native communities."[46] Participants were to identify "the reasons for the disparities between what men have achieved in the United States and what other men have achieved in Germany."[47] The program was a quintessential reflection of American culture, pure, pop, and political. American culture was assumed to have two underlying transactional "hypotheses." First, individualism is "achievement," and, second, informed voluntary choice, aware of the "consequences of the alternative choices," provides the greatest advantage, "individually and collectively."[48]

German POWs' instruction fostered upward mobility for a polity in which all mobility would be horizontal for some time and in which classes had been eliminated or were being informally developed as the black market grew and engagements with the occupiers increased. For Germans who had exerted themselves for a dozen years, the program also offered a strange and hollow-sounding prospect: the contention that "the dominant American reaction is ... that this is a world in which effort [related to 'moral purposes'] triumphs."[49]

Rebuilding Germany, physically and intellectually, required efforts different than those a machine-driven war had demanded. American soldiers, always, it seemed, rotating, offered a cultural insight into America. The fluidity of their presence, their seemingly indefatigable—if often indecorous —changeableness and interchangeability, provided a moving background, a "rear projection," against which German society appeared stable, despite all obvious signs to the contrary. The most interesting incubators of American culture were certainly not those ordinarily associated with it. Given the shortage of food, warm places, and jobs for Germans, and the American sense that armies had better uses of soldiers, it is not surprising that mess-halls figured prominently as locales for Americans and Germans to confront one another. Here the lowest recruit or the NCO who had been "busted" could find a still more abject human, one to whose country that reduction in rank had happened. And the German could observe the variety and disposability of provender.

Two Cultural Agents

American music, standing between popularity and prestige,[50] contributed to German culture through jazz, bebop, the blues, and finally rock. Doubtless, the first years after the war could well be described in terms used to describe bop:

> passages of flowing motion with frequent changes of direction and no obvious sequences; in contrast, abrupt beginnings and endings, with a feeling of impatience, self-consciousness, wry humor, brief emphasis on an occasional outburst of dissonant, chromatic harmony, and no pausing to enjoy its resolution.[51]

Jazz was inexpungable. This distinctly American idiom had influenced pre-Nazi German music; it now emerged as a three-pronged expression of popular culture: it marked a limited acceptance of American music, expressed the desire for unrestraint, and made the black unmenacingly visible.[52]

Americans, often sharing German *snobbisme* regarding American music, used German audiences to authenticate their talents by playing the German masters. Sometimes their musical experimentation seemed slender when the entire German existential question was one of experimenting, with little inclination left over for the "tradition of American experimentalism."[53]

Somewhat on the other side of the aesthetic continuum, the American musical was of modest importance, especially when it could be seen as errant prodigy, whether by imitation or emigration, of the operetta. But in many cases, concert halls served a practical function: they were more places in which to keep warm and to socialize. More than composition, American styles of performance were significant. The Seventh Army Symphony, for instance, "[surpassed] a number of major European orchestras in tonal homogeneity and technical ability."[54]

Wartime American songs, which continued to be popular afterwards, although quite different in melodic content from the German, echoed the escapist intent of German romanticism. Nazi romantic music was essentially communal and sought to destroy the private sphere. Much American popular music reflected yearning without aspiration. Still, as enwrapped in a short song, "love affirmed the self in a precarious world where human life had become a cheaper commodity, and time, therefore, a more precious one."[55] Even despite restrictions on the ownership of radios and other obstacles to songs' availability, because GIs hummed, whistled or sang them, and because so many Germans were, even while fraternization was prohibited, in close contact with Americans, American popular songs quickly became a "background and mood stimulus, [and mediated an historical] past along with [one's] private or existential one... ."[56]

Still further along the intellectual-cultural continuum and standing in total contrast to even *avant-garde* music, is the detective story. For all its popularity among Americans, it seems not to have been a significant cultural factor in the "Americanization of Germany."⁵⁷ The following are purely speculative, but suggest why there has been no German cultural impregnation by America in this form.

The reason lies in the very essence of the detective story. The art of self-tormenting [wrote Dorothy L. Sayers]

> is an ancient one... . Man, not satisfied with the mental confusion and unhappiness to be derived from contemplating the cruelties of life and the riddle of the universe, delights to occupy his leisure moments with puzzles and bugaboos.... It may be that in them he finds a sort of catharsis or purging of his fears and self-doubts.⁵⁸

Two German cultural manifestations, the Third Reich as a polity and the war it lost, collided to make the detective story unacceptable as a cultural vehicle of authority.⁵⁹ Terror, the Gestapo's "novel form of government," as Hannah Arendt described it, or as the "incalculability" of the nightly bombing raids and of allied armies, had lost its appeal. It could no longer serve as "delicate torture at its most refined."⁶⁰ Of terror one could not say that it is "never more agonizing than when we invent it in our minds for use upon ourselves."⁶¹ For a while, terror was beyond invention.

Disclosures about concentration and extermination camps compelled Germans to admit what they knew all along.⁶² The revelations, had they been confined to the fear a detective-mystery generates, might have been bearable. But Nazism and the war, demonstrating what one might do when one's own fears are mobilized, at once transcended and undermined the mystery's *terror*. This rendered it unentertaining. Literature's mere cerebral engagement had been fused with *horror*. Horror mixes with "fear or dread ... repugnance and loathing."⁶³ America's cultural influence became authority when it stimulated the awareness that horror had occurred.

Nazism dulled ethical and intellectual faculties.⁶⁴ Loss of the war and the occupation awakened Germany. Daily chores kept it awake. In this atmosphere, the detective story assumed a level of abstract irrelevance. For Germany had just passed through the ultimate criminal story, but one in which the criminal was known. As the detective story "must pose a question (whodunit?) and must answer that question,"⁶⁵ the detective story was superfluous.

One may recall that the pre-Hitler detective story probably reached its high-point with the terror and ghastliness of the child-murderer in "*M.*" The killer is known *ab initio*. His capture involves a chase by police and criminals. The latter, fearful that their respectability will be tarnished, pursue, capture, and try the killer.⁶⁶

Nazism perfected terror. The system it begot was one from which there was "no retreat, however sheltered, to which horror [could] not penetrate."[67] Nazism, no mere literary genre, was the *ultimate crime*. But after the war, in the language of the detective story, it became a "mere crime story, in which the incidents—tragic, horrible, even repulsive—form the actual theme, and the quality aimed at is horror—crude and pungent sensationalism."[68]

In addition, the experiences between 1933 and 1945 began as terror and deteriorated into horror, which "imposes no structure but rather an emotion, a feeling."[69] Nazis documented their successes. Records made it unnecessary to seek "Clues[,] traces of guilt which the murderer leaves behind."[70] Unlike clues, the documented acts were individual and then aggregate "proof of guilt"; the sorts of "deductions" that make detective stories interesting were unnecessary.[71]

There is also a political reason the detective story did not prosper. It may best be described as institutional. The detective story works only if two inseparable assumptions are made: first, that a crime has been committed and, second, that, until the culprit is captured and tried (or confesses), he is innocent. The notorious *Fragebogen* of the early postwar years, however, reflected a very different set of pervasive assumptions. Democracy was not fostered by, but was a condition precedent to, the detective story as a cultural form. Also, early postwar conditions did not encourage this form of diversion, lest it encourage questions as to the form, substance, and justice of the occupation, or even encourage Germans to ask whether they were being fairly treated, or might themselves be innocent. And the detective story was problematic for the fledgling democracy in another way as well: for twelve years Germans had been taught to distrust everyone, save those approved by their leaders, and to trust those leaders to supply the essential elements of the detective story: alertness and active intelligence. In the detective story "the reader's job [is] to keep his wits about him, and, like the perfect detective, to suspect *everybody*."[72] If the detective story mixes "puzzles and violence,"[73] both Nazis and victors would have reason to eschew its publication, albeit on different grounds.

Further Thoughts on Culture as Authority

Germans recognized both the possibility of a cultural mimesis and the ambiguity confronting such awareness:

American ideas ...[were] rejected almost instantaneously...not so much because they [came] from the "occupiers" but because of the feeling that anything new [was] all right for the United States but not for an old country; all right for a rich country but not for a poor country; all right for people who have youth and health and faith, but not for a people who have become disillusioned and cynical about general concepts of right and wrong, democracy and patriotism.[74]

American cultural influences eventually became worrisome when they were tied with such increasingly contentious notions as re-armament and "reunification."[75] After August 13, 1961, American influence often frightened Germans because it reflected a question long at issue in Germany, namely, whether unification was a desired goal.[76]

Paul Tillich distinguished between the "predominantly vertical thinking in Europe,"[77] and the "horizontal" cast of American thought. Victory and occupation meant the possible propagation of the domestically successful "American way of life." Europe was "feudal"; America reflected "the progressive actualization of the infinite possibilities in man's dealing with nature and himself."[78] In other words, Europe was hierarchical; America was egalitarian. This meant that "the European danger [was] a lack of horizontal actualization; the American danger [was] a lack of vertical depth." While, according to Tillich, America was satisfied with "making man better,"[79] Nazi Germany sought to create a new man. In fact, at war's end America wanted more than to improve man; it sought to make him over and, for a moment, Germany provided the clay with which to attempt this.[80] Germany, rather than sparking a missionary American zeal, inspired the initial policy of encouraging Germans to recognize their defeat and bear an occupation whose purpose was the extirpation, not simply the epuration, of Nazis and Nazism. Americans, "with their pragmatic-positivistic mentality were no match for the Germans; thus their deNazification and reeducation process was not exactly a success."[81]

As their cultures confronted each other, Germany and the United States, were diatonic scales. American military victory and the authority that bestowed were the major scale. Germany, once again defeated, was the enduring minor. The United States had to overcome a cultural as well as political orientation that Nazism and its culture were simply a "lesser evil" and "a temporary and partial forfeiture of democratic liberties."[82] By rejecting this palliation at the start, the triple cultural concerto, *pure, pop, and political,* could in diverse but intersecting ways become sufficiently *authoritative* to produce a transactional atmosphere.

This atmosphere was needed to overcome the passivity of arguing that "the German people were forced to endure this dictatorship for twelve years, a period sufficiently long to destroy any illusions about that form of government."[83]

Rather than a passive culture, Nazism was electrically politicized. America's primary cultural political task was not simply to counteract an "unpolitical"[84] escapist disposition, but to prevent an aversion-politics. American cultural eventually policy reflected an awareness of this task and, indirectly, sometimes unintentionally, created an atmosphere in which "apathy and abhorrence of politics" could be counteracted.[85] The *Amerika Haus*, German-American friendship activities, "Law Day" ceremonies, among other transactional diversions, served this purpose well on an ad hoc basis. The early loathing of politics was calmed less by ethical considerations than by West Germany's *embourgeoisement*, which began with the currency reform of 1948 and the Marshall Plan.[86]

Americans and Germans understood that the U.S. victory, having not been America's alone, was imperfect. Both realized that the United States would engage in multiple transactions and that those among the wartime Allies and the public at home would precede those in Germany. Some shared interests remained among the Allies, which, together with the generally disturbed conditions, worked against intra-German transactions and did not, it seems, conflict with American policy.

The ability to enforce a democratic political culture was thought initially to be threatened less by what was occurring in the East than by "the danger ... that parliament [would] become the tool of ... special interest groups, that an inferior feudal order with a parliamentary veneer" would emerge.[87] While this did not develop, the fear was resuscitated after 1990.

Again, post-unification Germany experiences an ironic anxiety about German culture first felt after 1949. Then it was not so much that division would become a manner of thinking, but that the European idea would overwhelm "civic and federal ... issues."[88] Echoes of this would be heard after 1990.

Americans felt themselves culturally "disinherited."[89] Their cultural values included this disendowment. But they could now authenticate America through a mixture of humane impulses (fidelity to ideas of the *novus ordo seclorum*) tempered by pragmatic imperatives (a singleminded toughness "forced" on them by the intractable old world).[90]

For the American intellectual the opportunity in Germany was no less compensatory than for the American political actor: the opportunity (concealed as a necessity) to play a role. For the latter it was to engage in

Realpolitik, for the former to find "that republic of letters which he carried in his heart [and which] did not exist in his own country."[91] Thus, intellectuals, too, often in uniform, contributed to the "ambulatory," carpetbag culture. As American might extended into Germany's innermost niches, the intellectual, purveyor of "pure culture," served multiple purposes. He could soften the harshness of policy or build ties with other intellectuals. But ultimately, he, relying only on products of the intellect, could not convey authority.

A cultural transformation had occurred, not merely between Americans and the Germans, but within individual Germans themselves. Nazism, it could finally be admitted, offended and threatened not just those who fled. Unless one assumes that no cognitive dissonance existed among Germans in the years 1933–1945, that no one pondered over the fate of Jews, and that none of the standard responses to these issues (the unpraiseworthy inner emigration, lying, denial, rationalizing, and ultimately forgetfulness) existed, one must accept that many conducted themselves as sleepwalkers, narcotized by their own ethical uncertainty, by a harmony of Nazi ideas with their own, and finally by the presence of Nazi terror.[92] The improbability of such blankness remains a cultural issue that no transaction could obviate.

Conclusion

Germany initially resembled a desert strewn with the relinquishments of war, of defeated modern civilized life. Many curious things happened. For instance, as the process of displacement hardened, a pattern of squatters' claims, not unlike that now encountered in the aftermath of the Cold War, developed. This foretold the repetition of a pattern well-known throughout history: each successive wave (or "avalanche") of migrants posed problems for those who had already established themselves in the new society. Often not even the existing residents had a legal claim to the property on which they lived. In Germany in 1945 another difficulty existed: the property on which the displaced located themselves had not even belonged to the people on whom they now made demands, for it had, in many cases, been taken from Jewish owners before the war. What fortitude it must have taken not to allow the initial *apatrides* to stay where they had first settled and lodged themselves. None may have thought of themselves as pioneers, nor were they seen as such; yet, in a sense, they were just that. And being thus, their culture confronted the American.

Until then few pioneers had experienced, and then lost, the very qualities that had marked the rise of an urban, capitalist culture. Furthermore, previous pioneers, footsoldiers of an advancing culture trod upon what they rationalized as "unclaimed" land, or were themselves instruments of displacement, if not its victims. In 1945, only a minority of the displaced persons encountered by Americans and their culture were urban capitalists or on the way to becoming capitalists. But there were enough of them to suggest the possibility of an additional urban proletariat; some no doubt thought of becoming urban capitalists. In fact, many did move from a *pushcartel* into the bourgeoisie.

In Germany, America's cultural transactions and the Cold War, more by happenstance than intention, fostered a society which, because of its materialism, its uncertain attitude toward its past, and the suddenness with which it is periodically startled by events—most recently in 1989—now confronts the first real test of America's largely shapeless cultural legacy.

What is striking about American culture is not that it had no deep and long effect on Germany. What is striking is that it had an effect when an effect was necessary and that effect, however unintended, was generally benign. Further, the culture, for reasons having more to do with its politicization than its purity, knew when to withdraw or accepted its absorption and turned to other matters.

American culture *never sought anything*. American *policy* and *commercial* interests used, or attempted to use, values and visions constituting our material and intellectual cultures to achieve certain goals. This is the essence of American culture.

Culture, pure and pop, was continually repoliticized. It produced a paradoxical reaction. The numerous, often contradictory, reasons for America's mixed cultural influence reflect the tense intersection of the constituents of American and German culture: "symbols, beliefs, values, norms, sanctions, and artifacts,"[93] and recent experience with them. But these are themselves rooted in culture, and Americans could not simply replace these constituents, for, in addition to being culture-bound, they were necessary for stability and predictability. By virtue of what Americans dismissively understand as *culture*, American policy left to art, music, theater, literature, cinema, science, education, and commerce the task of addressing that necessity.

In many ways, Tillich's distinction between vertical Germany and horizontal America was and remains facile. Unification has made Germany a more horizontal polity. The question is: Did American popular and political culture contribute to deepening and mooring German attachment to the stable political order that has been suddenly expanded to the new Federal states? And beyond that, how much did American culture contribute to expectations in the new Federal states about the conditions and consequences of unification? Therein, ultimately, lies much of the effectiveness of American culture, pure, pop, and political.

The conclusion is that the ability of West German culture simultaneously to transact and serve as authority—as American culture had done—is diminishing. But vis-à-vis East Germany, West Germany acts more victorious in a dubious victory than America did in a real one. Much of the difficulty lies in the differences between the two victories. That in 1945 began with transformational urges, but it ended as a series of often coincidental transactions; that of 1990 was really the last in a particular series of transactions. Germany is still moving through the transformational phase with its destructive impulses. These impulses include rooting out, often vengefully, even the nonpolitical culture. Nominally, the present situation involves one people, a portion of whom brings the rest face-to-face with the last previous moments of shared experience, and another portion of which is accustomed to having its decisions accepted, many of which were shaped by transactional, disposable, material American culture.

Notes

1. These terms are used by James MacGregor Burns to describe two forms of leadership. Burns, *Leadership* (New York: Harper & Row, 1978), pp. 4 *passim*. As used in this discussion, transaction means a series of one-by-one exchanges, complete in themselves, which help create a climate in which the number, quality, and frequency of such exchanges might reasonably be expected to increase.
2. The reasons Americans so long believed that American culture satisfied two criteria of authority—being lasting and having desired, not contradictory, effects—are themes for another discussion and reflect American culture itself. Briefly, they have to do with an overestimation of American culture's ability to permeate the German. The reasons also have to do with the expectation that Americans knew what being a Nazi meant, and that either all Germans were Nazis or none were; with the intrusion of the Cold War; with the assumption that by forgoing more extreme forms of denazification one made Germany a better ally against the Soviet Union; and with the greater qualities implied by democracy. German culture's recuperability from nazism was underestimated because we had, and still have, no reliable means of determining to what extent nazism itself was a product of German culture. Also, Americans needed, in unstable times, to believe their culture made a difference.

   It is also true that there was no real imperative to question the authoritative quality of American cultural influences. Their presence seemed, in classically American terms, "self-evident truths," precisely because of the unchallenged assumption that Soviet cultural influences in the East were foreign and negative, while American in the West were authentic, which is to say in harmony with what being German meant. The German Democratic Republic's political and economic decomposition of 1989 provided the excuse to do what might have been done earlier: to reexamine the cultural question freed of ideological ballast. Once that was eliminated, other things became apparent, one of which was the possibility that, if there was a German cultural element that endured nazism, World War II, German division, and Soviet-enforced cultural orthodoxy, perhaps the American influence, too, was other than was long believed. This chapter can only make some initial points to address this.

3. At the beginning of the period under discussion (1945–1946) this ability, in the organizational, rational arena, lay with the occupying forces. The relativity, however, was not so much vis-à-vis the defeated as it was in regard to nature, the non-political actor whose "decisions" involving disease, death, and demography required an inventive improvisation that reflected much of the United States' culture.

4. Political culture is "the pattern of cognitive, valuative, and affective orientations toward *political* objects." Arend Lijhart, "The Structure of Inference," in Gabriel Almond and Sidney Verba, eds. *The Civic Culture Revisited* (Boston: Little, Brown and Company, 1980), p. 38.

5. Joint Chiefs of Staff Directive (hereafter, JCS) 1067 (1945) addressed primarily political questions and only obliquely addressed cultural questions.

6. JCS Directive 1779, July 11, 1947.

7. This throwaway quality is seen in West Germans' attitude toward the new Federal States, whose existence at the moment of unification reflected the West's sense that all that was the East was disposable. The Federal Republic and its institutions were meant to be *provisional*. This oft-told tale need not be recounted. The manner in which unification occurred—by simply drawing the mantle of the West over the East—rendered the Federal Republic permanent. The culture of disposability remained. The German Democratic Republic was jettisoned by people on both sides of the former border, which thereby gained a measure of legitimacy it had lacked previously: the GDR's citizens *ci-devants* quickly regretted the predictable course events took, and the West argued that the GDR's swift disassembly was necessary for a variety of reasons. The *Treuhandanstalt*, which superintended the liquidation of properties in the new Federal States, illustrates this perfectly. Until unification, the one German state (West Germany) was a permanent improvisation; the other was improvisationally permanent. Citizens of the erstwhile German Democratic Republic, rather quickly regretting having thrown as much *away* as they had thrown *off*, found a new measure of resistance against western "occupation," in such oddities as the "Trabi," East Germany's much-ridiculed primary automobile.

8. Margery Carpenter, "American Investment in German Universities, *The Journal of Higher Education*, 24, 1953, 72.

9. Ibid.

10. Nazi cultural politics provides an example of this standard, namely the notorious *entartete Kunst*. Americans permitted politics to invade esthetics and encouraged elevation of conceivably medi-ocre art, for example, because Nazis had condemned it.

11. Ernst Fraenkel and Karl Dietrich Bracher, *Staat und Politik* (Frankfurt am Main: Fischer Bücherei, 1957), p. 172.

12. In fact, of course, these communities have been productively *and* fatally fused. Perhaps only Jewish, French, and Russian fates have been quite so intertwined with the German.

13. Hans J. Morgenthau, *Politics among Nations*, rev. by Kenneth W. Thompson (New York: McGraw-Hill, Inc., 1993), p. 143.

14. Gordon Craig, *The Germans* (New York: Penguin Books, 1991), p. 10.

15. One need not wander into organismic or corporativist theories of the state to recognize that states have "body" and "character." It is one of Nazism's (minor) legacies that, along with other helpful explanatory tools, it befouled the use of these two terms.
16. This repetitive tendency helps explain why some persist in speaking as though these were *natural* qualities.
17. This means "there is something to the idea that countries, like individuals, have personalities, and that, whatever the formal methods employed for their expression, those personalities should not be unduly suppressed." John Rockewell, *All American Music: Composition in the Late Twentieth Century* (New York: Alfred A. Knopf, Inc., 1983), p. 23.
18. Emigres sought to expunge elements of the culture that had cast them out. Often, as exemplars of the nascent American culture, they sought to engraft it to the German culture. Americans saw in the war a chance finally to cut themselves loose from the German influence. In neither case, although for different reasons, did the effort succeed.
19. Alfred Jarry, a *fin de siecle* author, poignantly observed that "we have not destroyed everything if we do not destroy even the ruins" ("Nous n'avons point tout demoli si nous ne demolisson meme les ruines"). Quoted, Michael Bendeikt and George E. Wellwarth, *Postwar German Theater* (New York: E. P. Dutton & Co., 1968), p. xii. Authority in much of what would become West Germany initially lay with United States' efforts to determine how much and what to destroy. In the end, even if the will to destroy had been stronger, events blunted it.

    There were *cognitive* reasons not to follow Jarry's dictum. (How can one remember what is essentially a palimpsest but whose mnemonics are necessary, lest one become a people without memory? Or how is one to distinguish oneself from the ruinous impulses of those one replaces?) There are *political* reasons (how can one explain the superiority of one's own—victorious—system and encourage more than mere mimetics if no record is left of the discredited system?) There are *historical* reasons (how is one to narrate and account for change, and presumably progress if all has been destroyed?). There are *ethical* reasons (how is one to gauge one's own passage through morally turbulent times if even ruins were destroyed?). There were also *economic* reasons (how is one to justify the complete destruction in terms of costs?). In this case, there were instances in which the Nazis themselves stopped short of cultural eradication while approaching extinction of those who produced the culture. *Ex nihilo nihil fit.*

    More complete destruction than was militarily necessary, it was always suspected, would have stiffened German resistance to postwar cooperation. Such destruction was also proscribed by the Just War Doctrine. Even so, collateral cultural damage occasionally violated that doctrine.
20. We say "organized people" to distinguish Germans (under a foreign rule, but with an identity) from those whose experiences in death, slave, and concentration camps, or even as products of *Lebensborn*, had made them political amnesiacs.
21. To have demolished all would have made recollection impossible. In an enforced amnesia, one could not "recognize that the perspectives then were in no way as open as it would appear to an idealized memory. The future had begun. In Yalta, in Potsdam. The alleged *tabula rasa* was in fact written on." Hans Schwab-Felisch, "Einleitung," in Hans Schwab-Felisch und Hans Werner Richter, *Der Ruf* (Munich: Deutscher Taschenbuch Verlag, 1962), p. 12.
22. The discussion began after 1989 when conscious—but thoughtless!—efforts were made totally to discredit the German Democratic Republic's culture, pure, pop, and political. A predictable paradoxical reaction, an *Ostalgie*, set in.
23. Johan Huizinga, *Homo Ludens* (Boston: Beacon Press, 1955), p. 1.

24. Clyde and Florence Kluckhohn, "American Culture: Generalized Orientations and Class Patterns," in Lyman Bryson, Louis Finkel-stein, R. M. MacIver, *Conflicts of Power in Modern Culture* (New York, Harper Bros., 1947), pp. 113–114.
25. Pitirim A. Sorokin, *Man and Society in Calamity* (New York: E. P. Dutton and Company, Inc., 1943), p. 156. What, Meinecke aside, was the "German catastrophe"—defeat, Hitler, or Germans' incapacity to rid themselves of him?
26. Ibid. Here "some become brutalized, others intensely socialized. [Some] lose their sense of honor; others are ethically and spiritually reenforced .... In certain respects calamity is destructive in all fields of culture; in other respects it proves a stimulating and constructive force, making for a cultural Renaissance." Ibid., p. 156. The disjunction of society and brutalization is, however, mistaken in the Nazi case, an issue which confronted Americans immediately upon entering Germany. The fusion of brutality and socialization could also be found among Nazism's victims. Cf., John Sack, *An Eye for an Eye* (New York: Basic Books, 1993).
27. Maurice R. Davie, *Refugees in America* (New York: Harper & Brothers, Inc., 1947), p. 395.
28. Still there is, among Germans and non-Germans, a perdurable tendency to mourn primarily the loss of intellectuals, who are in any case, a minority. Lamented is a possible extinction of potential Einsteins, not the real destruction of present people. Once again, at least as applied to one subject of Nazi destruction, the issue is the survival of the "exception Jew," where the "exception" is the survivor. In 1945, a deadly emancipation had taken place, disastrously paralleling post-Napoleonic Germany. "'Exception Jews' were once again simply Jews, not exceptions from but representatives of a despised people." Hannah Arendt, *The Origins of Totalitarianism*, new ed. (New York: Harcourt Brace Jovanovich, 1973), p. 61. Americans were not exempt from seeing Jews as "despised people." One thinks of General George S. Patton.
29. While this suppleness contributed to West Germany's success-full transformation, it has encouraged the *hauteur* many East Germans sense in West Germans. The most interesting chapter of postwar West German history may have been the period between 1945 and 1955; it appears also to be the most neglected. Yet it set the tone and shaped the attitudes governing Germany today. If West Germans were made more aware of the first decade after World War II, they might have more understanding for their new *Mitbürger*.
30. Paul F. Lazersfeld, "Mass Culture Today" in Norman Jacobs, ed., *Culture for the Millions? Mass Media in Modern Society* (Boston: Beacon Press, 1964), p. xxi.
31. Not all emigres were involved in this nastiness. The work of composers like Kurt Weill, whose *Dreigroschenoper and Aufstieg und Fall der Stadt Mahagonny* incensed even non-Nazi Germans, would thereafter be broken by a European and an American caesura. While his "Schickelgruber" was biliary wartime lumpishness, other compositions reflected "the sea change" at its best.
32. Emigres' personal animus often neutralized them and rendered them useless in the occupation. If these people, often far more valuable than their squabbles suggested, were examples of Germany's recent political culture, including Weimar, they and it offered little onto which to latch if one sought a stable democracy. Neither Nazism nor the war stilled pre-war animosities. In fact, as Germany's collapse neared, tensions between refugee groups intensified. Remorse about what had happened to Germany, rather than sorrow at what had happened to individuals moved to the intellectual foreground. Publication of Hannah Arendt's *Eichmann in Jerusalem* was the watershed for the Jewish refugees. Early signs of this may be read in emigres' *Tagebücher* or other anthologies. Cf. Klaus Mann, *Brief und Antworten, 1922–1949* (Reinbek bei Hamburg, 1991).
33. Carl Zuckmayer, an open letter to Erika Mann, "Aufbau," in Peter Haertling, *Ich war für all das zu Müde* (Hamburg: Sammlung Luchterhand, 1991), p. 126.

34. Ibid., p. 126. But the sense, *les incertitudes allemandes*, was encouraged by experience, and Zuckmayer could write, "... no decent German would wish to exclude himself from sharing in responsibility for the guilt in which Germany ensnared itself." Ibid., p. 128. Some have argued that the number of such refugees was too small to affect policy. Expertise and tenacity may reasonably have compensated for numbers.
35. H. Stuart Hughes, "Second Thoughts on an Old Relationship," *Confluence*, vol. 1., no. 3, September 1952, p. 23.
36. Ibid.,p. 24.
37. Paul Tillich, *Theology of Culture* (New York: Oxford University Press, 1959), p. 163.
38. Burkhardt Roeper, "The Realization of Democratic Ideals in Germany," *Confluence*, vol. 1, no. 2, June 1952, p. 22.
39. Ibid.
40. Unfortunately, the question of what is genuine or authentic lies at the heart of Nazism and its efforts to render Germany and Europe *judenrein*. And, of course, the authenticator is a dominant cultural figure. One thinks of Martin Heidegger. Clarity was needed as to what were "genuine" German values. Needed, too, was "continuity between 'old and new' and ... harmony between 'faith and reason.'" Vincenzo M. Kuiper, letter to the editor, *Confluence*, vol. 1, no. 2., p. 87.
41. Cf. George Orwell, for example. In terms of an image, Germany defied even the physical improbability, as when Munich's Deutsche Museum in the first year after the war, housed, alongside its cultural contents, displaced persons, the remnants of expiring cultures. It is a consequence of war, defeat, and victory, that the victor will act as though culture were a physical "thing."
42. Radio Free Europe once reported that it was "easily understandable that these splendid boys [of the Seventh Army Symphony Orchestra] win our sympathies faster than all the nuclear divisions which are ready to defend us."
43. Heleno Sano, *Die Verklemmte Nation: zur Seelenlage der Deutschen* (Munich: Knaur, 1992), p. 12.
44. Edwin Casady, "The Basic Assumptions of Democracy as Presented to German POWs," in Lyman Bryson, Louis Finkelstein, R. M. MacIver, *Conflicts of Power in Modern Culture* (New York, Harper & Brothers, 1947, p. 229.
45. Ibid.
46. Ibid. A similar program was housed at Wilton Park, England.
47. Ibid.
48. Ibid. In a word, the American political culture consists of individual survival in collective freedom balanced by collective survival with individual freedom.
49. Clyde and Florence R. Kluckhohn, op. cit., p. 109. Certainly, Germans long held that this was closer to *moralism* than to moral behavior.
50. Cf. William W. Austin, *Music in the 20th Century* (New York: W. W. Norton, 1966), p. 502.
51. Ibid., p. 289.
52. Jazz, the marriage of political and religious, thus potentially contrary, thrusts, results in "discipline within freedom." Ibid., p. 275. Germans, once they overcame—if they ever did—their attitude toward blacks, discovered that this dialectic was possible. They also discovered its entertaining side. For *some* blacks the popularity of jazz meant temporary release from being a mere cast of entertainers, or an "entertaining caste," (Ibid., p. 689) both of which were still essentially vestiges of slavery. Germans in these *Unterhaltungs* regarded blacks as exotic.
53. Rockewell, *All American Music*, p. 49. Rockewell says John Cage owed much to Meister Eckhart. Especially since unification, Cage's "insistence that ... the listener ... 'created' a musical experience" and that a composer "had permission to do any

damn fool thing [he] wanted to" became not only a point of esthetic discussion, but decidedly political and iconoclastic, and included Charles Ives' music as well. Ibid., p. 57.

54. *Stuttgarter Zeitung*, quoted in *Stars and Stripes*, September 28, 1956, p. 11.
    At home, Americans, who had been decidedly ambiguous toward German music after World War I, rediscovered it after World War II. Several reasons may be adduced. The numbers of emigre composers, performers, and musical educators—and those who would listen to them—were, for obvious reasons, higher after 1933. As more musicians had traveled between the wars, their reputations and contacts preceded their emigration. Jazz had penetrated European compositions. Some composers went beyond adopting American themes and adapted American lyrics. Weill composed a score for four poems by Walt Whitman; Paul Hindemith set Whitman's "When Lilacs Last in the Dooryard Bloom'd" to music. Exiles, conducting local orchestras across the United States, or leading national ensembles on radio, helped change Americans' attitudes toward German music, especially that which was not Wagnerian.
55. Robert Bamberger, Introductory notes to accompany *We'll Meet Again: the Love Songs of World War II* (The Smithsonian Collection of Recordings, n.d.), p. 8.
56. Frederick Jameson, *Postmodernism: or the Cultural Logic of Late Capitalism* (Durham, N. C., Duke University Press, 1991), p. 299. Our citation in no way suggests acceptance or even understanding of postmodernism.
57. The western novel and its like had, of course, long been a favorite German entertainment. The two extremes here were Karl May, who had never been to America, and Friedrich Gerstäcker, who had. More often than not, one suspects, Americans were considered cowboys riding herd over forces of evil, not detectives following clues to solve crimes. The western on film was popular as an acceptable form of conflict and, perhaps more important, gave a Germany wedged, frozen, and compressed into a "rump state," the illusion of expansiveness. Like so much of the cultural activity, the western was escapist.
58. Dorothy L. Sayers, "The Omnibus of Crime," in Howard Haycraft, *The Art of the Mystery Story* (New York: Simon and Schuster, 1946), pp. 71–72.
59. It is correct: Germans do read detective stories; the contention may be illustrated by Edgar Wallace. But this is not the point. This form of literature was not culturally received as authority. Only later did Germany spawn an indigenous detective canon. When the detective story emerged, its reader, suspected of being *degenere superieur*, hid, as Gordon Craig observed, the detective behind a wall of Thomas Mann.
60. James Sandoe, "Dagger of the Mind," in Howard Haycraft, *The Art*, 251.
61. Ibid.
62. For instance, in 1934, the opening lines to *Flüsterwitz* were: "Lieber Gott, mach mich stumm/daß ich nicht nach Dachau kumm!" During the war the ten-stanza variation on "Ten Little Indians," *Zehn kleine Meckerlein*, concluded, after nine *Meckerlein* had disappeared: "Ein kleines Meckerlein/liess diese Verse sehn. Da sperrt man es in Dachau ein, und jetzt … sind's wieder zehn."
63. Sandoe, "Dagger, 250. "Horror may recur but it cannot be sustained; it dulls the senses. … It is too anesthetic." Ibid., p. 251.
64. The detective story or mystery is said to "offer … the reader … an intellectual satisfaction." R. Austin Freeman, "The Art of the Detective Story" in Haycraft, *The Art*, 11. It is also "a work of imagination, demanding the creative artistic faculty; on the other hand, it is a work of ratiocination, demanding the power of logical analysis and subtle and acute reasoning; and … there must be a somewhat extensive outfit of special knowledge." Ibid., p. 9.
65. Sandoe, "Dagger," 251.

66. The film's original title, *Mörder unter uns* was changed to avoid bruising Nazi sensibilities. A 1946 film with almost the same title, *Die Mörderer sind unter uns*, was a production of DEFA, in East Germany.
67. Sandoe, "Dagger," 251.
68. Freeman, "The Art," 9. We will not here discuss the difference between Hannah Arendt's "banality of evil" and the exploitation of that evil by a variety of media.
69. Sandoe, "Dagger".
70. Marie F. Rodell, "Clues," in Haycraft p. 264. This is not the place to compare the guilt an individual murderer *may* feel and its presence or absence in the German case. Also, documents were not "traces of guilt," but evidence of Nazi virtue.
71. "The amateur [here the citizen of a democracy] who reaches the solution ... with his freedom to think, act and criticize," unwelcome then because he could uncover official crimes, seems more in vogue after 1990. Exposing Nazis was an American activity, before it became a German one. Howard Haycraft, "Dictators, Democrats, and Detectives," in Haycraft, *The Art*, 316–317.
72. Sayers, "Omnibus," 98, fn.
73. Joseph Wood Krutch, "Only a Detective Story," in Haycraft, *The Art*, p. 181.
74. Carpenter, "American Investment," 107–108.
75. We place reunification in quotation marks. The term is totally at odds with what Germany ever officially sought, what might have been possible, or what came about in 1990. The Germany that might have qualified as "reunited" was that with the frontiers of 31 December 1937 and this has not existed since 1945. Germany's "second unification" is an apt phrase, if one wishes to be historically accurate.
76. The entire question of sensitivity to population problems is cultural and has cultural effects. Once settled, although largely by definition only, displaced persons no longer played a role. The massive shifts of populations since 1945 inured Americans and Germans to the injuries of homelessness, a factor rekindled after 1989. American and German development of a language to avoid talking about homelessness has fostered an entire Western carpetbag subculture which is statistically called the "underclass."
77. Tillich, op. cit., p. 167.
78. Ibid., p. 163.
79. Ibid., p. 168.
80. Both Germany and America had once taken the concept of *novus homo*, which to the Romans meant an upstart, and made a virtue of it. In this we find a root of cultural differences that the U.S. sought to address after World War II. The Nazis reflected the upstart's impertinence, while the American mirrored his inventiveness. If it was to be more than material, this inventiveness would have to be tested after the war. One ordinarily had precedents on which to fall back to help one anticipate, recognize, and respond to problems. Not so after World War II.

Although she did not, to my knowledge, address the question, an observation of Hannah Arendt's, as phrased by Elizabeth Young-Bruehl, is applicable here. "New beginnings carry with them an element of arbitrariness and contingency which is dizzying: when a new regime is launched, there is a traditional temptation to mask the unpredictability with an appeal to the past. The 'foundation legends' do not picture freedom, they invoke a repetition, a return to a paradise lost." Elizabeth Young-Bruehl, "Reflections on the Life of the Mind," in Lewis P. Hinchman and Sandra K. Hinchman, eds, *Hannah Arendt: Critical Essays* (Albany, N. Y.: State University of New York Press, 1994), pp. 348–349.

The arresting issue is, whether the United States ever contemplated the irony of her task. Was it not natural that she should view matters from her own experiences, and hence culture? Were Americans, in Germany, attempting to "found... 'Rome anew,'" or to "found... a 'new Rome'"? Hannah Arendt, *On Revolution* (New York: The

Viking Press, 1965), p. 213. It appears that, to the extent the dichotomy is applicable, some wished for a "new Rome," while the practicalities of the situation limited them to resurrecting "Rome anew" and cleansed. There could be no "beginning of a specific national history." Ibid. For without the old "specific national history," nothing confronting the United States, and the other Allies for that matter, made sense.

81. Sano, *Die Verklemmte Nation*, p. 12. It is interesting, in passing, to note how important a vowel can be: a mere a distinguishes denazification from *denazi fiction*. Yet, the pragmatism referred to was not all Germans experienced with Americans. Commenting on a performance of the Seventh Army Orchestra, one public official marveled: "Everyone knows Americans can produce cars, but this—gesturing toward the orchestra—this is hard to believe." Audiences were astounded "to see privates and corporals play classical music on such a high artistic level." *Stars and Stripes*, September 28, 1956, p. 11. The orchestra that year performed 55 concerts, attended by 60,000.

82. Roeper, "Realization," 15.

83. Ibid.

84. Unpolitical is a translation of the German *unpolitisch* which amounts to making a political creed out of the rejection of politics. Thomas Mann gave currency to the term during World War I. As Fritz Stern once said, there are "political consequences" to being unpolitical.

85. Roeper, "Realization."

86. Ibid., pp. 17–18.

87. Ibid., p. 20.

88. Ibid., p. 21.

89. Cf. H. Stuart Hughes, "Second Thoughts on an Old Relationship," *Confluence*, vol. 1, no. 3, September 1952, 19.

90. Despite their largely replenishable material wartime exertions—or because of them—Americans, exuding inferiority vis-à-vis their images of Europeans—excluding only occasionally the emigres, about whom they maintained their skepticism—reflected what they believed Europeans, often embodied in emigres, thought of Americans. At the end of the war American material and social inventiveness was thought to be critical, and "American social inventions [were taken to be] the most distinctive and meaningful contributions made by the United States to the totality of world culture." Kluckhohn, "American Culture," 114. This authority-undermining self-disparagement reflects American culture's susceptibility to reduction as simply utilitarian: to make "the lot of the common man ... easier" and to advance the equality of opportunity. Ibid. Interestingly, a European emigre, Ernst Krenek, reflecting European skepticism about democracy in the United States, made a typically pragmatic point when he commented that "it has been said that God must have loved the common man because He made so many of them. A different opinion [is] that God does not seem to have particularly loved the common people, or else he would not have made them so common. [This reflects] a wholesome revolt against the all-too-readily accepted assumption that everything that appears in overwhelming majority is sanctified by its multitude." Quoted, Rockewell, op. cit., pp. 22–23. Yet, Germans today often regard American pragmatists as cultural exemplars.

91. Ibid., p. 22.

92. See also Sano, *Die Verklemmte Nation*, 11. For tainted German intellectuals to associate with Americans was seen as an act of cleansing. As the case of Hannah Arendt and Martin Heidegger suggests, there were inexplicable lapses when the association seemed entirely to ignore, without condoning, the German intellectuals' complicity.

93. Thomas R. Dye, *Power and Society*, 6th ed. (Belmont, CA: Wadsworth Publishing Co., 1993), p. 41.

9. Equality, Difference, and the *Grundgesetz*:
Women, Families, and the Federal Republic's Basic Law*

Robert G. Moeller

The Basic Law *(Grundgesetz)*, the constitutional foundation for the Federal Republic of Germany adopted in 1949, articulated an explicit response to the past of National Socialism, to the social dislocation of the immediate postwar period, and to the present of global conflict between East and West. It defined those fundamental civil rights destroyed by the Nazis and, from the perspective of West Germans, denied other Germans across their eastern border in the "Soviet Zone of Occupation." The Basic Law also drew on the democratic tradition of the Weimar Republic, while seeking to avoid the structural weaknesses of the Weimar constitution, which had made it possible for the Nazis to seize power by legal, electoral means. An examination of the Basic Law can thus illuminate the exercise in political introspection through which West Germans confronted their past by defining their future.[1]

Included in this process were lengthy discussions of the status of women and the family. These topics were addressed directly in the debates over women's equality (paragraph 2 of Article 3) and the need

---

*In much abbreviated form, this article presents arguments developed by Robert G. Moeller in *Protecting Motherhood: Women and the Family in the Politics of Postwar West Germany* (Berkeley: University of California Press, 1993). Because of space restrictions, I have attempted to keep references in the version presented here to a minimum.

for the constitutional guarantee of the state's protection of motherhood and the family (Article 6). Unlike other areas of economic and political reconstruction, the Allies did not attempt any direct influence on this part of the process of recovery and self-definition; this was an aspect of postwar reconstruction where Germans made their own history, if not under circumstances of their own choosing.[2]

Postwar public opinion polls reflected both the profound disinterest of most Germans in the deliberations of the Parliamentary Council, the body charged with drafting the Basic Law, and the general political apathy of West Germans after the experience of the Thousand Year Reich.[3] However, the Parliamentary Council's debates over the status of women and the family's future were exceptions to this rule of detachment from formal political life in the early postwar years. In their final form, both Article 3 and Article 6 were shaped in part by the mobilization of public opinion. Women and the family attracted widespread attention in ways that questions of federalism did not. These were concerns that directly touched every German's life.

Discussions of women's equality with men and the status of the family illuminated points of intersection and divergence in the conceptions of gender relations held by women and men, by Christian, Free, and Social Democrats. Analyzing the debates around these issues can thus tell us much about how West Germans viewed the reconstruction of gender as an essential part of the general project of recovery and rebuilding after defeat in war and the end of National Socialism.

Postwar West Germans were particularly concerned by the perceived "crisis of the family," which was brought on by extended separations of soldiers from their wives and children, the high rates of adult male death in the war, the difficulties of postwar reunions under circumstances of continued privation, and high rates of divorce. Sociological studies of the family concluded that it was largely thanks to women's efforts that the family had survived the "collapse" of 1945 to emerge as the basis for psychological and political rebuilding. However, there were also signs that women's efforts in the war and the postwar period represented a "forced emancipation" that placed tremendous pressures on the family. Thus, although the family was one of the few societal institutions to emerge from the rubble, identified as a repository of uniquely German values that had withstood the extraordinary strains of the war and postwar years, social observers emphasized that it, too, was at risk.[4]

The war had also left an ideological rubble that West Germans needed to clear away. After 1945, Germans felt compelled to address the legacy of Nazi misogyny, racist pronatalism, and attempts to subordinate families to the priorities of the state.[5] In a new democratic Germany, it was essential that women enjoy the rights to full political participation, which the Nazis had so radically abridged. Politicians and social commentators also emphasized that it was crucial to restore a domestic sphere, safe from state intervention, where women could once again devote full attention to their most important responsibilities as wives and mothers of *private* families, not families subordinated to the priorities of the Führer or the *Volk*.

It was against this background that the Parliamentary Council set about defining those parts of the Basic Law that affected women and the family. In the initial guidelines for the *Grundgesetz* that emerged from discussions of delegates from the Allied-occupied zones at Herrenchiemsee in 1948, women and the family received no mention. Some postwar state constitutions had guaranteed women civil equality, and in some cases this was extended to wage equality as well. But in the outline for discussions of the Basic Law handed on to the representatives in Bonn, it was thought that women were adequately covered by a language that ensured all citizens equality before the law and banned discrimination of all sorts.

By the time the Parliamentary Council completed its deliberations, however, the Basic Law included the explicit promise that "men and women have the same rights." This victory represented a giant step beyond the equal rights clause of the Weimar constitution and a triumph for the Social Democratic party (SPD) and mobilized public opinion in what the SPD's Frieda Nadig called "the battle for equal rights."[6] The chief general in this battle was the SPD's Elisabeth Selbert, a member of the party's postwar executive committee, a representative in the state parliament in Hessen, and one of only four women delegated to participate in the deliberations of the Parliamentary Council. Selbert, an expert in constitutional affairs, had completed her legal training in 1929 and had practiced criminal and civil law in the Third Reich, living a contradictory existence as a lawyer within a political system that suppressed her political beliefs and discriminated against her sex. She had come to Bonn as an expert on the problem of reconstituting the court system and establishing a national framework for judicial review, but when it became apparent that women's equal rights would not automatically be included in the Basic Law she quickly shifted her priorities and became the SPD's principal advocate of constitutionally securing gender equality.[7]

In the debates of the Council, Selbert emphasized the SPD's historic commitment to the principle of the equality of the sexes, but she also invoked a more immediate past, painting an image of the "woman, who during the war years stood atop the rubble and replaced men at the workplace" and who, on this basis, "has a moral right to be valued like a man." All "ifs, ands and buts" must be eliminated, insisted Selbert, particularly given the demographic legacy of the war, the "surplus of women," which, she calculated, left "170 women voters for every 100 men ... and made the voice of women as voters ... essential for the acceptance of the constitution."[8] The SPD also emphasized that a firm commitment to women's rights was a crucial step toward overcoming the misogynistic legacy of National Socialism.

Selbert's arguments confronted the opposition of the Christian-Democratic/Christian-Social coalition (CDU/CSU) and the Free Democratic Party (FDP). Her critics feared that extending equality to all aspects of relations between women and men—public and private—would necessitate an immediate, thoroughgoing reform of the explicitly patriarchal provisions of the 1900 civil code (*Bürgerliches Gesetzbuch*). Free and Christian Democrats agreed that measures necessitating revision of the existing family law extended well beyond the mandate given the Parliamentary Council.

The CDU/CSU also stressed that a language of unqualified equality would violate the "natural" boundaries of female-male difference. Equality should not erase "those nuances created by nature, which require a different treatment." Hermann von Mangoldt, a CDU representative from Schleswig-Holstein, provided examples to illustrate this abstract principle. "Mentally less well-endowed children" and the "mentally ill," argued Mangoldt, were groups that required special schools and treatment. Other examples included "the gypsy, who wanders around, [and] can be subjected to certain, special legal regulations." Citing the experience of the United States, Mangoldt pointed to a political tradition in which the dominance of the intellectual legacy of the French revolution made it necessary to make public declarations of full equality. "But essentially," he maintained, "suspended above all laws in the United States is the idea that we cannot and will not ever permit ourselves to be flooded by a foreign race (von einer fremden Rasse überfremdet werden) ... [I]n the laws regulating immigration they state: We must preserve the dominance of the nordic race in the USA."[9]

Coming little more than three years after the destruction of the outspokenly racialist regime that had subordinated gypsies to very special regulation indeed and that had defined mental illness to include many whose insanity was opposition to National Socialism or possession of arbitrarily defined "asocial" qualities, such analogies are jarring; they reveal that in Germany certain ideological persuasions had not been destroyed by Allied bombs. Moreover, in the context of the debate over equal rights for women, they indicated that natural differences between women and men were to be equated with immutable racial characteristics that required special legal treatment. Sexual difference—like race and ethnicity for Mangoldt—was natural, immutable, and cause for special legal provisions. The proclamation of unrestricted equality of women and men thus would represent no less than a violation of nature.

The initial rejection in early December 1948 of the SPD's call for an unequivocal language of equality by the majority in the Parliamentary Council prompted a wave of petitions, which dramatically amplified Selbert's demand for women's equal rights with men. "Public opinion," which scarcely registered elsewhere in the debates of the Parliamentary Council, weighed in decisively against the CDU/CSU's and FDP's unwillingness to accept full equality for women. Middle-class and socialist women's organizations alike delivered one message: the constitution should include a specific acknowledgement of women's equality with men in all aspects of life.[10]

This massive response prompted opponents of Selbert's formulation to retreat hastily when the Parliamentary Council again took up debate over Article 3 in January 1949. Those speaking for the conservative coalition and FDP now proclaimed their complete commitment to constitutional guarantees of the equality of women and men and denied that they had ever wanted anything else.

Even as she could be confident that her position would carry the day, however, Selbert took great pains to reassure her colleagues that for her party equality was based on a recognition of sexual difference and the need for special treatment of women in some situations. "Equality of rights," she explained, "is founded on an equality of worth, which acknowledges difference." Thus, provisions for maternity represented no preferential treatment for women but rather the means necessary to compensate women for the extraordinary burdens they bore because of their "natural obligations as mothers."[11] Properly understood and enforced, equality would not lead to *Gleichmacherei*, the arbitrary levelling of difference invoked by CDU/CSU critics, who argued that it was this sort of equality that existed in the "Soviet Zone of Occupation." There, they charged, the "mechanistic" implementation of equal rights served only to emancipate women to work alongside men in all jobs. Such equality would lead to the destruction of the family, as women were compelled to work in occupations for which they were unsuited, and would deny women the possibility of fulfilling their obligations as wives and mothers. Such fears, Selbert maintained, were totally unfounded, and she took care to dissociate herself and her party from allegations of communistic levelling.

By emphasizing the importance of sexual difference, Selbert also claimed to distance herself and her party from "women's righters" *(Frauenrechtlerinnen)*, bourgeois feminists often dismissed with this term of opprobrium. According to Selbert, women's righters, unlike women organized in the SPD, claimed that women should be equal because in no crucial respect were they different from men. On this score, Selbert resolutely rejected a position that was represented by no one at the Bonn deliberations, nor, for that matter, by any part of the German bourgeois women's movement. The brand of Anglo-American feminism which insisted that sexual differences between women and men were of no social or political consequence and that equality should be based on the common *humanity* of women and men had never found a substantial audience in Germany. But Selbert's denunciation of the specter of "women's righters" did serve to underscore that for the SPD there was to be no contradiction between espousing a politics of equality and insisting on the significance of difference.

Presenting the line consistently advanced by Social Democrats, Selbert emphasized that equality did not mean forcing women to become like men; rather, acknowledging difference was completely compatible with equal rights for women. Equality should include a woman's right to pursue wage work, but in many cases married women might choose not to work outside the home. In no way did this make them inferior to their husbands, explained Selbert, because "the obligation to educate the children and run the household, in short to perform sociologically valuable labor, is the equivalent of the husband's obligation to support the family *(Unterhaltspflicht)* ... The work of the housewife is sociologically of the same worth as the work of the woman employed [outside the home]."[12] To be sure, sociological function did not draw the same line between women and men as the biological difference described by Mangoldt. But for Social Democrats, separate could be equal.

From this perspective, Selbert affirmed, it would still be essential to undertake a thoroughgoing revision of the existing family law. This consequence of Article 3 was unavoidable, but it should not be a cause for dismay or anxiety. The patriarchal order underwritten by the *Bürgerliches Gesetzbuch* was inconsistent with a new Germany's commitment to the equality of all its citizens; the civil code was long overdue for a complete overhaul. Completing that project would take time, and the Parliamentary Council stipulated that the Bundestag would have until April 1, 1953 to finish the task. While some CDU representatives shared Adolf Süsterhenn's view that the failure to meet this timetable would lead to "circumstances of complete lawlessness,"[13] a majority accepted Social Democratic arguments that setting a deadline was the only way to ensure that equality in principle would become equality in practice.

As the debates over Article 3 made clear, any discussion of women's rights immediately raised questions about the family and conceptions of women's responsibilities as wives and mothers. The discussions of Article 6 made equally explicit that any discussion of motherhood and family raised questions about women's rights. Particularly vehement in insisting that the Basic Law incorporate specific guarantees of parental authority and the integrity of the family were the forces of political Catholicism, represented by parts of the CDU/CSU. The highest ranks of the Catholic clergy and a range of church-related lay organizations forcefully reminded their political representatives that the constitution must guarantee the family's protection, enshrine the sanctity of marriage, and underscore the rights of parents over children; here, too, "public opinion" affected the deliberations of the Parliamentary Council.

Championing parental authority and "protection" for the family in the Parliamentary Council were Süsterhenn, the Cultural and Justice Minister for Rheinland-Pfalz, and Helene Weber, a veteran of the Catholic middle-class women's movement and Center party politics in the Weimar Republic. They were joined by the postwar Center party, that part of the Weimar political organization of the same name that had not been absorbed into the CDU/CSU. Represented by only two delegates in the Parliamentary Council, the Center, still strongly allied with political Catholicism, took a firm stand in favor of anchoring a Christian vision of the family in the Basic Law. Helene Wessel presented the Center's position in debates over the constitutional protection of the family.

In Weber's formulation, the family was not a product of a "cultural order." Rather, it "belongs to the natural forms of association, [and] it cannot be compared to economic or social associations. The family is the basis of all associations, of the existence of the nation and the state."[14] The nature invoked by Weber was defined not by biology, culture, or society, but by a divinely endowed order, which predated all state forms and to which states must accommodate themselves. The natural rights of the family set limits to the authority of the state; it was the responsibility of the state to guarantee the survival of this natural institution, to afford it "particular protection." Weber's arguments were fueled by the resurgence of "natural law" thought among conservative Catholic circles in the postwar period. These groups explained the catastrophic outcome of National Socialism as the inevitable terminus of a process of secularization that had its origins in the French Revolution. The destruction of the Third Reich cleared the ground for rebuilding Germany on a Christian basis. This, in turn, implied political guarantees for "prepolitical" institutions, particularly the church and the family.

For Weber and Süsterhenn, the CDU's primary advocates of these views, there was no question of what constituted a family. Weber's natural family was one in which "the wife is free for the life of the family." Women's increased participation in the wage labor force threatened to make this impossible. While conceding that in the unsettled circumstances of the late forties, there might be instances where wives earned more than husbands, Weber rejected this as inappropriate, the temporary product of extraordinary circumstances. Protecting families in the postwar world thus implied eliminating such social threats to nature and reestablishing families on the basis of a male wage sufficient to support children and a non-wage-earning wife.[15]

The SPD's Frieda Nadig, a regional secretary of the Social Democratic welfare organization "Workers' Welfare" *(Arbeiterwohlfahrt)*, and a member of the North Rhine Westphalian state parliament, was quick to point out that this view of the family had little to do with nature and amounted to a denial of social reality in postwar West Germany. Nadig reminded her colleagues "of the surplus of seven million women, which we now have. If we consider that this surplus of women is constituted primarily of those between 22 and 45, then we know that an extraordinarily altered form of association for life *(Lebensgemeinschaft)* will emerge. We must take into account that in the future we will have a Mother-Family."[16] The consequence was a far broader definition of what constituted families and the need to guarantee the legal equality of "legitimate" and "illegitimate" children.

Selbert, so outspoken on women's equal rights, had much to say on this topic as well. She asked rhetorically, "Is the bourgeois [*bürgerliche*] marriage the only form of living together toward which we should aspire?" With Nadig, she insisted on recognizing "the new forms of organizing existence demanded by ... the consequences of the war and economic necessity." While calling for the "protection and maintenance of the bourgeois family," she argued that the "'Mother-Family' assume a place alongside bourgeois marriage." Along with married women, unmarried mothers deserved full legal rights over their children and the "full protection of the state." In fact, it was precisely unmarried motherhood that was founded on a "high sense of responsibility and qualities of moral character."[17]

The CDU/CSU coalition completely rejected these expanded conceptions of what might constitute a family. While admitting that postwar Germany was a society where many legitimate children might be denied a father, Süsterhenn explained that "this is not the normal state of affairs." To be sure, "in human history and in this and that cultural order, it is possible to identify different conceptions of family," but the natural family invoked by the Center, CDU, and CSU was that which existed "within the framework of a Christian-occidental [*christlich-abendländische*] or western cultural order [*Kulturordnung*], and in this order the family is always conceived of as a self-contained unit."[18]

Süsterhenn needed to make no clearer that for the CDU/CSU, the natural family, this "self-contained unit," was part of a political order that was defining itself in terms of another strategy of containment and alliance with a Western order on political and economic as well as cultural levels. Demarcating the border around the "Christian-occidental" family, a natural family where children had fathers and mothers, was another part of demarcating boundaries between West and East.

Behind the CDU/CSU and Center pressure to insert a specific conception of the family into the Basic Law was yet another agenda—extending "parental rights" to allow parents to determine the religious orientation of schools and the appropriate training for public school teachers. These demands had been standards in the repertoire of Center party politics since the emergence of organized political Catholicism at the national level in the 1870s, but the necessity of guaranteeing "parental rights," explained Weber, was more self-evident than ever after the experience of National Socialism, "which has increased our sense of responsibility in all such questions."[19] "According to the words of Hitler," Wessel reminded her colleagues, "National Socialism wanted to steal children from their parents for the good of the state."[20] Returning them to their proper place and preventing any similar state intervention in the future meant allowing parents to determine the denominational nature of the schools their children attended.

The deadlock between SPD and CDU/CSU was ultimately broken by the FDP. Theodor Heuss, speaking for his party, categorically rejected extending parental rights to the determination of a school's religious character. While he sympathized with the defensive reaction against the Nazi past, "when children were forced into organizations," he also insisted that state governments should retain the power to determine school policy. Extending parental rights over schooling had origins not in nature but in the nineteenth-century struggle of political Catholicism to establish state-funded Catholic schools. Combined, the forces of the FDP and SPD could defeat the attempt to expand parental control over the schooling of their children, potentially erasing the boundary between church and state, and the CDU's leader, Konrad Adenauer, counselled compromise on this issue lest the conservative coalition create an unbridgeable gap between itself and political liberalism in the realm of "cultural policy" *(Kulturpolitik)*.

On the question of constitutional guarantees for the family's protection, Heuss was far more willing to find common ground with the CDU/CSU. Avoiding the question of exactly what constituted a family, he agreed that this form of social organization deserved guarantees of its integrity. His initial concern that a discussion of the family would involve the state in questions of "morality or tradition and biology" gave way to his acceptance of bolstering the family as part of the psychological response of a generation that had experienced the "violation (*Vergewaltigung*) of family life under National Socialism." Beyond this, guaranteeing the constitutional protection of the family was for Heuss a declaration with no specific content; it was a principle the FDP could support, but its significance was largely symbolic.[21]

Heuss's assessment proved to be well off the mark. As debates over the reform of family law and women's status in the fifties made abundantly clear, anchoring the family in the *Grundgesetz* was not only symbolic; it provided clerical spokesmen and conservative Catholic and Protestant politicians with a constitutional weapon to combat measures to establish the equality of wife and husband within marriage. Appeals for establishing women's equality within marriage based on Article 3 were answered with invocations of the constitutional pledge of the family's protection based on Article 6. Opponents of equal rights for women charged that in natural families, wives were subordinate to husbands. Married women's obligations to husbands and children set limits to women's individual rights to equality. As late as 1957, when the Bundestag finally passed a revised family law, fathers were still accorded the last word over their children's welfare in cases of irreconcilable parental disputes. It was left to the federal constitutional court to overturn this provision, insisting that ensuring a woman's equality meant recognizing her status, "precisely in that area—motherhood—where her essence is most deeply rooted and where she realizes herself."[22] It was not until two decades later, with another revision of the family law in 1977, that a wife's employment outside the home was no longer contingent on fulfillment of her marital and family "obligations" and that complete equality between husband and wife was the law of the land.

To be sure, the tension between notions of female equality and female difference, defined in terms of women's relationships to husbands, children, home, and hearth, was not new in postwar West Germany; at least since the late eighteenth century, the link between woman and family has structured all discussions of women's social and political status in Europe and North America. However, the inclusion of these topics in the agenda of the Parliamentary Council suggests how central they were to a discussion of the foundations for a new Germany. As the debates over the *Grundgesetz* made clear, the process of postwar reconstruction and recovery from the devastation of the Thousand Year Reich included reflections on how best to reestablish "woman's place."

In its final form, the *Grundgesetz* captured the conflicting images of women in the postwar period—of women's capacities and achievements, on the one hand, and of women's vulnerability and need for protection within families, on the other. The Basic Law did not reconcile these conflicting visions or resolve the tension between demands for equality and demands for an acknowledgement of difference; rather it explicitly locked them into place.

Debates over women's equality also outlined the political languages that were available in the postwar world for describing equality and defining the boundaries between equality and difference. They revealed that there was no unanimity over what defined families or what constituted the natural difference between women and men. Nature, difference, and the family were sometimes rooted in biology, sometimes in society and sociological function, and sometimes in a preordained, prepolitical divinely endowed religious order. It was on the ideological terrain marked off by these competing alternatives that the political discussion of women and the family would take place in the Federal Republic's early history.

As its arguments in favor of Article 3 made clear, the Social Democratic party by 1949 had all but abandoned its legacy from Friedrich Engels and August Bebel, according to which women's equality with men would ultimately be accomplished by women's entry into the wage workforce. For the postwar SPD, such conceptions embodied a "false equality" that "levelled" sexual difference and granted women equal rights only when they were in no way different from men; this was an ideological position that had become the exclusive property of those other Germans across the eastern border of the Federal Republic.

As Selbert also underscored, for Social Democrats a West German conception of equality diverged from the position of some Anglo-American feminists, who argued that sexual difference was of little significance in defining women's equal rights. A brief comparison with the debate over equal rights for women in the post-World War II United States illustrates where German and some American feminists diverged and highlights the framework within which postwar West Germans attempted to reconcile the concept of equality with the concept of a distinct female nature. Immediately after the war, the United States Congress took up a proposed constitutional amendment according to which "Equality of rights under the law shall not be denied or abridged by the United States, or by any State, on account of sex." In this context, feminist proponents of the amendment confronted a strong feminist opposition led by the Women's Bureau, a federal agency housed in the Department of Labor, which was solidly backed by trade unionists, the League of Women Voters, church groups, and the American Association of University Women. These opponents feared that equal rights would eliminate the protective legislation for women workers won by trade unionists. Demands for special treatment were justified by acknowledging that women were different because of their role as mothers; protection for women was part of a commitment to protection for families. Feminist proponents of an unrestricted conception of equal rights argued that legislating special treatment created an image of women not only as different but also as vulnerable, needy, and dependent.

When the Equal Rights Amendment came to a vote, it won a simple majority but not the two-thirds required for the Senate to approve a potential amendment to the United States constitution. In an uncomfortable alliance with probusiness Republicans and antilabor southern Democrats, some well-organized feminist activists succeeded in defeating a language of equal rights for women proposed by other well-organized feminist activists. The United States Congress was not ready to "amend motherhood," to repudiate a definition of sexual difference according to which women's equality with men would always be modified by their reproductive capacity.[23]

Three years later, an even stronger language of equal rights became part of the West German Basic Law, but the most vocal advocates of women's equality did not come even close to proposing the equal rights position of those American feminists which others feared would "amend motherhood." The feminist position that downplayed gender difference and emphasized the unrestricted equality of women and men as the basis for women's equal rights did not exist in German feminism before 1933; it was not imported into German politics by the forces of Allied occupation after 1945; and it was introduced by Selbert into discussions of the Basic Law only so that she might forcefully reject it. The equality that Selbert advocated was an equality that "acknowledge[s] difference." As debates over gender equality and family law reform in the conservative, restorative climate of the fifties would make clear, it was a short step from this acknowledgment of difference to an overwhelming ideological emphasis on woman's primary, if not exclusive, role as wife and mother.

The Parliamentary Council's deliberations over Article 6 provided clear indications of another political language that would fundamentally shape discussions of women's status and the family in the early history of the Federal Republic and that indicated the abiding influence of political Catholicism in postwar West Germany. Although competing conceptions of what might constitute a family still appeared in discussions of the Parliamentary Council, it was apparent that for the CDU/CSU only one type of family should exist. To be sure, in the Bonn Republic, Christian Democrats would leave the confessional "tower" that had still contained the Center party during Weimar, but the debates in the Parliamentary Council indicated that, on the ostensibly apolitical questions of the family and women's status, Christian Democracy would remain particularly susceptible to conservative Catholic influence.

Laws alone cannot construct social reality. However, the measures defining women's status articulated in the Basic Law are important because they brought into sharp focus competing conceptions of how best to reconstruct gender difference in the wake of National Socialism. They identified the family and woman's status as central concerns of the postwar era and framed the agenda for the political discussion of these issues in the Federal Republic's first decade.

Notes

1. There are numerous treatments of the Basic Law. For an introduction, see Peter H. Merkl, *The Origin of the West German Republic* (New York: Oxford University Press, 1963); and Werner Sörgel, *Konsensus und Interessen: Eine Studie zur Entstehung des Grundgesetzes für die Bundesrepublik* (Stuttgart: Klett, 1969). On the politics of women's equality in debates over the Basic Law, see the overview in Anna Späth, "Vielfältige Forderungen nach Gleichberechtigung und 'nur' ein Ergebnis: Artikel 3 Absatz 2 GG," in Anna-Elisabeth Freier and Annette Kuhn, eds., *"Das Schicksal Deutschlands liegt in der Hand seiner Frauen": Frauen in der deutschen Nachkriegsgeschichte* (Düsseldorf: Schwann, 1984).
2. This generalization is based on my search for signs of direct Allied influence on West German attitudes toward gender relations in the archives of the British forces of occupation in the Public Records Office (Kew) and materials from the Office of Military Government U.S. in the Bundesarchiv (Koblenz). Although the "Women's Bureaus" established by the British and the United States provided informative reports on the reemergence of organized political life among German women, they ultimately reveal more of American and British conceptions and misconceptions of Germany than of direct Allied influence on German political attitudes. In this assessment, I diverge from the emphasis of Hermann-Josef Rupieper, "Bringing Democracy to the Frauleins: Frauen als Zielgruppe der amerikanischen Demokratisierungspolitik in Deutschland 1945–1952," *Geschichte und Gesellschaft* 17 (1991): 61–91. See also the assessment of Rebecca Boehling, "'Mütter' in die Politik: Amerikanische Demokratisierungsbemühungen nach 1945. Eine Antwort auf Hermann-Josef Rupieter," *Geschichte und Gesellschaft* 19 (1993): 522–29. Rupieper's exhaustive study of U.S. policy in the period 1949–1955 suggests virtually no American interest in the West German reform of the family law and the formulation of social policies affecting women and the family. See Rupieper, *Der besetzte Verbündete: Die amerikanische Deutschlandpolitik 1949–1955* (Opladen: Westdeutscher, 1991).
3. Elisabeth Noelle and Erich Peter Neumann, *The Germans: Public Opinion Polls 1947–1966* (Westport, Ct.: Greenwood, 1981), 227; and Anna J. Merritt and Richard L. Merritt, *Public Opinion in Occupied Germany: The OMGUS Surveys, 1945–1949* (Urbana: University of Illinois, 1970), 307.
4. For a useful summary of these studies, see Dieter Wirth, "Die Familie in der Nachkriegszeit: Desorganisation oder Stabilität?" in Josef Becker, Theo Stammen, and Peter Waldmann, eds., *Vorgeschichte der Bundesrepublik Deutschland: Zwischen Kapitulation und Grundgesetz* (Munich: Wilhelm Fink, 1979), 193–216.
5. See, e.g., Gabriele Czarnowski, *Das kontrollierte Paar: Ehe–und Sexualpolitik im Nationalsozialismus* (Weinheim: Deutscher Studien Verlag, 1991).
6. Parlamentarischer Rat, Stenographischer Bericht, Zehnte Sitzung, May 8, 1949, 225.
7. Deutscher Juristinnenbund, ed., *Juristinnen in Deutschland: Eine Dokumentation (1900–1984)* (Munich: J. Schweitzer, 1984), 95–102.
8. Parlamentarischer Rat, Hauptausschuss Bonn, Bonn 1948/49 (hereafter PR, HA), 17. Sitzung, December 3, 1948, 206–207.
9. Parlamentarischer Rat, Ausschuss für Grundsatzfragen (hereafter PR, AfG), 26. Sitzung, November 30, 1948, 46–47, Bundesarchiv (hereafter BA), Z5/34.
10. See, e.g., Ines Reich-Hilweg, *Männer und Frauen sind gleichberechtigt* (Frankfurt am Main: Europäische Verlagsanstalt, 1979), 22, 147.
11. PR, HA, 42. Sitzung, January 18, 1949, 539–541.
12. Ibid., 541.
13. PR, HA, 39. Sitzung, January 14, 1949, 488.

14. PR, AfG, 29. Sitzung, December 4, 1948, 96, BA, Z5/34.
15. PR, AfG, 26. Sitzung, November 30, 1948, 60–61, BA, Z5/34.
16. PR, HA, 21. Sitzung, December 7, 1948, 241.
17. Quoted in Marianne Feuersenger, *Die garantierte Gleichberechtigung: Ein Umstrittener Sieg der Frauen* (Freiburg im Breisgau: Herder, 1980), 50; and "SPD Frauentag in Wuppertal," *Neuer Vorwärts* 1, no. 11 (September 11, 1948), 6; and comments at SPD Reichsfrauenkonferenz, reported in *Genossin* 11 (1948), 123.
18. PR, AfG, 29. Sitzung, December 4, 1948, 52, BA, Z5/35; and HA, 21. Sitzung, December 7, 1948, 243.
19. PR, AfG, 29. Sitzung, December 4, 1948, 36, BA, Z5/35.
20. PR, HA, 21. Sitzung, December 7, 1948, 246.
21. PR, AfG, 29. Sitzung, December 4, 1948, 7, BA, Z/35, 7–9, 61–65; PR, HA, 21. Sitzung, December 7, 1948, 247. And on Adenauer's position, Rudolf Morsey, "Adenauer und Kardinal Frings 1945–1949," in Dieter Albrecht, et al., eds., *Politik und Konfession: Festschrift für Konrad Repgen zum 60 Geburtstag*, (Berlin: Duncker & Humblot, 1983), 497–98; and Hans-Peter Schwarz, *Adenauer*, Vol. I, *Der Aufstieg: 1876–1952* (Stuttgart: Deutsche Verlags-Anstalt, 1986), 593–94.
22. *Entscheidungen des Bundesverfassungsgerichts*, Vol. 10 (Tübingen: J.C.B. Mohr [Paul Siebeck], 1957), 78.
23. Cynthia Harrison, *On Account of Sex: The Politics of Women's Issues, 1945–1968* (Berkeley: University of California Press, 1988), 7–23.

10. Cinema, Spectatorship, and the Problem of Postwar German Identity

Heide Fehrenbach

> Spectatorship is not only the act of watching a film, but also the ways one takes pleasure in the experience .... Spectatorship refers to how film-going and the consumption of movies and their myths are symbolic activities, culturally significant events ... Spectatorship is not just the relationship that occurs between the viewer and the screen, but also and especially how that relationship lives on once the spectator leaves the theater.[1]

The story of West German cinema has often been told as an extension of World War II, in which military defeat was merely the prelude to a much more serious economic and cultural emasculation by Hollywood. Hollywood's postwar thrust into the West German market, it has been claimed, stunted the development of a native national cinema by monopolizing domestic screen time, shutting West German films out of the international (and especially European) market, and colonizing the consciousness of West German citizens by transforming them into American-style consumers.

Without attempting to construct a new narrative, I would like to share aspects of my research that question this interpretation, and in the process shed some light on identity construction after Hitler. To begin, I will need to shift the investigation away from the American incursion and focus instead on the responses of native elites in church and state to postwar film viewing and the newly established "Americanized" model of film censorship in order to reveal the challenges these elites expected American forms of commercial culture and control to pose for German reconstruction. I will conclude with a consideration of actual postwar film-viewing behavior among West Germans and speculate on some of the meanings film spectatorship may have had for postwar German identity.

CINEMATIC CONTROL AND SOCIAL ORDER: GERMAN IDENTITY IN A COLD WAR WORLD

After 1945, Germans were confronted with the task of national redefinition, of creating a new communal identity untainted by associations with the Nazi past. This was not an easy or uncontested process, nor was it confined to the political sphere. Some of the most fervent clashes over postwar reconstruction occurred in the putatively "apolitical" realm of culture, where politics could run rampant precisely because hard-nosed political scientists and economists considered it a tertiary sphere.

In the West, heated debates over the limits (as well as the social and moral implications) of the new democratic order frequently were played out in the cultural arena, where state and church officials could appeal to their traditional authority. While these officials relented to the process of political democratization, they remained resistant in the area of cultural—and specifically cinematic—control.

Because of the enormous popularity of film viewing in the first postwar decade and the putative psychological potency of the medium, official struggles to censor film and influence production constituted a significant chapter in native attempts at national and social reconstruction. In the aftermath of Hitler and Goebbels, censorship was treated—by both Occupation officials and native elites—as an important tool for political socialization and social control. And in an emerging Cold War world, cinematic representation attracted particular attention as a powerful participant in ideology construction.

During the Occupation, the American Military Government established the principles upon which a reconstructed West German cinema eventually would be based. These included political goals such as the denazification of industry personnel and the abolition of state control over film production and censorship, as well as economic liberalization in the form of free competition, open markets, and industry decartelization. In a democratically reconstructed Germany, film was to be subjected only to the putatively nonideological dictates of the market economy. State control was condemned by the American occupiers as a totalitarian practice—thus, the Nazi model of the state-sponsored, state-regulated film monopoly (which found its culmination in the 1942 creation of UFI) was to be extirpated.

Over the course of 1946–1948, during a protracted period of negotiation, American Information Control officers were able to impose this vision on the other Western zones. Nearly concurrently, they founded a German film producers association in the American zone, and during the last two years of the Occupation worked with it to establish the principle—based upon the Hollywood Hays Office—of industry self-censorship. German film producers in the American zone were initially skeptical regarding the success of this model because it contradicted the traditional prerogatives of the German *Länder* and churches in the area of cultural control. American Information Control officials promised some modification but urged the producers to act while they were under the protection of the U.S. Military Government. The message, then, was clear: German filmmakers were to present the new West German government with an institutional fait accompli.

As military occupiers, American officials were able to impose the principle of industry self-censorship and secure the formal assent of the German *Länder* and churches to participate, through minority representation, in the new national film censorship body, *Die Freiwillige Selbstkontrolle der Filmwirtschaft*, which began operation in July 1949. This organization represented a compromise between American principles and the interwar German model. It introduced self-regulation by the film industry members, who American officials considered free from ideological bias due to both stringent licensing practices and their single-minded pursuit of profit. At the same time, the American occupiers recognized that if the new censorship legislation was to outlive the Occupation, it would need the support of state and church elites, and thus modified exclusive industry self-regulation to include these interests.

Despite the acquiescence of the state cultural ministries, Dr. Walter Keim of Bavaria, head of the Standing Conference of Cultural Ministers of the German States, made it clear that he considered the agreement a "temporary expedient."[2] Throughout the Occupation, church and state officials—with substantial support from parents and educators—voiced grave concerns regarding the social role of film in the new democracy and the moral consequences of a cinematic culture dominated by purely commercial interests. At the heart of their efforts was a concern about the "laxity" of film control under the Occupation, and the unlimited access by all sectors of the German population—and especially youth—to the Allies' films.

Prior to 1949, the Bavarian cultural ministry, in particular, had made a number of ultimately unsuccessful plays to enact local censorship which, they argued, would be more responsive to cultural norms and religious values than that practiced by the Western Allies. The Christian churches, too, embarked on a course of unprecedented activity in film matters—founding official film offices, appointing film commissioners, and publishing film journals to advise congregants on the merits all films released in West Germany. The point was to influence consumer behavior and mitigate the social and cultural impact of commercial cultural products and practices.[3]

While elite efforts to control the social effects of film are as old as the medium itself and unique to neither Germany nor the postwar period, the disrupted social order of the defeated and occupied country intensified the perceived gravity of the cultural challenge. Conservatives in church and state feared the social effects of an open market, particularly given their strong desire to encourage "normalized" gender and family relationships after the war. After 1945, social "contagion" was no longer identified as issuing from ethnic or religious groups alien to a racially superior *Volksgemeinschaft* as during the Third Reich. Rather, it appeared in a form more difficult to control: the unmediated influence of cultural products that touted the merits of consumerism and individual fulfillment. At stake was the issue of who would exercise cultural sovereignty within Germany's borders, who would define the nature of the new German nation.

The fear that godless, materialist culture would accompany democratization and spell the death of a culturally discrete, capitalist West Germany was widespread among churchmen and conservative state leaders. One Catholic bulletin praised the absence of erotic decadence in the Soviet media, commenting pointedly that one shouldn't be surprised if those "unbroken youths someday become masters of the lustful boys" in the West.[4] And in 1950, Cardinal Faulhaber announced the position of the Catholic Church in his "Appeal for the Protection of Youth and the Security of the *Volk*," which denounced the circulation of "trash and smut" and demanded its regulation. Faulhaber warned that social decay was the result of the dangerous "pluralism of values" in a democracy that knew no limits. When "public morality" was being corrupted, he argued, it would be "inconceivable and irresponsible to conceal it with the cloak of democracy." Catholic bishops concluded that "the time had come, after years of dissolute living and lawlessness, to once again make decency and morality felt."[5]

The decisive campaign was fought in early 1951, when activist priests led armies of schoolboys onto the streets across West Germany to protest Willi Forst's film, *Die Sünderin* (The Sinner), demanding a new public morality and the "protection of our women's honor." The demonstrations culminated in the widespread stinkbombing of offending theaters and the disruption of screenings by the release of white mice. In the midst of the uproar, Cardinal Frings issued a pastoral statement from his archbishopric in Cologne calling on all Christians to boycott the film. Clergy in Füssen went one step further and refused to hold Sunday church services, perform weddings or funerals, or allow the ringing of church bells for the duration of *Die Sünderin*'s run in local theaters. By spring, the film was banned in dozens of towns across West Germany—including the new capital, Bonn.[6]

Far from representing an isolated attempt at film censorship by conservative clergymen, this incident embodies a number of significant issues for German postwar reconstruction. My reading of the *Sünderin* affair indicates that German churchmen were motivated by more than a predictable moral squeamishness to the film's first postwar female nude scene. They considered their mobilization an act of national "self-defense" against grave cultural threats—something the Protestant film commissioner emphasized when he "cried out from a plagued heart," inquiring "who will help hinder such spiritual murder of our young people and women, tested by suffering, and our broken-bodied men?" He was reacting to the way the film resonated with wartime dislocations in social and gender relations that he, and others in influential positions, perceived as dangerous to German reconstruction in the West.[7]

The film concerns the story of Marina (Hildegard Knef) who, after a short but significant life of prostitution, finds love and redemption with one man and ultimately affirms her fidelity to him by surrendering her life to join him in death. The film opens just before Marina commits suicide in the arms of her dying lover, Alexander. Exclaiming, "Oh my God, I've killed you," she initiates a series of flashbacks that answers the question of why she killed the man she loved.[8]

Marina, we learn, was a high-class call girl in a posh Munich nightspot when she first encountered a drunk and staggering Alexander being forcibly bounced from the bar. Overwhelmed with pity, she took him home, realizing the next day that he is "from a good family." A flashback to her own sad family life reveals an unemployed but once-prosperous father, a materialist and unfaithful mother, and a stepbrother who seduces the girl Marina by offering her money for sexual favors. Thus begins a short—but highly profitable—life of prostitution for Marina, until she meets Alexander, and realizes that "love means giving, never taking."

Life with Alexander is not without problems, however. We learn that he was an officer in World War II whose decline began with defeat. A malignant brain tumor that is causing a gradual loss of sight both destroyed his career and led his wife to abandon him. He carries sleeping pills so he can choose the time of his death. Marina attempts to avert this event by prostituting herself, first to sell one of Alexander's paintings and then, when his condition worsens, to raise money for his surgery. As luck would have it, her customer in the latter case turns out to be Alexander's doctor, who, realizing the situation in the nick of time, declines the encounter and orders the operation.

Marina and the recovered Alexander begin a new life in Vienna. These days are happy, with Alexander painting "as if possessed," until one evening he is blinded by a sudden relapse and convinces Marina to administer the fatal dose of pills. Drinking champagne before the fireplace, Alexander dies slowly, unaware that Marina has also taken the pills and is dying in his arms. She whispers, "I love you. I'm coming darling."

The film disturbed for a number of reasons, but most significantly because, while Marina did not fit the role of victim, Alexander did. The figure of Alexander emphasizes the instability of German masculinity, and his death hints at the futility—or even failure—of a reconstruction based on old, familiar terms. Alexander is the cinematic incarnation of Werner Hess's "broken-bodied man," set off by a self-reliant woman. Marina literally pulls him from the gutter and provides him with the means and self-respect to resume his career as an artist. His survival and success result entirely from Marina's efforts and volition. In its treatment of masculine and feminine roles, then, *Die Sünderin* could be read as an allegory of postwar German gender relations and illustrated that German masculinity had lost its potency.

In the aftermath of World War II, the German man was a real social problem, and the patriarchal family seemed on the verge of extinction. Four million German men had been killed in the war, nearly 12 million were held in prison camps at the end of hostilities, and by 1950, even with the return of most POWs, almost one-third of all German households were headed by divorced women or widows. Husbands returning home after years away in the war or prison camps often experienced disappointment following their long-awaited reunions. Men described their shock at meeting not the young, amiable, and soft-spoken wives who inhabited their fond memories, but women rendered haggard, hardened, and self-reliant as a result of the war on the home front. For in order to survive, women learned to provide for themselves and their children despite food rationing, nightly bombing raids, evacuations, epidemics, even brutalization and rape.[9]

While many women reported gaining a sense of confidence and self-sufficiency by surviving harrowing times, men's experiences of military defeat and imprisonment frequently resulted in physical and mental debilitation, and feelings of profound dishonor and despair. And homecoming did nothing to boost men's severely flagging self-esteem. For they entered a baffling new world where survival depended on ration cards, illegal black market deals, scavenging, gardening, long hours of waiting in line—and the efforts of women and children. In oral histories, women described the contributions of children as young as ten years old as "indispensable" to the household economy during the starvation years of the Occupation, but often complained about their hapless husbands who wouldn't or couldn't work. It seemed, then, that the war had emasculated men and masculinized women.

Women continued the exhausting work of subsistence into the postwar period and became the primary providers of the family household. And many quickly tired of caring for husbands and fathers who returned from the war to assume a dependent, unproductive status in the household—especially when these same men ignored the changed circumstances and attempted to reassert themselves as domestic decisionmakers and disciplinarians.[10]

By the early years of the Adenauer era, continuing signs of female independence were condemned in the press and discouraged through social policy. Public censure of female independence extended to the sexual as well. And since social crisis coincided with military defeat and occupation, these discussions were phrased in terms of national identity: German women were vilified for having had sexual relations with "enemy" soldiers. Commentators often neglected to distinguish between rape and prostitution or to acknowledge the miserable material circumstances that drove many women into temporary prostitution. Social workers in Aachen, for example, bemoaned the "grievous moral confusion" of girls who "propositioned foreigners in order to secure the enjoyment of food or consumer goods." By portraying women as selling themselves for "meager material advantages," such rhetoric resurrected the presumed connection between consumption and femininity and insinuated that German women were unfaithful partners and egotistical materialists. From here it was a short step to shifting responsibility for Germany's national humiliation. The men may have lost the war, but women were represented as sabotaging the reconstruction through their unsympathetic demeanor and promiscuous behavior.[11]

Critics of *Die Sünderin* transferred these accusations to the character Marina and attacked her as a prostitute and murderess. Indeed, what is striking in the film is not Alexander's determination to die but his decision to relegate to Marina the task of administering the fatal dose—and her willingness of accept that responsibility. For her action indicates that she, too, recognizes the psychological and social implications of Alexander's loss of sight. Throughout the film, Marina is spurred into action in the face of dire situations; tilted camera angles visually underscore the abnormality of such scenes. During periods depicted as "happy," the camera is righted and Marina becomes passive and ornamental, deferring to Alexander, who, recovered and strong, takes command of both their relationship and his career. Alexander's successful surgery initiates a striking montage of images, blending medium close-ups of Alexander with overlaid, nude sketches of Marina that prominently feature her bared breasts. As the sketches flash before our—and Alexander's—eyes, we hear Marina's voice addressing her lover. "You had to paint nudes. You had to start from the beginning; to see with other eyes." Eyes, that is, of a man in control, whose reassertion of self fixes Marina as an object of visual enjoyment and sexual fantasy. Thus, Alexander *must* die when he permanently loses his sight. For loss of sight means more than loss of livelihood: it signifies loss of aesthetic and sexual control and the negation of masculinity.

Ultimately, of course, identity in the film was permitted to remain neither ambiguous nor problematic. *Die Sünderin* exposed gender instability only to resolve it in a way that reinforced conservative social ideology. The aesthetic death scene at the end serves to "right" the skewed world of male impotence and gender inversion. The healing properties of heterosexual love have transformed Marina, causing her to renounce her solitary existence and self-centered materialism and to devote herself fully to her man. She sacrifices herself willingly for Alexander, and without his knowledge. Thus female martyrdom brings gender redemption and the containment of once-threatening sexuality—as the camera pans, for the closing shot, to the wall above the fireplace and the framed portrait of the nude "sinner," now safely dead.

Critics, however, disregarded this transformation and read the film strictly as a challenge to the traditional notions of morality and monogamy. One symptomatic review in the *Katholischer Film-Dienst* denounced the film's "positive romanticization of prostitution" and expressed concern that young women would be tempted into emulation, since the film suggests that "a prostitute can earn DM 4,000 in the course of a few hours."[12] Marina did not represent the "responsible" postwar consumer who would stimulate Ludwig Erhard's social market economy by saving her pfennigs to purchase a family refrigerator. Rather, she threatened German regeneration through her rampant consumerism and unregulated female sexuality. Thus critics were disturbed as much by the effects of the medium as by its message. Films like *Die Sünderin*, which openly thematized sexuality, were perceived as a grave danger to social normalization. Film was no mere entertainment, but a powerful school for inappropriate socialization.

What is more, church and state officials—and secular film critics—agreed that it was women and youth, not "broken-bodied" German men, who were most susceptible to the attractions and insidious influences of commercial film culture. Women were accused of attending movies avidly, unselectively, and "often with babies in their arms." As a result, some state officials argued that mothers could not be trusted to regulate their own—let alone their children's—film attendance.[13]

"Empirical proof" of the dangers inappropriate film viewing presented to "youth and the young democracy" was supplied by the Catholic journal *Filmdienst*, which published an infrared photo of a juvenile movie audience, accompanied by the following text:

> Grimacing children who have clasped their hands in front of their faces in alarm and horror; eyes wide open, the stare of fright, faces of the ruins, such as those photographed during the war among soldiers who staggered into the trenches during an attack.

The sensational commentary and bald analogy to soldiers' frontline experience called forth fears of irreparable psychological damage and behavioral problems. Such hyperbole was not uncommon, at least in Bavaria, where a letter from the Unified Citizens Committee of Schwabach requested state subsidies for the production of "worthwhile" films, since "all the money that one would wish to spare today will have to go toward prisons in the future."[14]

In the midst of increasing rhetoric of family dysfunction and social collapse, Catholic politicians in the Christian Democratic Union (CDU), supported by Cardinal Frings, demanded that the family become the building block of the new German democratic order. Advocating a political renewal based upon God's "natural law," the CDU, in a successful bid to become the governing party of postwar West Germany, advertised its support for the patriarchal family as the reversal of the "immoral materialism" that plagued Germany's past and present.[15]

The family was to serve an important cultural function in postwar West Germany. As Robert Moeller has suggested, it "embodied a critique of the ideological alternatives" provided by National Socialism and East German Communism: "In the confused categories of totalitarian theory, ... the family could serve as a vehicle for anti-Nazi *and* anti-communist rhetoric."[16] Yet the politicized discourse of film control also reveals that West German leaders sought to protect Germany from the social and moral implications of commercial culture, which they identified with democratization and Americanization. The normative family, then, was to provide a bulwark against three ideologically unappealing alternatives —the Nazi, the "Commie" and the so-called "Ami."

Given the larger international forces at work, social conservatives considered it a matter of national life and death to ensure the maintenance of a separate cultural identity. And although Adenauer steered the Federal Republic firmly along the path of political integration with the West, German elites displayed a pronounced ambivalence toward cultural integration. They pushed instead in the direction of a cultural *Sonderweg*, or special path.

What emerged from the *Sünderin* episode was the reintroduction of state regulation of film and consumer behavior, a kind of "discriminatory paternalism" of male supervision through state agencies. Self-sufficient wives and disrespectful, precocious children had to be tamed in order for German men to achieve a stable, uncontested masculine identity and reemerge as self-assured patriarchs. The assumptions underlying protective legislation were based on a generalized desire to remake autonomous and productive women and children into wayward or vulnerable victims who *could* be reformed and protected by revitalized German men. By the early 1950s, then, the "normalization" of gender and generational relations was considered a matter of national survival. Cultural representations that questioned the efficacy or implications of this agenda were therefore harshly condemned by church and state leaders.

State cultural ministries used *Die Sünderin* as the pretext to pressure the film industry into modifying the American model of industry self-censorship to include a stronger "public voice." The final settlement established a parity between industry and public representatives. The public voice was now represented by one member each from: the religious community, the state ministries of culture, the federal youth office, and for the first time, the federal government.[17]

Over the course of 1951, the churches, too, were able to wage a successful attack against the prevailing values of commercial culture and in the process bolster their own authority. Catholic bishops sought to subvert the commercial success of films like *Die Sünderin* by constructing their own "highly organized consumer groups"—in the form of Christian film leagues—to do battle with the "highly organized film industry." In late 1951, film leagues were founded in every West German diocese and required members to take an oath promising not to attend films rejected by the Catholic Film Commission. They were designed to pressure the industry to acquiesce to the taste of the Christian consumer.[18]

The film industry strenuously protested the film leagues, the solicitation of oaths, and posting of Catholic film ratings on theater showcases as infringements on constitutionally protected democratic freedom. But the Catholic press responded that membership was voluntary, and reminded the industry that film leagues were an invention of "America— the classic democracy," where they had functioned for 20 years. Thus one American model of organization was borrowed to counter another.[19]

What's more, the strategy worked. Within two months, national film league membership mushroomed to one million. By 1954, Christian film leagues boasted four million members—nearly three times the combined membership of all German political parties. A negative rating in the Catholic film journal typically resulted in slack business for the film outside of the major German cities. Thus, the strength and economic impact of this consumer group pressured the film industry to produce films that were morally and socially unobjectionable to the Catholic Film Office throughout the 1950s.[20]

This trend was reinforced by a system of financial credits extended to film projects reviewed by state and federal economics ministries. The purpose of the credits was to address the industry's financial problems and encourage the production of films that could compete on the international market—all part of a larger program intended to stimulate national economic growth and increase export revenues. By the early 1950s, then, the state again became involved in film production; and since the credit committees scrutinized scripts, cast, and technical personnel, they could—and did—influence film content, style, and commercial appeal. Most West German film companies, moreover, lacked an adequate source of financing; as a result, in 1951, the first year of operation, 75 percent of all feature films were supported by state or federal funds. Thus credit programs reintroduced formal state influence over cinematic production and strengthened the voice of the state regarding the types of films realized.²¹

This voice was not, however, one of moral authority. Since the film credit programs were designed as economic stimulus packages, state and federal ministries of economics sought to circumvent cultural and moral concerns and rebuffed attempts by cultural ministries to participate in the decision-making process. In response, state cultural ministries created another type of economic incentive for the film industry and dispensed it according to ideological criteria. In 1951, the German *Länder* created a Film Rating Board of the German States (*Die Filmbewertungsstelle der Länder*), which possessed no mandatory authority over film content, but was authorized to grant significant tax breaks to films determined to be either "valuable" or "especially valuable."²²

In practice, the credit commissions and rating board encouraged the production of a technically competent—but provincial—style of filmmaking which satisfied some state and church officials, but reinforced the scorn of serious film critics and the indifference—indeed disinterest—of international distributors and audiences. In fact, the peculiarly German genre of the *Heimatfilm* became the staple domestic fare of West German cinema during the 1950s. Fully one-fifth of all German productions were devoted to this genre, which celebrated the natural beauty of the Black Forest or Lüneberger Heide, featured close-knit communities and townsfolk in traditional dress, and contained the requisite festival celebrating local or religious traditions from an unproblematic—and unmarred—past. Moreover, *Heimatfilme* were extraordinarily successful commercial products, topping the list of box office smashes through 1955.

Rather than facilely assume an appalling lack of taste among postwar West German audiences, I would like to take another look at that most popular—if critically ridiculed—genre of *Heimatfilm* in order to both investigate possible reasons for its immense audience loyalty and assess its cultural significance. In doing so, I follow the lead of Janet Staiger, who recently suggested that "what we are interested in ... is not a so-called correct reading of a particular film but the range of possible readings and reading processes at particular moments and their relation ... to groups of historical spectators."²³

The following discussion, then, is intended to be suggestive rather than exhaustive. The point of this somewhat inexact exercise is to puzzle out the meanings that German audiences attached to their consumption of films and to speculate on the relation of these meanings to both the process of identity construction and the historical context that framed their lives.

HEIMATFILM AND POSTWAR FILM SPECTATORSHIP: BACK TO THE FUTURE?

As Alon Confino has recently argued, *Heimat*, since its modern incarnation in the late nineteenth century, has served as an "integrative symbol" which "endowed the nation with continuity and causality": a shared past, that is, and shared meaning. *Heimat* celebrates the local, the mundane, the domestic; it refers to geographical place of birth, but also the peculiar landscape, dialect, customs, and traditions attached to that locality. As such, it has a strong emotional component, since it is invested with all of the sentimental content of one's childhood. Encompassing both communal and personal identity, it denotes homeland, home, and hearth—with all of their myriad meanings and emotional associations.[24]

Contrasted with the masculine and martial connotations of "fatherland" and "nation," then, *Heimat* represents a feminized communal ideal. As Confino has suggested, fatherland and nation "could go to war, while Heimat could never do that. Heimat was something one fought for, never something that participated in battle." Since the turn of the century, *Heimat* was imagined as the sentimental separate sphere that, for Germans from both ends of the political spectrum, offered "respite from everyday social and political conflicts."[25]

By its very definition, then, *Heimat* was something that could—and would—survive political fluctuations and military defeat. Indeed, the decade after World War II witnessed the penning of a plethora of paeans to Mother *Heimat*. According to one contemporary, "one cannot speak enough of Heimat: it is something like heaven ... the original comfort from which all else flows ... let the world do as it will—the Heimat loves and confirms you without question, as its child."[26]

Symbolizing the unchanging, "essential," even spiritual German nation, *Heimat* became a central cultural construct in the early postwar period. At once consoling, forgiving, and rehabilitative—as Celia Applegate has emphasized in her book on the subject—it was used to facilitate the messy process of political and moral reconstruction. "Pulled out of the rubble of the Nazi Reich as a victim, not a perpetrator," it was designated the bedrock upon which the new democratic nation would be based and "came to embody the political and social community that could be salvaged from the Nazi ruins."[27]

In postwar West Germany, *Heimat* represented a new political and cultural orientation. Public presentation of the beauty of the German landscape, color shots panning the distinctive natural treasures of the provinces reassured West Germans that their "new state was not all that bad."[28] *Heimat* solved two postwar dilemmas with great economy: it provided an affirmative representation of the German nation and at the same time jettisoned the unsavory aspects of the German past.

Heimatfilm offered the German public escape on a number of levels. First, and perhaps even foremost, it provided a temporary escape from the cares of unemployment, inadequate (and often ugly, hastily erected) accommodations, and the rubble-strewn vistas of the urban landscape. *Heimatfilm* highlighted German flora and fauna, but its entertainment value was based upon a broader range of visual spectacle. *Heimatfilme* were produced, after all, for the commercial market; and the overwhelming success of its first issues meant that films like *Schwarzwaldmädel* (Black Forest Girl, 1950) and *Grün ist die Heide* (Green is the Heath, 1951) established the standards and contours of the cinematic genre. In the hit film, *Grün ist die Heide*, audiences were treated to an extended sequence filmed inside the circus big top, complete with clowns, comedy routines, acrobats, magicians, and animal acts. In this case, performance really does become little more than pleasurable distraction from both the problems internal to the film's plot and those, more pressing, concerns located outside the walls of the cinema.

Heimatfilme also showcased musical performance; indeed no film was complete without a handful of traditional *Volkslieder* and sentimental hits, which were simultaneously marketed on radio and records. The music served to cement the bonds of the cinematic community or celebrate the budding romance of the leading stars, and thus played a more integral role in the narrative. Folk songs appear as a part of oral tradition, passed from generation to generation according to a cyclical calendar of local celebration. Thus, they underscored the idea that *Heimat* grew out of a historic cultural heritage grounded in the affective ties of matrimony, family, and community. At the same time, however, many *Heimatfilme* employed popular Nazi-era stars and cinematic conventions (such as the musical and operetta). Through their sentimental content and modern form, then, *Heimatfilme* allowed audiences to indulge in nostalgia—or fantasy—about a happier communal or individual past by *simultaneously* affirming cultural traditions forged across a hazy *longue durée* and recalling the personal pleasures of film spectatorship during the Third Reich.

While stressing the interplay between past and present, *Heimatfilme* are nonetheless riddled with gaps, ellipses, and silences. They emphasize history and tradition, but only in their vaguest form; they contain few specific references to the recent historical past. *Heimatfilme* never mention politics and are stone silent on National Socialism; yet references to the war do appear—albeit in the most oblique form—in a couple of the most popular films.

In *Grün ist die Heide*, for example, the action revolves around a dutiful daughter (played by Soja Ziemann) and her father, a former Pomeranian landowner (Hans Stüwe), who have been driven west by the war, taken up residence in their relatives' country manor on the unscarred Lüneberger heath, and are trying to adjust to their new *Heimat* when the film opens. The father, Lüder Lüdersen, vastly complicates the process of assimilation by his uncontrollable compulsion to hunt deer—the one aspect of his life that he is unwilling to surrender. In their new homeland, hunting is prohibited; and Lüdersen is tracked through the woods to the manor by the new forester, Walter Rainer (Rudolf Prack), who promptly falls in love with Lüdersen's daughter, Helga.

The war, then, is part of the unportrayed past. Like a natural catastrophe, it has no author but unsettling repercussions: the unexplained loss of Helga's mother, the need to accept new authority, new laws, and a new life. The war's aftershocks need to be weathered, and the nonnative male self needs to be disciplined to ensure the reemergence of social and emotional equilibrium. Indeed, the film (and a farewell speech by Lüdersen toward the end of the film) repackages German refugees, like himself, as the war's true victims, in need of forbearance and understanding. In the end, the success of postwar reconstruction is dependent on the test of male character, which fortunately in this case, after a lot of vacillating, appears to hold up.

In fact, a specific sort of male character emerges in these films: an ideal type of romantic lead who will take Germany into the future. Like the forester, Walter Rainer, the ideal German has a code of honor. He is law-abiding to a point, but not to a fault. In *Grün ist die Heide*, Walter resists having Lüdersen arrested for poaching out of concern for the shame it will bring Helga. Instead, he is satisfied when Helga promises to leave the province and move to the city with her as yet undisciplined dad. Thus the dilemma is resolved, and Walter avoids becoming yet another unfeeling civil servant "just following orders." A bit of legal latitude goes a long way after National Socialism, and Walter is intended to be perceived as a principled humanitarian, a man with a heart—something that signals his difference from the Nazi film hero.

Other films were even bolder in resurrecting a moral masculinity, since this was accomplished by explicit reference to the recent German past. *Am Brunnen vor dem Tore* (At the Fountain near the Citygate), a popular *Heimatfilm* from the 1951/52 season also starring Soja Ziemann, introduces us to Kurt Kramer, the humble but handsome owner of a gas station on the outskirts of scenic Dinkelsbühl. After assisting Inge (Ziemann), a charming damsel-in-distress, Kramer unwittingly becomes embroiled in a love triangle with her and her ex-fiancée, a British pilot she met during the Occupation. The love triangle, then, has national-political complications and is played out in a most interesting way. To begin with, the young men never overtly compete for Inge's affections. In fact, until the very end, Robert, the English pilot, has no idea that Kurt is in love with Inge because Kurt's sense of honor will not allow him to make his emotions plain to either her or Robert. The reason is the bond of friendship Kurt feels for Robert. When we first see Robert, he has stumbled upon Kurt's station and stops for gas. The shop, however, is empty, Kurt is nowhere to be seen, and Robert's eyes are drawn to the wall where a broken propeller blade is mounted. Kurt enters and an intent Robert questions him about the blade. Is it from a fighter? Yes, answers Kurt, an English Spitfire. Where did it come from? How did he get possession of it? Kurt shrugs off the questions, "Oh, it's a long story." But when Robert insists, Kurt matter-of-factly relates how he was on his twenty-fifth mission when he hit an English fighter which went down. He landed his plane next to it and could see that the pilot was unconscious, so he pulled him from the burning craft. Robert urges Kurt to look closely at him. "I," announces Robert, "am that pilot. And I've been searching for you all over."

In this remarkable and understated scene, the German pilot is redeemed as the unsung hero, a humble guardian of human life who returns to his modest living after the war. The experience of the war becomes the glue that seals their friendship, and Kurt is congratulated for displaying compassion within the context of an impersonal war. The exchange between Robert and Kurt suggests that the hostilities were not, after all, personal, since they are not mentioned beyond the fact of the attack. The rescue, however, he performed as a man; and Kurt appears all the more likeable because he is clearly an unboastful, reluctant hero.

In offering audiences a new model of moral masculinity, *Heimatfilme* tended to set the romantic hero against an older rival for the desired woman's affections. In *Am Brunnen*, for example, an older local notable, Herr Straaten, watches warily as Inge's friendship with Kurt develops and later mourns the news that Robert has returned to renew his engagement with her. We learn that Straaten intercepted Robert's letters to Inge from England, which led Inge to assume the engagement was off, and even worse, that he perpetrated an art theft that has been unjustly attributed to Inge's brother. When Kurt discovers Straaten's crime, the older man confesses and asks his accuser to look closely at the stolen portrait, which bears an uncanny resemblance to Inge, who, in turn, resembles his beloved dead wife! His compulsive and dishonest behavior, then, was the result of an overwhelming emotional need to regain an irretrievable past.

Straaten makes amends first symbolically, then sacrificially. He secures Kurt's permission to attend the annual local festival already underway and unexpectedly assumes the role of the Swedish general who, during the Thirty Years War, spared the city at the pleading of the local children. Entering on horseback through the city gate, Straaten is confronted by Inge, shepherding a mass of children. After listening to her heartfelt plea for mercy, Straaten abruptly altering the script and lifts the startled Inge to meet his lips in a tender kiss. Releasing her, he gallops off and returns home, where Kurt is awaiting him. Excusing himself one last time, Straaten exits the room and we hear a gunshot. In a last redeeming move, he has dispatched himself and his criminal past. His suicide becomes the noble act that expiates the sins of the father, as the sound of his gunshot is drowned out by a drum roll that draws the visual action away from his personal tragedy and back to the festival, where the parade is underway. At that moment, Straaten and his act tellingly evaporate; the film chronicles neither the news nor the reception of his death. There are no messy remnants, no repercussions, no need to examine the meaning of the act; the past simply and mercifully disappears.

Straaten represented an imperfect and aging masculinity that needed to be surmounted. The past has been depoliticized and "softened" into a personal failing, a generational miscalculation. Straaten's tragic flaw is that he had no feel for what was appropriate to the present. He was mired in the past; he couldn't adapt, forget, move on. He had to pass into the past to liberate the present.

Yet *Heimatfilm* offered German audiences more than just the romantic triumph of the son and a new generation of moral masculinity. *Heimatfilme* also recognized the *pathos* involved in release from the past, something that may account for their popularity with older viewers. For even when the older man doesn't die—as in the smash hit comedy, *Schwarzwaldmädel* (1950), in which an elderly Black Forest *Kapellmeister* is rejuvenated when a young woman becomes his temporary housekeeper—the moment of realization that his affections have been misplaced is one of poignancy, not humor. Moreover, this moment again coincides with a local festival, and the old man is encouraged to "come sit with us old folks; we'll watch the young people dance." As the enchanting Bärbel (Ziemann) dances with a young artist, Hans (Rudolf Prack), the camera comes to rest on the *Kapellmeister* who lowers his eyes and sings sorrowfully: "You can ponder it for a long time, but then your heart will break." Thus the generational eclipse is portrayed as personally painful but necessary; the past must be cleared away before the present can thrive unencumbered.

Recent studies have commented on the recurrent theme of male generational conflict in *Heimatfilme*, but as yet no attention has been paid to the related phenomena of father-daughter relationships or the problem of the missing mother. *Heimatfilme* of the early 1950s focused on the romantic or familial dilemma of an attractive yet compassionate young virgin who enlivens and inspires her elderly admirers. In *Schwarzwaldmädel*, Bärbel's entry into the *Kapellmeister*'s household—to fill in as housekeeper while her spinster aunt takes a rare vacation—is set against a prior comic scene in which the domineering aunt interrupts the composer's work and his beloved cigar-smoking with her incessant, overzealous cleaning. Bärbel, in contrast, transfixes him with her fresh beauty, hums through her light tidying, and inspires him to interrupt work on a hymn to play a waltz on his piano, which in turn provokes her to dance. Characters like Bärbel are loyal, non-judgmental caretakers, whose youth releases them from responsibility for the past—although not initially for their older charges. As midwives to the future, they promise a fresh start. They are nurturers, but also soft and vulnerable. Uniting the desirable with the maternal, they spark an optimism for the future in a way that tired old mothers couldn't.

The nature of this much-thematized femininity merits a closer look. In the tellingly titled *Schwarzwaldmädel*, when we first spy Bärbel she is wearing a charming dirndl. She is not, however, in the Black Forest village but at a masquerade party in the resort town Baden-Baden, where, we later learn, she works in a jeweler's shop. At the masquerade, she bumps into the artist, Hans, who upsets her basket of apples. Bending to help her collect the fruit, Hans asks, "Are these real *(echt)*?" The answer is that they are, and so of course is she—*ein echtes Mädel aus dem*

Schwarzwald—whose youthful beauty and guilelessness render her somehow more "authentic" (and therefore more desirable) to the ennui-ridden Hans than his sometime girlfriend, Malwina (Gretl Schoerg), a sophisticated nightclub singer with a predilection for expensive jewelry. Immediately and predictably, Bärbel sparks in the cosmopolitan artist a romantic interest so unfamiliar in its earnestness that he follows her to the Black Forest.

Bärbel holds out the promise of a regeneration that is as much communal as personal. Her portrait by Hans, in fact, becomes the basis for a poster that advertises the upcoming village festival where she ultimately is crowned "festival bride." Pure and genuine, she symbolizes the very essence of *Heimat* and serves as the center of a communal celebration of tradition, renewal, and optimism. Toward the end of the film, her image—fixed not only on paper but in Hans's mind—draws him back to the Schwarzwald from Baden-Baden a second time. The return to *Heimat*, then, becomes a quest to retrieve Bärbel and the values she embodies.

The film, however, is no wholehearted paean to provincialism. In fact, a village innkeeper who changes hats to become mayor at this moment, police chief at that, draws chuckles for both his jealous monopoly on authority in the community and his energetic efforts to marry off his daughter to a wealthy city-dweller. The trappings of *Heimat* are not fully immune from merry-making either, for although the village *Heimatmuseum* is the site of Bärbel and Hans's first kiss, it is also associated with the *Kapellmeister*'s misplaced affections and a man's comic transvestite transformation into an elderly female villager in traditional dress. Finally, although we meet Bärbel in the more cosmopolitan Baden-Baden, she nonetheless beats out the dutiful (but comically diminutive, shrill-voiced, and barrel-bodied) daughter of the innkeeper as festival bride.

Thus, it seems, *Heimatfilm* was not an exhortation to return to either the golden past or to simple village life. In fact, Bärbel is rewarded for her "echt" nature even before she leaves the masquerade in Baden-Baden, when a raffle ticket that Hans has bought her wins her the party's grand prize: a shiny red Ford! It is in this very Ford that she sets out for the provinces of the Black Forest. And in case we are unsure about what to make of this pricey acquisition, we are offered a shot of her gray-haired Hausfrau landlady bubbling over with excitement at Bärbel's good fortune as she wishes her tenant a good trip. Moreover, it is behind the wheel of the Ford, with the convertible top down and the *Kapellmeister* in the passenger seat, that Bärbel first charms his heart—to the tune of a waltz on the radio. This, then, was the desired postwar German woman: a portrait of female vitality that could straddle the past and future, that could speak to—and reconcile—both.

Heimatfilme suggested to female audiences that their role in German regeneration did not necessitate a return to their mothers' lives. In fact, they were fêted for being somehow different, and better. They could run an inn, work in a store, enjoy desired goods and travel—and still not capitulate to materialism or allow it to distract them from what was truly important. Bärbel's car quietly disappears from view after it has worked its magic by transforming her into a *modern* woman sporting traditional values. Moreover, when Bärbel and Hans embrace in dance at the end of the festival (and the film), we never question that it will result in matrimony and never doubt that they will return to Baden-Baden. Thus, these films assure us that *Heimat* is something you carry with you—provided you remain within national boundaries.[29]

Although *Heimatfilm* was considered family entertainment, anecdotal and industry sources suggest that German women were especially keen consumers of the genre.[30] While a breakdown of audience demographics is unavailable, there may be reasons why women in particular were attracted to the genre. Women, as we have seen, were posited as the libidinal center of the *Heimatfilm*'s universe; they were the vortex around which all action, concern, and fantasy swirled. Yet they were no mere objects of desire. They received both cognizance and credit for their efforts at caretaking, were lauded for their loyalty and strength, and drew sympathy for their substantial contributions on the home and work front. The *Heimatfilme* under discussion all shared, and showed, a common feature: a working woman who struggled to construct a life as well as a home, who was as strong-willed and determined as she was sweet— and whose men noticed and admired this state of affairs. Moreover, the films rehabilitated the German man as an attentive, sensitive, and compassionate mate, and suggested that he could provide a stable home life in the midst of an anxiety-ridden (and divorce-prone) reality. *Heimatfilme* may well have appealed to women's romantic and consumerist fantasies, but they also must have appealed to their need for recognition and security. And women doubtlessly found no cause for complaint that their celluloid counterparts were celebrated as the genuine basis for the postwar moral and social order.

Heimatfilme held out a fantasy for the future. They showed what a *Wohlstandsgesellschaft*, or prosperous society, would look like "long before it became a reality for the broad German public." In these films, unlike real life, housing, clothing and food were never the object of concern. *Schwarzwaldmädel* and *Am Brunnen vor dem Tore* featured worlds untouched by material want, in which the begging of musical vagabonds is politely and generously answered with free food, beer, and social acceptance. In this case, mendicancy was romanticized as a lifestyle choice,[31] and the freedom of the road becomes a metaphor for self-realization in the developing democracy of plenty.

Heimatfilm, in its peculiar postwar form, emerged and peaked at a specific historical moment: a period of political and economic uncertainty, emotional and social upheaval. In 1950, the year of *Schwarzwaldmädel*'s release, the unemployment rate stood at 11 percent and refugees constituted almost 17 percent of the population. When the genre (and movie attendance in general) began its gradual decline in 1956, the unemployment rate was under 4 percent, wages were up between two-thirds and three-quarters over their 1950 level (freeing most households from destitution for the first time in German history), the five-day work week had been instituted, and consumer goods like refrigerators, vacuum cleaners, washing machines, and phonographs were making their way into German homes. The *Wohlstandsgesellschaft* was becoming a reality. Indeed, *Heimatfilme* themselves seemed to change with the times; those produced after mid-decade struck some as little more than advertisements for domestic tourist destinations.[32]

* * *

"It still astounds," wrote one recent commentator on *Heimatfilm*, "how quickly these films found their audience of millions despite the competition from Hollywood."[33] But I have tried to suggest that their commercial success was the outgrowth of a particular time and form of address. After all, *Heimatfilm* could—and did—address German audiences as potential consumers, but Hollywood never addressed German audiences as Germans, with reference to their national past, present, or future.

Through the mid-1950s, *Heimatfilme* showed sensitivity to the postwar emotions of nostalgia, loss, and personal pain. Like their youthful heroines, these films were good-natured in their treatment of flawed characters, all of whom were likeable because they were fundamentally good-at-heart. None was intentionally hurtful, deceit and deception (like that of Herr Straaten's) were attributed to unhealed psychic wounds; criminal acts were psychologized and forgiven.

Thus *Heimatfilm* focused on the postwar healing process, but confined it to an emotional or spiritual exercise and doled out sympathy in generous portions. The genre enticed millions of German viewers with a vision of the future in which Germans could regain both their prosperity and their pride. *Heimatfilme* guaranteed personal and national redemption, forgiveness and forgetfulness; they offered the postwar German viewer, that is, something that Hollywood films could not.

For a short period of time between 1950 and 1956, *Heimatfilm* became the reigning West German film genre, and the West German film industry experienced a little "golden age" on the basis of this sure moneymaker. But it was precisely the national nature of *Heimatfilm* that prevented it from being an attractive export product. This triumph of cinematic provinciality represents a striking cultural about-face from Goebbels' grand plan to beat Hollywood at its own game by surpassing the "quality, cultural boldness, and feel for the modern" of American products in order to both dominate international markets and shape consumer identities. As Victoria deGrazia has argued in a different context, "exceptional familiarity with Americanism, even outright imitation, was not considered antithetical to forming a self-consciously nationalist mass culture"; and in this case, Goebbels sought to reproduce Hollywood's formula in order to advertise Germany's superiority. Yet despite his dogged diatribes—and instructive screenings of American films—he never quite succeeded in retraining German filmmakers. If German films played to an estimated one billion viewers in over 8,400 cinemas across Europe by 1942, Goebbels could thank the German *Reichswehr*. The expansive market for Germany's films died with its military hegemony. Like the fabled secret weapon, the secret formula for international cinematic success never materialized.[34]

After the war, Hollywood did win a large share of the German market. But the heyday of *Heimatfilme* indicates that the American film product dominated neither the West German market nor the consciousness of most German consumers through the mid-1950s. First-rate Hollywood films like "Gone with the Wind", "Rebecca", and "The Lost Weekend," for example, played well in larger German cities among adult audiences. And if they received favorable reviews by word of mouth and the press, they did well in towns and outlying areas as well. But there was no out-and-out American domination of the market in the ten years between 1945 and 1955 for a number of reasons.[35]

First, because of military occupation, lingering political resentments, and what one German contemporary called an "anti-reeducation consciousness" that "didn't find it necessary to receive instruction from a foreign military." Interwar fascination with American culture faded once it became associated with the unilateral policies of military government and doctrinaire didacticism. U.S. intelligence reports through 1946 indicate that Germans resented the heavy-handedness and moral finger-pointing of early reeducation attempts. As a result, American officials gradually retreated from this strategy—due both to its lack of success and the changing needs of an emerging Cold War world. By late 1946, they realized that liberal democracy would be easier to swallow as entertainment and looked to Hollywood to do their work.

The eight major Hollywood film companies promised full cooperation with the American agenda for German reeducation, and then took their time sending old, fully amortized films that had not yet been screened in Germany. Until the currency reform in mid-1948, U.S. imports lagged behind both French and British since profit remained unconvertible to hard cash. And although Hollywood films did the best business in 1947 Berlin—where the public had access to the offerings of all four Allies—surveys showed that they had little following in places like Schleswig, where British films dominated the screen. Moreover, for each report attesting to the popularity of American films there is another that suggests they irritated German audiences with their "carefree escapism," incomprehensible humor, and primitive subtitles. As one industry member recounted, "Hollywood films had no better start in postwar Germany than British or French films." And German re-releases from the Weimar and Nazi periods surpassed imports in popularity (nearly 70 percent of Germans polled in 1951 said they preferred domestic films) due to the absence of language barriers and the presence of familiar stars. Preference appears to have been linked to educational and social status: while three-fifths of viewers from the lowest educational level preferred German films, only one-half of those with "mid-level" education and one-third of "highly educated" Germans expressed the same preference.

After 1948, with currency reform and the return of commercial distribution, annual American imports more than doubled and Hollywood began sending quality features like *The Best Years of Our Lives* and *The Bells of St. Mary's*. But since money was now valuable—hence scarcer—there was a noticeable shift in consumer behavior. As an industry insider put it: Germans "stopped going to the flicks and started attending films." Germans, that is, began making informed choices about the films they saw, and demanded a certain level of quality. This perception may have been fueled by the marked shift in the class composition of the audience. Industry insiders noted an increase in attendance by the newly "pauperized" educated classes as well as those of higher socio-economic standing. Doctors, lawyers, civil servants, white-collar workers, university students—who, until recently, had preferred the theater—were now lured to the cinema as much by the engaging programs as by the cheaper admission prices. These groups also constituted a large proportion of the audience for quality American films.[36] But I would be reluctant to classify them as willing subjects for cultural Americanization—since studies suggest that, while they were avid consumers of *quality* films, they exhibited no firm preference for the products of any particular nation. Cinephiles at German universities, in fact, typically developed a firm fascination for French films. After Hitler, cultural cosmopolitanism was embraced by educated Germans as an antidote to what one cinephile hyperbolically called "the twelve years of international isolation and internment" during the Third Reich. It became the badge of "enlightened" new Germans, who sought to shed the chauvinism of their shameful past.[37]

Yet that doesn't tell the whole story. The German market, like most modern commercial markets, was segregated not only according to class and education but also according to generation and gender. While the most avid—and frequent—film-goers were under the age of 40, the most avid—and faithful—audience for Hollywood films was young and male.

In mid-sized cities and smaller towns, young men between the ages of 18 and 30 would dominate the audiences of the late show on Saturday, which typically featured Hollywood westerns, crime films, and "sensational" films. The same shows would often be screened at Sunday matinees for another, more youthful, male audience of *Volksschüler*, apprentices, and workers between the ages of 10 and 16. The most beloved stars among this set included Errol Flynn, John Wayne, Alan Ladd, Rita Hayworth, and later Marilyn Monroe, Marlon Brando, and James Dean.[38]

By the mid-1950s, young Germans began to identify German film with their parents and the National Socialist past: it seemed outmoded, authoritarian, and thoroughly unacceptable in comparison to the more "modern" impulses from America. Gerhard Bliersbach's reminiscences of his youthful film attendance during the 1950s suggest that it served as an expression of autonomy—and a challenge to postwar styles of socialization. He described the noise and excitement of an audience unencumbered by parents. As the

Hollywood film was about to roll, the cinema-owner issued a "German call to order"—but to no effect. Bliersbach continues:

> Here, adults were powerless. We screamed, we groaned, we clapped, we moaned, we rejoiced. What I loved about American films was to be able to mature to a fast-paced tempo and a happy ending; it had the speed of my daydreams. Like no other cinema, Hollywood captured the strains of adolescence—the anxieties and conflicts, the fantasies and desires.[39]

Moreover, Bliersbach indicates that, as in previous generations, young Germans looked to Hollywood for a new model of male identity: "The virile stars taught a masculine lesson: Cary Grant, Robert Mitchum, Tony Curtis, Victor Mature. American actors possessed a physical presence, that their German counterparts lacked."[40]

Bliersbach claims to have rejected German films (and particularly *Heimatfilme*) because he detected in them an unsure—or inadequately developed—masculinity. He complains of an unnaturally prolonged bonding to mother-figures and an insufficiently oedipal response to fathers: "I was disturbed by the physical ineptness of West German actors. These weren't real men. But rather mommy's little boys, who give way at the first sign of rough-housing."[41] In fact, in the most popular *Heimatfilme* of the early 1950s, the male lead does vacillate at the first sign of resistance and is quick to capitulate to competition from an older man for the love of the desired woman. The happy ending that ultimately unites the young couple results from a twist of fate or fortuitous intervention, not the volition of a German hero.

Since World War I, American culture periodically had been looked to as the source for a modern model of male subjectivity. The process of crossing the Atlantic for cultural clues to aid gender development was not an innovation of the 1950s. In the early 1920s, for example, young male intellectuals celebrated American culture for its "naturalness" and unreflected self-confidence, which made earlier Wilhelminian culture appear effete—particularly in view of the recent military humiliation. Bertolt Brecht, among others, admired the American boxer as the expression of a vital masculinity who embodied the "myth of the heroic": he was "hard, tough, and trained to the core" and held out the promise of cultural and self-renewal. Under Hitler, American culture was again employed as a basis for a new male identity—this time to counter the discipline and drilled conformism of the Hitler Youth. Urban working class youths congregated in renegade groups like the "Edelweiss Pirates," "Navajos," and "Roving Dudes" and set out on camping trips to flee the supervision of school and state. While away, they shed their received identities and transformed themselves into rugged individuals modelled on their favorite cowboy or gangster hero. Thus Hans would become "Texas Jack"; Dieter, "Alaska Bill"; and Klaus, "Whiskey-Jonny."[42]

American culture had remained a consistent tool of generational protest against the specific form and content of male socialization since the Weimar period. In the aftermath of Germany's second defeat in just over a generation, German boys who came of age under Adenauer again turned to American stars for yet another "radically modern" model of masculinity. This time the sources of inspiration were Montgomery Clift, Marlon Brando, Bill Haley, Elvis Presley, and James Dean: young men with a working class aura who, through their casual clothes and self-assured bearing, projected a romantic, rebellious macho—an attractive (yet generation- and class-specific) brand of individual freedom and self-expression.[43]

Many German teenagers admired the youthful, confident, uninhibited—even "informal"—masculinity embodied in their favorite Hollywood stars. Set against the cultural stereotype of the socially formal, physically stiff, "soldierly" German male, it spoke to them of adventure and sexual discovery, freedom from restriction and want. The beloved German fan magazine of the 1950s, *Bravo*, featured Marlon Brando on its cover in the summer of 1957, when the star was visiting the Federal Republic to film *The Young Lions*. A medium close-up of Brando in a sporty shirt and civilian hat dominated the page, flanked by two minute shots—pushed to the upper and lower corner margins—of Brando in character, uniformed as a Nazi officer. The caption declared approvingly: "Brando is such a casual civilian, he feels fundamentally ill-at-ease in any uniform." As the physical expression of disorderly and unconstrained masculinity, Brando and other American male stars of that era embodied a physical and cultural ideal that struck some postwar youth as more honest and enticing.[44]

Limited evidence suggests that by the late 1950s teenage girls, too, felt themselves to be affected by this generational struggle. One woman recalls:

> An often-heard sentence from my life in the 'fifties: "turn down the radio, Daddy's working." Elvis Presley versus my father. Superficially, my father won. But the upbeat, provocative, stimulating music quietly wormed its way into my dreams. Elvis supplied my fantasies for a future as woman and wife ... with a crucial explosiveness. An alarming but hidden explosiveness that ... recurred as I put on my first pair of nylons and high-heeled shoes.[45]

Like their young male counterparts, some teenage girls turned to American-style culture and consumer goods to construct new social and sexual identities. In this case, Hollywood stars like Rita Hayworth, Ava Gardner, and Marilyn Monroe may have offered German girls a mature and sexualized feminine ideal that attracted precisely because of its difference from the maternal—and infinitely more respectable—brand of *German* womanhood showcased in *Heimatfilme*. What Jackie Stacey has argued for female film-goers in postwar Britain may well apply to young women in 1950s West Germany, that "Hollywood stars were ... contested terrains of competing cultural discourses for femininity. ... [T]he reproduction of self-image through consumption was perceived as a way of producing new forms of 'American' feminine identity which were exciting, sexual, pleasurable and in some ways, transgressive."[46]

By the mid-1950s, then, West German teenagers began to seek a transformation of identity through a "transformation of the body." And although attention to how the body is "clothed and presented" has been a central signifier of a girl's maturation to adult femininity in consumer societies, by the late Adenauer period, young West Germans of both sexes began to alter their appearances as a way to experiment with alternative identities. Self-transformation, moreover, rapidly translated into social practice as a highly visible minority of young Germans offered themselves for public display (and widespread public censure) by consciously manipulating the cultural meanings and national associations of dress and demeanor. Thus, consumption, personal style, and leisure activity took on symbolic significance as young Germans employed American culture, in a variety of ways, to mark their difference from received notions of German identity. With the advent of the *Wirtschaftswunder* and increased disposable income, then, American-style consumption became a weapon of choice in the postwar generation's protest against parental prescriptions for proper socialization.[47]

As Bliersbach has observed, "American cinema had no sense of shame." To a growing number of youth in the late 1950s who were no more than toddlers in 1945, American films represented both an escape from a reprehensible German past *and* a disavowal of German fathers who, Bliersbach argues, "have never been especially presentable"[48]—and became even less so in the aftermath of National Socialism.

NOTES

1. Judith Mayne, *Cinema and Spectatorship* (New York: Routledge, 1993), 1–2.
2. Walter Keim, "Die Freiwillige Selbstkontrolle der deutschen Filmwirtschaft," *Kulturarbeit* 9 (1949): 193.
3. Charles Ford, *Der Film und der Glaube*, trans. P. Pascal (Nuremberg: Glock & Lutz, 1955). Also Heide Fehrenbach, "The Fight for the 'Christian West': German Film Control, the Churches, and the Reconstruction of Civil Society in the Early Bonn Republic," *German Studies Review* 14 (February 1991): 39–63.
4. Quoted in Julianne Eisenführ, *Die Sünderin. Geschichte und Analyse eines Kinoskandals* (Unpublished Magisterarbeit, Universität Osnabrück, 1982), 281.
5. Akten des Bayerischen Ministerium für Unterricht und Kultus, Bayerisches Hauptstaatsarchiv (hereafter BayHStA) MK 51766. Memos dated 11 June 1951, 20 June 1951, and 26 July 1951. Also "Bischöfe fordern Jugendschutz-Gesetz," *Münchner Merkur* (24 March 1950).
6. "Hirtenwort des Kardinals Frings gegen den Spielfilm *Die Sünderin*, 28. Februar 1951", quoted in Klaus-Jörg Ruhl, ed., *Frauen in der Nachkriegszeit, 1945–1963. Dokumente* (Munich: Deutschen Taschenbuch Verlag, 1988), 115–116. Also Eisenführ, *Die Sünderin*, 249–295; *Filmblätter* #4 (26 January 1951), 78; and an except from *Der Spiegel* #26 (1951) that appears in Ursula Bessen, *Trümmer und Träume. Nachkriegszeit und fünfziger Jahre auf Zelluloid* (Bochum: Studienverlag Dr. N. Brockmeyer, 1989), 184.
7. From a film review by Werner Hess in the *Evangelischen Filmbeobachter* 3 (1 February 1951); also Cardinal Frings' Palm Sunday address quoted in Eisenführ, *Die Sünderin*, 299.
8. For an expanded discussion of this film, see Heide Fehrenbach, "*Die Sünderin* or Who Killed the German Male? Early Postwar German Cinema and the Betrayal of Fatherland" in Sandra Frieden, et al., eds. *Gender and German Cinema. Feminist Interventions:* Vol. II. (Providence: Berg Publishers, 1993), 135–60. See also Fehrenbach, *Cinema in Democratizing Germany. The Reconstruction of National Identity in the West, 1945–1962*. (Chapel Hill: University of North Carolina Press, forthcoming).
9. Doris Schubert, *Frauen in der deutschen Nachkriegszeit*, Vol. I (Düsseldorf: Pädagogischer Verlag Schwann-Bagel, 1984), 34. Ute Frevert, *Women in German History*, trans. Stuart McKinnon-Evans. (Providence: Berg Publishers, 1988), 257–58, 263–64. Robert Moeller, "Reconstructing the Family in Reconstruction Germany: Women and Social Policy in the Federal Republic, 1949–1955," *Feminist Studies* 15, #1 (Spring 1989): 137–169.
10. Sibylle Meyer and Eva Schulze, "'Als wir wieder zusammen waren, ging der Krieg im Kleinen weiter'. Frauen, Männer und Familien im Berlin der vierziger Jahre" in L. Niethammer and A. von Plato, eds., *"Wir kriegen jetzt andere Zeiten." Auf der Suche nach der Erfahrung des Volkes in Nachfaschistischen Ländern. Lebensgeschichte und Sozialkultur im Ruhrgebiet 1930 bis 1960*, Vol. 3. (Berlin: Verlag J.H.W. Kietz Nachf., 1985), 305–26. Also Barbara Willenbacher, "Zerrüttung und Bewährung der Nachkriegs-Familie" in M. Broszat, et al., eds., *Von Stalingrad zur Währungsreform. Zur Sozialgeschichte des Umbruchs in Deutschland*. (Munich: Oldenbourg Verlag, 1990), 595–618.
11. Der Publizist Walther von Hollander über Ehezerrüttung, Ehetrennung, Ehescheidung, 1946" and "Die Lage der Jugendlichen in Aachen, 1947," in *Frauen in der Nachkriegszeit*, 31–34 and 37. Frevert, *Women in German History*, 258; Annemarie Tröger, "Between Rape and Prostitution" in J. Friedlander, B. Wiesen Cook, et al., eds., *Women in Culture and Politics: A Century of Change*. (Bloomington: Indiana Uni-

versity Press, 1986), 105–112; Erika Hoerning, "Frauen als Kriegsbeute. Der Zwei-Fronten-Krieg. Beispiele aus Berlin" in "Wir kriegen jetzt andere Zeiten." On social policy toward women and the family, see Moeller, "Reconstructing the Family"; also Moeller, "Protecting Mother's Work: From Production to Reproduction in Postwar West Germany" in *Journal of Social History* 22, #3 (Spring 1989): 413–437; and more recently Moeller, *Protecting Motherhood. Women and the Family in the Politics of Postwar West Germany* (Berkeley: University of California Press, 1993).
12. Klaus Brüne, review of *Die Sünderin* in the *Katholischer Film-Dienst* (2 February 1951) reprinted in Hilmar Hoffmann and Walter Schobert, eds., *Zwischen Gestern und Morgen. Westdeutscher Nachkriegsfilm 1946–1962.* (Frankfurt: Deutsches Filmmuseum, 1989), 356. For the specific criticisms of the working committee of the Freiwillige Selbstkontrolle der Filmwirtschaft, see Eisenführ, *Die Sünderin*, 226–27.
13. BayHStA MK51766. Letter from Regierungspräsident, Oberbayern, to Bayerisches Staatsministerium für Unterricht und Kultus, 4 March 1947.
14. BayHStA MK 51766. Letter from the Schulrat, Schulamt Rosenheim, to the Schulreferat, Stadtrat Rosenheim, dated 10 April 1951, quoting an article in *Filmdienst* 4, #5. Also letter from the Vereinigte Bürgerausschüße der Stadt und des Landkreises Schwabach to the Bayerisches Ministerium für Unterricht und Kultus, dated 8 May 1951. In addition, administrators of Catholic Girls School in Rosenheim, frequent complainants and lobbyists to Bavarian Cultural Minstry, assembled a catalogue of film-induced behaviors: "indifference to the educational influence of parents ... and every authority, lack of respect, and craftiness ... , rude behavior in public and against friends." They declared *Die Sünderin* an offending film and proposed that the Bavarian Parliament permit children under the age of 14 to attend only *Kulturfilme* and filmic fairytales, and to strictly control the types of films seen by those between the ages of 14 and 18. BayHStA MK 51766. Letter from Schulpflegschaft der kathol. Mädchenschule Rosenheim to the Bayerischem Landtag, 15 March 1951. A similar letter was sent by the Evangel.-luth Landeskirchenrat to the Bavarian Ministry for Education and Culture.
15. Moeller, *Protecting Motherhood*, 62–75 and 76–108.
16. Moeller, "Reconstructing the Family," 146.
17. For a discussion of the censorship body, see Johanne Noltenius, *Die Freiwillige Selbstkontrolle der Filmwirtschaft und das Zensurverbot des Grundgesetzes*. (Göttingen: Verlag Otto Schwarz, 1958). The same year, the federal government passed the *Jugendschutzgesetz*—a law intended to protect minors from the immoral influences of the mass media. Unsurprisingly, the most vocal opponents of *Die Sünderin's* exhibition were the law's most active proponents, with Bavarian Cardinal Faulhaber playing a leading lobbying role. The legislation hearkened back to the 1926 "trash and smut" law, sponsored by the Catholic Center-Nationalist coalition government in response to the perceived "sexual anarchy" and leftist cultural threats of that time. The Weimar legislation permitted Land ministries and youth offices to proscribe films and literature for distribution or display to minors under the age of 18. The new legislation, however, retained the age limit of 16 years imposed by the Americans for film censorship, which ensured that the problem of juvenile film attendance would remain a hot topic for research and lobbying by state youth offices into the late 1950s, when sustained public pressure from educational and religious leaders finally resulted in an increase in the age of unrestricted film attendance to 18.
18. Bühler, *Die Kirchen und die Massenmedien*, 42; also P. Max Gritschneder S.J., "Bilanz der katholischen Filmarbeit," *Petrusblatt* (15 July 1952).
19. Walter Keim, "Genießen wir Katholiken verfassungsmäßige Meinungsfreiheit auf dem Gebiet des Films?", originally published in *Münchener Katholische Kirchenzeitung* (5 and 12 March 1950), reprinted in *Film-Korrespondenz* 1/1950 (1 May 1950): 3–4.

20. Bühler, *Die Kirchen und die Massenmedien*, 42. Also "Die Filmdebatte des Bundestages" in *Filmforum* 3, #8 (1954): 5; "Die Ziele der Katholischen Filmliga" in *Nürnberger Nachrichten* (4 July 1951); "Hirtenwort der deutschen Bischöfe zur Filmfrage" in BayHStA MK51763. The Evangelical Church founded a similar organization, the *Filmgilde*, with less public fanfare and fewer members. See Werner Hess, "Evangelische Filmgilde" in *Kirche und Film* 21 (1 November 1951): 4.
21. Jürgen Berger, "Bürgen heißt zahlen—und manchmal auch zensieren. Die Filmbürgschaften des Bundes 1950–1955" in *Zwischen Gestern und Morgen*. Also Robert Liebig, "Filmbürgschaften aus Frankfurt" and Reinhold E. Thiel, "Filmförderung oder Schnulzenkartell?" in Herbert Stettner, *Kino in der Stadt. Eine Frankfurter Chronik*. (Frankfurt: Eichborn Verlag, 1984), 40–43 and 44–46.
22. Georg Roeber and Gerhard Jacoby, *Handbuch der filmwirtschaftlichen Medienbereiche*. (Pullach, 1973), 483–87. Herman Krings, *Was heißt wertvoll. Über Grundlagen und Maßstab der Filmbewertung*, 2nd ed. (Wiesbaden-Biebrich: Der Filmbewertungsstelle Wiesbaden, 1961), 14–17.
23. From Janet Staiger, "'The Handmaiden of Villainy'," quoted in Mayne, *Cinema and Spectatorship*, 67.
24. Alon Confino, "The Nation as Local Metaphor: Heimat, National Memory and the German Empire, 1871–1918" in *History and Memory* 5, #1 (1993): 73–74. Also, "Heimat" in Projektgruppe deutscher Heimatfilm, *Der Deutsche Heimatfilm. Bildwelten und Weltbilder. Bilder, Texte, Analysen zu 70 Jahren deutscher Filmgeschichte*. (Tübingen: Tübinger Vereinigung für Volkskunde, 1989), 15–32; and Celia Applegate, *A Nation of Provincials. The German Idea of Heimat*. (Berkeley: The University of California Press, 1990).
25. Confino, "The Nation as Local Metaphor," 73–74.
26. Wilhelm Michel, "Lob der Heimat," *Pfalz und Pfälzer* 1 (August 1950), quoted in Applegate, *A Nation of Provincials*, 235–36.
27. Applegate, *A Nation of Provincials*, 229 and 243–44.
28. Projektgruppe deutscher Heimatfilm, *Der deutsche Heimatfilm*, 82; and Claudius Seidl, *Der deutsche Film der fünfziger Jahre*. (Munich: Wilhelm Heyne Verlag, 1987), 66.
29. A number of *Heimatfilme*, in fact, thematize the threat of female emigration to the United States or England (as in the case of Inge in *Am Brunnen*). In all cases, the would-be expatriate remains in Germany and emigration is depicted not as a political or economic choice, but a psychological state of denial that would have dreadful emotional consequences for the emigrant as well as those left behind.
30. Willi Höfig, *Der deutsche Heimatfilm, 1947–1960* (Stuttgart: Ferdinand Enke Verlag, 1973), 135.
31. See Projektgruppe deutscher Heimatfilm, *Der deutsche Heimatfilm*, 82–84; and Gerhard Bliersbach, *So grün war die Heide. Die gar nicht so heile Welt im Nachkriegsfilm* (Weinheim: Beltz Verlag, 1989).
32. Werner Abelshauser, *Die langen fünfziger Jahre. Wirtschaft und Gesellschaft der Bundesrepublik Deutschland 1949–1966* (Düsseldorf: Schwann, 1987), 80–81. Also Kaspar Masse, *Bravo Amerika. Erkundungen zur Jugendkultur der Bundesrepublik in den fünfziger Jahren* (Hamburg: Junius Verlag, 1992), 65–69; and Projektgruppe deutscher Heimatfilm, *Der deutsche Heimatfilm*, 87.
33. Wolfgang Kaschuba, "Bildwelten als Weltbilder" in Projektgruppe deutsche Heimatfilm, *Der deutsche Heimatfilm*, 11.
34. Victoria de Grazia, "Mass Culture and Sovereignty: The American Challenge to European Cinemas, 1920–1960," *Journal of Modern History* 61 (March 1989): 66 and 78. Also David Welch, *Propaganda and the German Cinema 1933–1945* (Oxford: Clarendon Press, 1983); Erwin Leiser, *Nazi Cinema* (New York: Macmillan, 1974); and

Hans-Dietrich Schäfer, *Das gespaltene Bewußtsein. Über deutsche Kultur und Lebenswirklichkeit 1933–45* (Munich: Carl Hanser Verlag, 1981).
35. Ludwig Thome, "Der deutsche Filmbesucher," in *Internationale Film Revue* 1 (1951/52): 280. Helga Haftendorn, "Zusammensetzung und Verhalten des Filmtheaterpublikums in der Mittelstadt," in *Filmstudien* II (1957): 15.
36. Thome, "Der deutsche Filmbesucher," 279–80. Horst G. Feldt, "Der Ausländische Film in Deutschland," in *Internationale Film-Revue* 1 (1951/52): 274–76. Wilmont Haacke, "Filmkontrolle und Meinungsfreiheit," in *Kulturarbeit* 7 (1952): 125. Hans Abich, "Die Filmproduktion in Deutschland—Ihre Struktur, Ihre Hauptprobleme, Ihre Thematik," in *Internationale Film-Revue* 1, #4 (1951/52): 253–58. Haftendorn, "Zusammensetzung und Verhalten des Filmtheaterpublikums in der Mittelstadt," 20–21. OMGUS-ICD Opinion Surveys, "The Moving Picture Audience in AMZON," dated 28 April 1948, in the Erich Pommer Collection, Box B, #8 at the Cinema Library, University of Southern California.
37. Dieter Krusche, "Rückblicke und Ausblicke zum 10. Internationalen Filmtreffen" in *Filmforum* 10 (July 1956), quoted in Anna Paech, "Die Schule der Zuschauer. Zur Geschichte der deutschen Film Club Bewegung," *Zwischen Gestern und Morgen*, 237–38.
38. Haftendorn, "Zusammensetzung und Verhalten des Filmtheaterpublikums," 15–22; Bliersbach, *So grün war die Heide,* 40–41.
39. Bliersbach, *So grün war die Heide,* 38–40.
40. Bliersbach, *So grün war die Heide,* 41.
41. Bliersbach, *So grün war die Heide,* 53.
42. David Bathrick, "Max Schmeling on the Canvas: Boxing as an Icon of Weimar Culture" in *New German Critique* 51 (Fall 1990): 116 and 123. Detlev Peukert, *Inside Nazi Germany. Conformity, Opposition, and Racism in Everyday Life,* trans. Richard Deveson. (New Haven: Yale University Press, 1987), 145–74; as well as Peukert, "Youth in the Third Reich," in Richard Bessel, ed., *Life in the Third Reich* (New York, 1987), 25–40. See also Schäfer, *Das gespaltene Bewußtsein,* 137.
43. Maase, *Bravo Amerika,* 83–137.
44. Maase, *Bravo Amerika,* 115 and 113–14.
45. Maase, *Bravo Amerika,* 137, also 81, 96 and 118. Also Christine Bartram and Heinz-Hermann Krueger, "Vom Backfisch zum Teenager—Mädchensozialisation in der 50er Jahren" in Heinz-Hermann Krüger, ed., *"Die Elvis-Tolle, die hatte ich mir unauffällig wachsen lassen." Lebensgeschichte und jugendliche Alltagskultur in den fünfziger Jahren* (Opladen: Leske und Budrich, 1985), 81–101; and Jürgen Zinnecker, *Jugendkultur 1940–1985* (Opladenf: Leske und Budrich, 1987). Uta Poiger is currently studying the female response to American popular culture in both East and West Germany in her doctoral dissertation, *Taming the Wild West: East and West German Encounters with American Popular Culture, 1949–1962.*
46. Jackie Stacey, *Star Gazing: Hollywood Cinema and Female Spectatorship.* (London and New York: Routledge, 1994), 205.
47. Maase, *Bravo Amerika,* 96–101.
48. Bliersbach, *So grün war die Heide,* 53. And Maase, *Bravo Amerika,* Chapters 5–8.

NOTES ON CONTRIBUTORS

Volker R. Berghahn, John P. Birkelund Professor of European History, Brown University, Rhode Island.

Peter K. Breit, Professor in the Department of Politics and Government, University of Hartford, Connecticut.

Gordon A. Craig, Professor of Humanities Emeritus, Stanford University and *Honorarprofessor*, Free University of Berlin.

Heide Fehrenbach, Asst. Professor of History, Colgate University; currently holding a post-doctoral fellowship at the Rutgers Center for Historical Analysis.

Hermann Glaser, formerly Director of the Department for Educational and Cultural Affairs, City of Nürnberg; *Honorarprofessor* Technical University Berlin.

Gerald R. Kleinfeld, Professor of History at Arizona State University, Tempe, and Editor of *German Studies Review*.

Robert Moeller, Professor of History, University of California, Santa Cruz.

Dietrich Orlow, Professor of History, Boston University.

Uta Poiger is completing a PhD in History at Brown University on the influence of American popular culture on East and West German identities.

Reiner Pommerin holds a chair for Modern and Contemporary History at the Technical University of Dresden. His publications include *Der Kaiser und Amerika* (1986) and *Strategiewechsel. Bundesrepublik and Nuklearstarategie in der Ära Adenauer-Kennedy* (1992). He is co-editor of *Foreign Relations of the Federal Republic*, vols.I and II.

www.ingramcontent.com/pod-product-compliance
Lightning Source LLC
Chambersburg PA
CBHW071159070526
44584CB00019B/2858